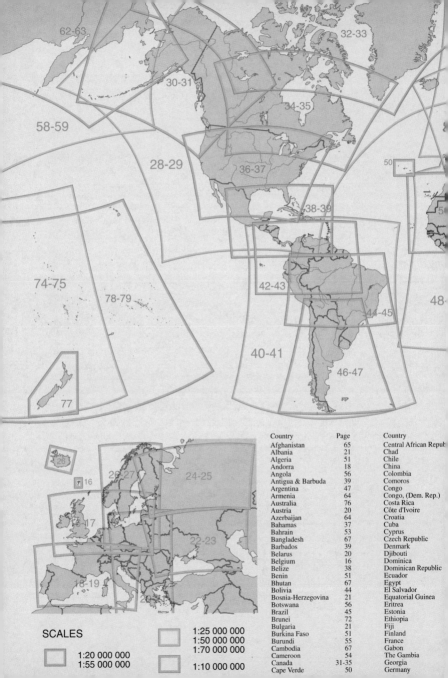

62-63   32-33

30-31

34-35

58-59

28-29

36-37

50

38-39

74-75

78-79

42-43

44-45

48-

40-41

46-47

77

26   16

26-27   24-25

16-17

22-23

18-19

SCALES

1:25 000 000
1:50 000 000
1:70 000 000

1:20 000 000
1:55 000 000

1:10 000 000

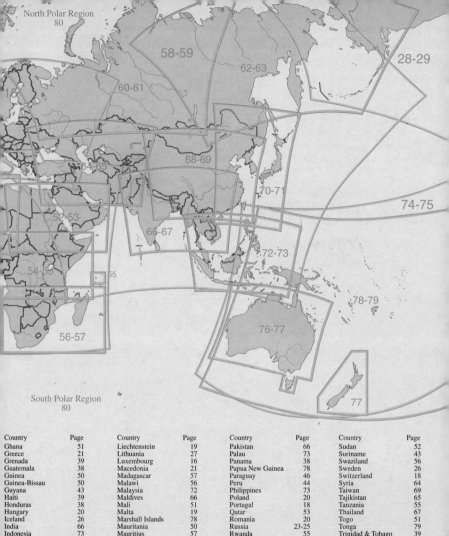

North Polar Region
80

58-59

28-29

62-63

60-61

68-69

64-65

70-71

52-53

74-75

66-67

72-73

54-55

55

78-79

56-57

76-77

South Polar Region
80

77

AA *Pocket*
World
Atlas

Atlas design and specifications:	Bo Gramfors, Ulla Durvall, Siv Eklund
Geographical environments artwork:	Tiziana Gironi
Production:	Lovell Johns, Oxford

Published by arrangement with Lovell Johns Ltd, 10 Hanborough Business Park, Witney, Oxfordshire OX8 8LH.

A CIP catalogue record for this book is available from the British Library.

ISBN 0 7495 2377 8

Copyright © 1996 Lovell Johns Ltd, Oxford, England
Revised and reprinted 1997, 1998, 2000
Copyright © This edition first published by The Automobile Association 2000
Printed in Italy by STIGE Turin

Published by AA Publishing (a trading name of AA Developments Ltd, whose registered office is Norfolk House, Priestley Road, Basingstoke, Hampshire, RG24 9NY. Registered number 1878835).

Flags authenticated by The Flag Research Center, Winchester, Mass. 01890, USA.

Front cover globe: Mountain High Maps ™ Copyright © 1993 Digital Wisdom, Inc.

P ainting a portrait of a person means catching looks, character, traces of experience and the changes it brings, atmosphere and - yes, the soul of that person.

When developing this atlas we have tried to do just these things. To paint a portrait of our Earth trying to capture its looks as seen from space; its character with all its Geographical Environments - rain forests, deserts and savannas; the traces of experience and change through our impact on communications, farmland, boundaries and the naming of places and also its soul as the planet we live on and care about.

In spite of its tiny size this World Atlas can give you a comprehensive picture, background, situation and facts about our planet. Together with the statistical section, the atlas also gives you an understanding of the world with its living conditions and opportunities for your fellow human beings either concentrated or scattered all over the surface of the Earth.

Use the Atlas as a travel companion, for 'armchair travelling', for facts and place finding or just as a good book.

To care about our Earth, its people, its Environments and its future is to gather information and knowledge and so understand and be able to influence its destiny.

Take your time to read your Atlas and get to know it.

The Earth is in your hands.

Bo Gramfors
1996

LIST OF CONTENT

MAP SECTION

THE WORLD

EUROPE

NORTH AMERICA

SOUTH AMERICA

AFRICA

ASIA

AUSTRALIA

POLAR REGIONS

INDEX SECTION

STATISTICAL SECTION

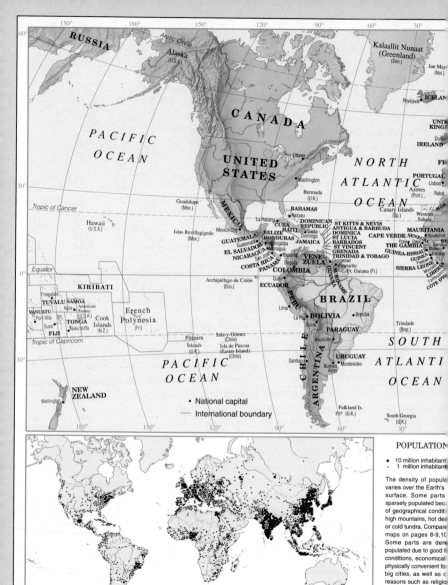

National capital
— **International boundary**

POPULATION

● 10 million inhabitants
· 1 million inhabitants

The density of popula
varies over the Earth's
surface. Some parts
sparsely populated bec
of geographical condit
high mountains, hot des
or cold tundra. Compare
maps on pages 8-9,10
Some parts are den
populated due to good I
conditions, economical
physically convenient fo
big cities, as well as o
reasons such as religi
ethnic grouping. Popula
growth is mainly centre
the already densely
populated areas.

6 THE WORLD, political

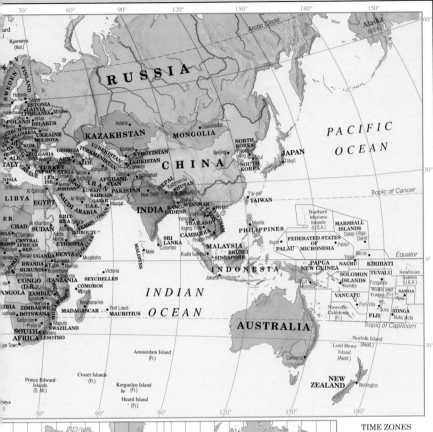

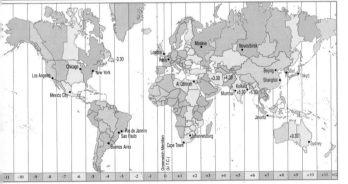

TIME ZONES

The Earth spins around its axis anticlockwise and completes one turn every 24 hours. As the world rotates it is day on the part facing the Sun and night on the side in shadow. As shown on this map, we have divided the Earth into 24 standard time zones. They are based upon lines of longitude at 15 degree intervals but mainly follow country or state boundaries. You can compare times around the world by using the map. For example; when it is 12 noon in London it is 5 hours earlier in New York or 7 am.

VAN DER GRINTEN'S PROJECTION

7

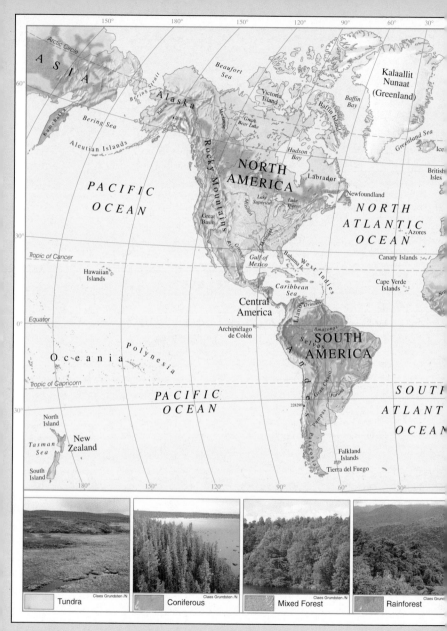

Tundra   Coniferous   Mixed Forest   Rainforest

8   THE WORLD, geographical environments

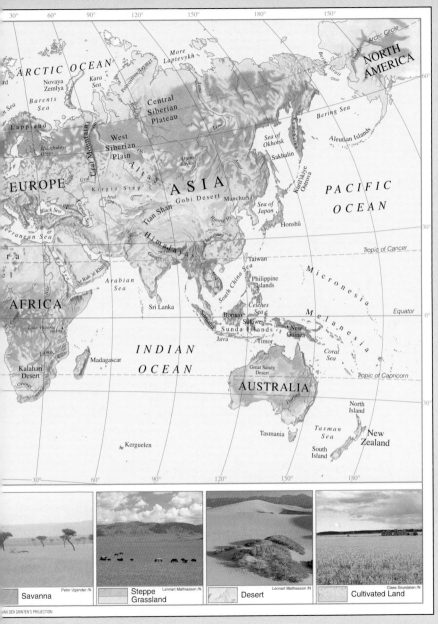

ARCTIC OCEAN

NORTH AMERICA

Arctic Circle

Novaya Zemlya

Kara Sea

More Laptevykh

Bering Strait

Barents Sea

Central Siberian Plateau

Bering Sea

Lappland

Ural Mountains

West Siberian Plain

Lena

Sea of Okhotsk

Aleutian Islands

EUROPE

Kirgiz Step

Altay

ASIA

Ozero Baykal

Amur

Sakhalin

Kuril'skiye Ostrova

PACIFIC OCEAN

Black Sea

Aral

Tian Shan

Gobi Desert

Manchuria

Sea of Japan

Mediterranean Sea

Himalayas

Huang He

Honshū

Tropic of Cancer

Red Sea

Arabian Sea

Ganges

Taiwan

South China Sea

Micronesia

AFRICA

Sri Lanka

Philippine Islands

Lake Victoria

Celebes Sea

Borneo

Sumatra

Sunda Islands

New Guinea

Melanesia

Equator

Kalahari Desert

Java

Timor

Coral Sea

Madagascar

INDIAN OCEAN

Great Sandy Desert

AUSTRALIA

Tropic of Capricorn

Darling

North Island

Kerguelen

Tasmania

Tasman Sea

New Zealand

South Island

Savanna	Steppe Grassland	Desert	Cultivated Land

Peter Ugander /N

Lennart Mathiasson /N

Lennart Mathiasson /N

Claes Grundsten /N

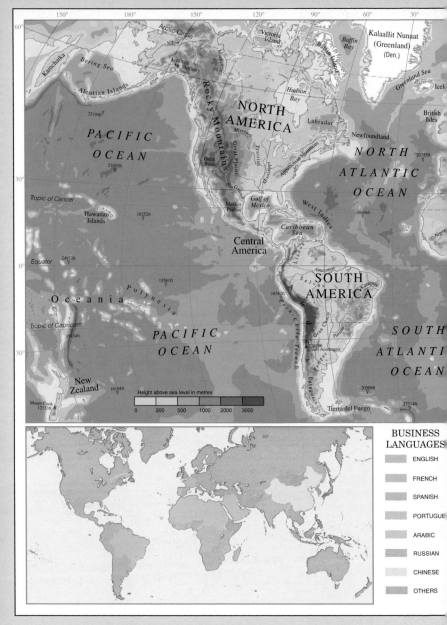

10 THE WORLD, physical, languages, religions

RELIGIONS

C - Catholic
P - Protestant
O - Orthodox

CHRISTIANS

ISLAM, Sunni Moslems
ISLAM, Shiah Moslems

BUDDHISM
SHINTOISM

HINDUISM

CHINESE RELIGIONS
(Confucians, Taoists etc)

☆ JUDAISM
◉ COPTIC CHRISTIANS

Sparsely populated areas

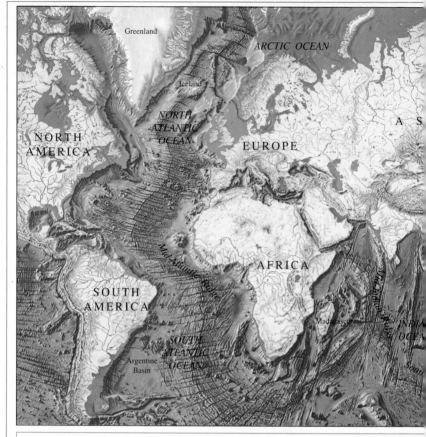

Greenland

ARCTIC OCEAN

Iceland

NORTH ATLANTIC OCEAN

NORTH AMERICA

EUROPE

A S

AFRICA

Mid-Atlantic Ridge

SOUTH AMERICA

Madagascar

INDIAN OCEA

Mid-Indian Ridge

SOUTH ATLANTIC OCEAN

Argentine Basin

Underwater landscapes

Topography of the ocean floor can be divided into two distinct features: the continental margins and the deep sea basins.

The character of the ocean basin depends on the extent to which sediments mask the crust and also the degree of volcanic activity. The sediments may be either pelagic or terrigenous. The latter are brought down by turbidity currents which are avalanches of silt and sand from the continental shelf. These powerful currents can cut channels in the continental shelf such as the Hatteras Canyon off North America and transport material thousands of kilometres.

On the continental shelf, sediments are affected by waves, tidal currents and changes in sea level.

a. Shallow areas are most accessible, they may overlie oil and gas bearing rock.
b. The continental slope defines the edge of the continental block.
c. Deep sea floors can be very flat with gradients less than 1:1000.
d. A Guyot is a submarine volcanic mountain with a completely smooth top.
e. Volcanic islands can be higher above the seabed than Everest is above sea level.
f. Mid ocean ridges. New oceanic crust is formed along these.
g. Atolls are extinct volcanoes which have been colonized by coral.
h. Deep sea trenches. Oceanic crust is destroyed under neighbouring plates.

ARCTIC OCEAN

NORTH
AMERICA

PACIFIC OCEAN

Aleutian Trench

North
Pacific
Basin

New Guinea

*Tonga
Trench*

SOUTH
AMERICA

AUSTRALIA

*Kermadec
Trench*

PACIFIC OCEAN

*Tasman
Basin*

an Ridge

*Mariana
Trench*

East Pacific Ridge

© HACHETTE/GUIDES BLEUS

Seabed treasures

In the deeper sea regions mineral exploitation has concentrated on manganese nodules. These lumps grow at rates of between 3-8 mm, .25 in each million years, and they are valuable for the copper, nickel and cobalt they contain. Granules vary in size and may be up to 150 mm, 6 ins in diameter.

On the continental shelves and near coastal regions placer deposits are often commercially viable. They consist of heavy mineral particles which have been weathered from locally occurring ore bodies and deposited on beaches and in estuaries. Gold is extracted from placer deposits off Alaska.

	Moderate coverage of manganese nodules		Nodules with >1% cobalt
	Extensive coverage of manganese nodules		Nodules with >35% manganese
•	Nodules with >1.8% nickel and copper	▲	Placer deposits

s   Metalliferous muds

13

EUROPE : Facts & Figures

AREA: 3,850,000 mi² / 9,900,000 km²

BIGGEST COUNTRY: Russia
Area (European):
1,663,859 mi² / 4,309,400 km²
Population: 147,231,000 (1998)

SMALLEST COUNTRY: Vatican State
Area: 0.17 mi² / 0.44 km²
Population: 1,000 (1996)

BIGGEST CITY: Paris
Area: 40mi² / 105 km²
(Metro. Area 185 mi² / 479 km²)
Population: 9,318,821 (1990)

HIGHEST MOUNTAIN:
Mount Elbrus, Russia
18,466 ft 5,630 m

% WORLD OIL PRODUCTION:
18.7% (inc. Russia)

NUMBER OF INHABITANTS:
727,000,000

POPULATION DENSITY:
82 per mi² / 32 per km²
Highest: Malta
3,025 per mi² / 1,168 per km²
Lowest: Iceland 7.8 per mi² / 3 per km²

LIFE EXPECTANCY AT BIRTH:
68.3yrs Male, 77yrs Female
Highest: Andorra 86yrs M, 95yrs F
Lowest: Russia 62yrs M, 74yrs F

MARRIAGE RATE per 1000 annually: 6.0
Highest: Lithuania 12.9
Lowest: Estonia 3.8

DIVORCE RATE per 1000 annually: 2.1
Highest: Russia 4.6
Lowest: Macedonia 0.3

MAIN LANGUAGES:
English, French, German, Russian

MAIN RELIGIONS (%):
55% Roman Catholic, 25% Protestant,
13% Orthodox, 7% Muslim

OLDEST UNIVERSITY:
Universitá degli Studi, Bologna, Italy
11th Century

LARGEST UNIVERSITY:
La Sapienza University, Rome, Italy
184,000 students

LITERACY: 94%
Highest: Finland, France,
Germany 100%
Lowest: Albania 86%

Sources: The Statesman's Yearbook 1998/99
UN Statistical Yearbook 42nd edition

Scale 1:25 000 000

| 0 | 250 | 500 km |

| 0 | 100 | 200 | 300 miles |

¹/₂ hour's flight ✈

LAMBERTS CONFORMAL CONIC PROJECTION

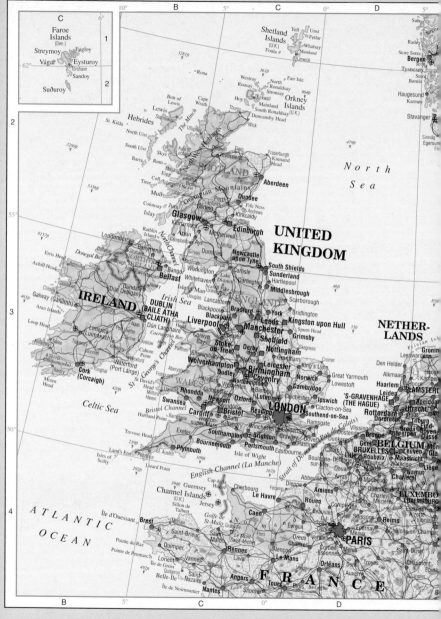

16 EUROPE, north-western

Scale 1:10 000 000

0	100	200	300	400	500 km
0	50	100	150	200	250	300 miles

½ hour's flight

ALBERTS CONFORMAL CONIC PROJECTION

18 EUROPE, south-western

Scale 1:10 000 000

| 0 | 100 | 200 | 300 | 400 | 500 km |

| 0 | 50 | 100 | 150 | 200 | 250 | 300 miles |

¹/₃ hour's flight

LAMBERTS CONFORMAL CONIC PROJECTION

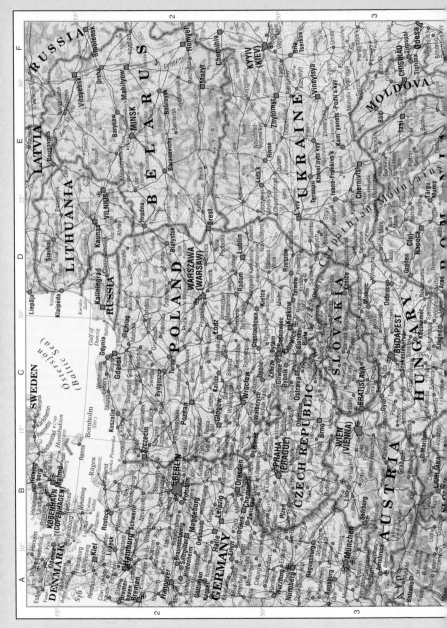

20 EUROPE, central and eastern

22 EUROPE, south-eastern

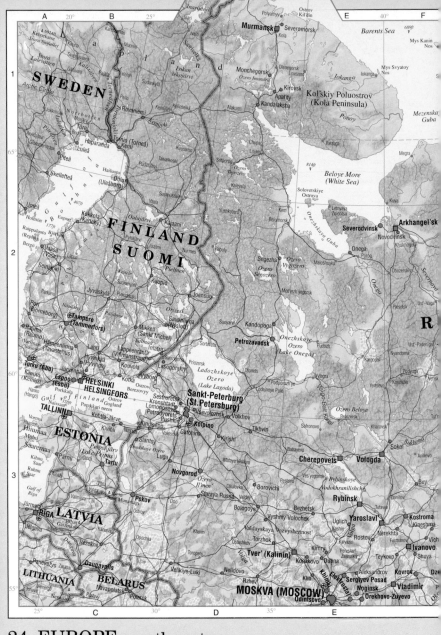

24 EUROPE, north-eastern

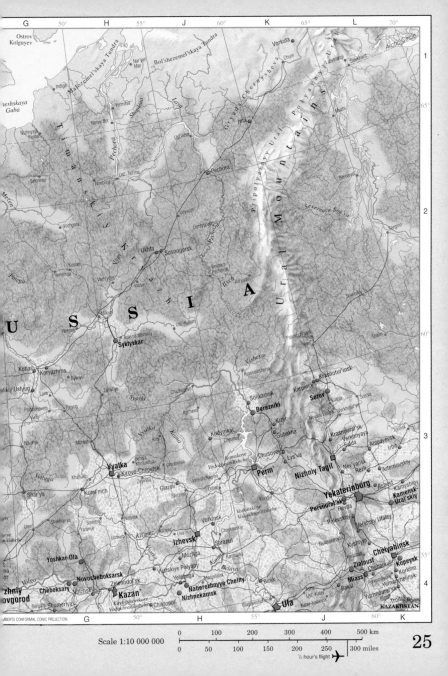

26 SCANDINAVIA

NORTH AMERICA : Facts & Figures

 AREA: 8,514,000 mi^2/ 22,050,000 km^2

 SIZE IN COMPARISON:
3rd largest continent

COASTLINE:
197,876 mi / 318,443 km
(including Greenland)

 NUMBER OF COUNTRIES: 23

BIGGEST COUNTRY: Canada
Area : 3,850,000 mi^2/ 9,970 610 km^2
Population: 30,194,000 (1998)

SMALLEST COUNTRY:
St Kitts-Nevis
Area: 101mi^2/ 261 km^2
Population: 42,000 (1996)

 BIGGEST CITY: Mexico City
Area: 571 mi^2/ 1,479 km^2 (Fed. Dist.)
Population: 16,900,000 (1997)

 HIGHEST MOUNTAIN:
Mount McKinley
20,303 ft, 6,190m
First conquered by:
Hudson Stuck, Harry P Karstens, 1913

 LONGEST CAVE SYSTEM:
under Mammoth Cave Nat. Park,
Kentucky, 348 mi / 560 km

 BIGGEST LAKE: Lake Superior,
32,140 mi^2/ 83,270 km^2

 LONGEST RIVER:
Mississippi 2,348 mi / 3,779 km

 HOTTEST TEMPERATURE:
56.7°C / 134°F, Death Valley, U.S.A.

 COLDEST TEMPERATURE:
-78°C / -172°F, valley of
Mackenzie River, Canada

 LENGTH OF ROAD NETWORK:
2,839,702 km / 4,569,932 km

LENGTH OF RAIL NETWORK:
293,815 mi / 472,838 km

 % WORLD OIL PRODUCTION:
20.0%

% WORLD GOLD PRODUCTION:
21.9%

 NUMBER OF INHABITANTS:
455,000,000

SOME ENDANGERED ANIMALS:

 Grey Bat   Polar Bear   Jamaica Ground Iguana   Giant Clam

Mexican Prairie Dog   Gila Monster

Red Wolf   Green Turtle   Desert Slender Salamander   Queen Conch

---

 **POPULATION DENSITY:**
36 per mi^2 / 14 per km^2
Highest: Barbados
1,574 per mi^2 / 608 per km^2
Lowest: Canada
8 per mi^2 / 3 per km^2

 POP. GROWTH PER ANNUM:
+1.4%
Highest: Costa Rica +2.9%
Lowest: Grenada,
St Kitts-Nevis -0.1%

 % MALE/FEMALE:
49.6% M, 50.4% F
Greatest difference:
Trinidad & Tobago
52.4%M, 47.6%F
Least difference:
Nicaragua 50.1%M, 49.9%F

 LIFE EXPECTANCY AT BIRTH:
73.6yrs Male, 80.3yrs Female
Highest:
Costa Rica 76yrs M, 79yrs F
Lowest: Haiti 59yrs M, 60yrs F

 MARRIAGE RATE per 1000 annually:
7.6
Highest: Cuba 17.1
Lowest: Dominican Rep. 3.6

 DIVORCE RATE per 1000 annually:
1.7
Highest: Cuba 6.0
Lowest: Guatemala,
Nicaragua 0.2

 AVERAGE SIZE OF HOUSEHOLD:
3.7
Highest: Guatemala 5.2
Lowest: USA 2.6

 MAIN LANGUAGES:
Creole, English, French, Spanish

 MAIN RELIGIONS (%):
66% Roman Catholic,
17% Protestant

 OLDEST UNIVERSITY:
Harvard University, Cambridge,
Massachusetts, 1636

 LARGEST UNIVERSITY:
State University of New York, USA
369,318 students

 LITERACY: 86%
Highest: Canada, USA 99%
Lowest: Guatemala 55%

Sources: The Statesman's Yearbook 1998/99
UN Statistical Yearbook 42nd edition

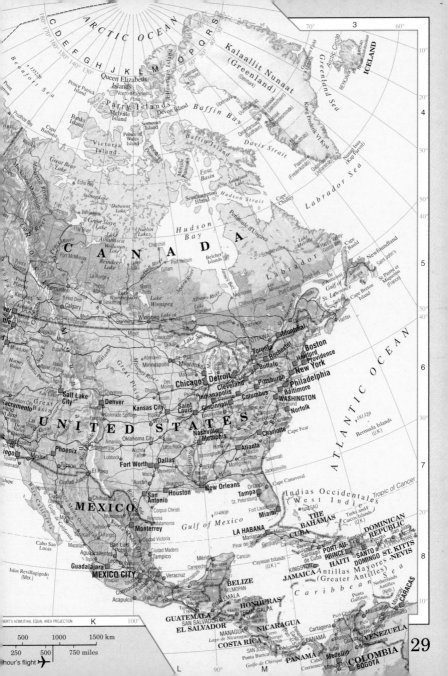

30 WESTERN CANADA and ALASKA

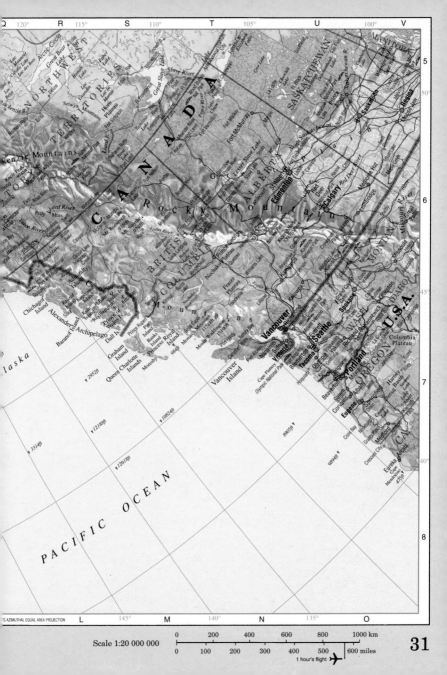

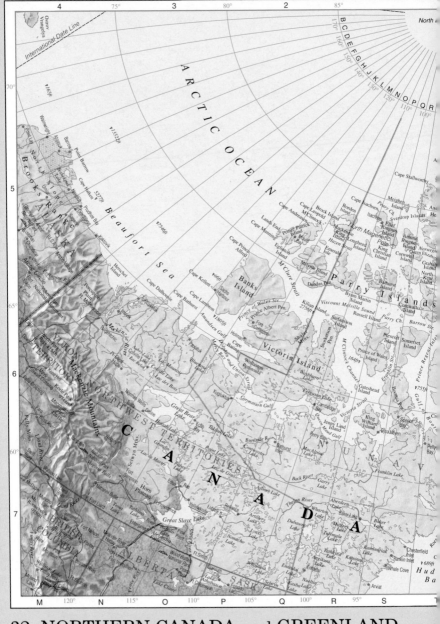

ARCTIC OCEAN

International Date Line

Brooks Range

ALASKA

Beaufort Sea

Banks Island

Parry Islands

Victoria Island

YUKON TERRITORY

Mackenzie Mountains

NORTHWEST TERRITORIES

C A N A D A

BRITISH COLUMBIA

ALBERTA

SASK.

N U N A V U T

Great Bear Lake

Great Slave Lake

Hud Ba

32 NORTHERN CANADA and GREENLAND

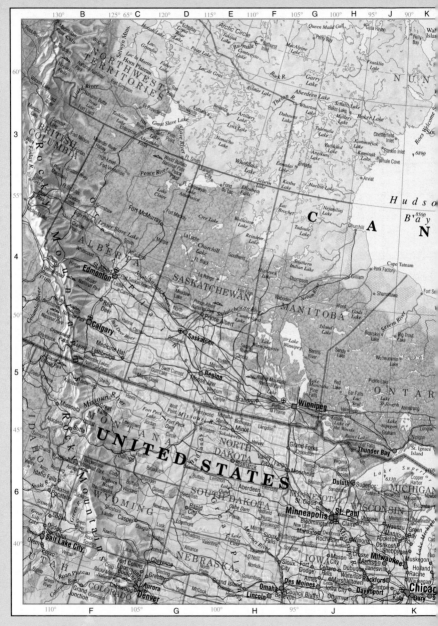

34 CANADA, eastern

Scale 1:20 000 000

| 0 | 200 | 400 | 600 | 800 | 1000 km |

| 0 | 100 | 200 | 300 | 400 | 500 | 600 miles |

1 hour's flight ✈

LAMBERT'S AZIMUTHAL EQUAL AREA PROJECTION

36 UNITED STATES

Scale 1:20 000 000

38 CENTRAL AMERICA

SOUTH AMERICA : Facts & Figures

AREA: 6,800,000 mi² / 17,700,000 km²

SIZE IN COMPARISON:
4th largest continent

COASTLINE: 19,884 mi / 32,000 km

NUMBER OF COUNTRIES: 12

BIGGEST COUNTRY: Brazil
Area : 3,286,739 mi² / 8,511,996 km²
Population: 165,158,000 (1998)

SMALLEST COUNTRY:
Suriname
Area: 63,256 mi² / 163,820 km²
Population: 443,000 (1998)

BIGGEST CITY:
São Paulo (Metro. Area)
Area: 3,070 mi² / 7,951 km²
Population: 16,800,000 (1997)

HIGHEST MOUNTAIN:
Cerro Aconcagua,
22,829 ft / 6,960 m

First conquered by: Matthias Zurbriggen,
14th January 1897

HIGHEST LAKE: Lake Titicaca
Height above sea level:
12,506 ft / 3,811 m
Depth: 1,214 ft / 370 m
Area: 3,200 mi² / 8,290 km²
Length: 100 mi / 161 km

BIGGEST LAKE: Lake Titicaca,
3,200 mi² / 8,290 km²

LONGEST RIVER:
Amazon, 4,080 mi / 6,570 km

MOST EXTENSIVE LOWLAND:
Part of Amazon Basin with large
rainforests covering some
1,930,502 mi² / 5 million km²

HIGHEST FALLS: Angel Falls,
discovered in 1935
Total fall: 3,215 ft / 980 m

LENGTH OF ROAD NETWORK:
1,488,150 mi / 2,330,508 km

LENGTH OF RAIL NETWORK:
50,150 mi / 80,706 km

% WORLD OIL PRODUCTION:
8.6%

% WORLD GOLD PRODUCTION:
8%

NUMBER OF INHABITANTS:
320,000,000

POPULATION DENSITY:
46 per mi² / 18 per km²
Highest:
Ecuador 114 per mi² / 44 per km²
Lowest:
Suriname 6 per mi² / 3 per km²

POP. GROWTH PER ANNUM:
+1.5%
Highest: Bolivia +2.3%
Lowest: Guyana +0.1%

% MALE/FEMALE:
49.8% M, 50.2% F
Greatest difference:
Uruguay 48.7% M, 51.3% F
Least difference:
Brazil 49.9% M 50.1% F

LIFE EXPECTANCY AT BIRTH:
66.4yrs Male, 72.9yrs Female
Highest: Chile 71yrs M, 78yrs F
Lowest: Bolivia 60yrs M, 63yrs F

MARRIAGE RATE per 1000 annually: 5.2
Highest: Chile 6.8
Lowest: Paraguay 3.6

DIVORCE RATE per 1000 annually: 1.4
Highest: Uruguay 3.2
Lowest: Chile 0.5

AVERAGE SIZE OF HOUSEHOLD:
4.2
Highest: Venezuela 5.4
Lowest: Argentina 2.7

MAIN LANGUAGES:
Dutch, English, French, German,
Italian, Portuguese, Spanish

MAIN RELIGIONS (%):
77% Roman Catholic, 4% Protestant,
5% Hindu

OLDEST UNIVERSITY:
University of San Marcos, Lima, Peru
1551

LARGEST UNIVERSITY:
University of Buenos Aires, Argentina
248,453 students

LITERACY: 89%
Highest: Guyana 67%
Lowest: Bolivia 81%

SOME ENDANGERED ANIMALS:

Maned Sloth

Orinoco Crocodile

Giant Tortoise

Golden Headed
Lion Tamarin

Pampas Cat

Marine Otter

Fur Seal

Mountain Tapir

River Turtle

Sources:
The Statesman's Yearbook 1998/99
UN Statistical Yearbook 42nd edition

42 SOUTH AMERICA, northern

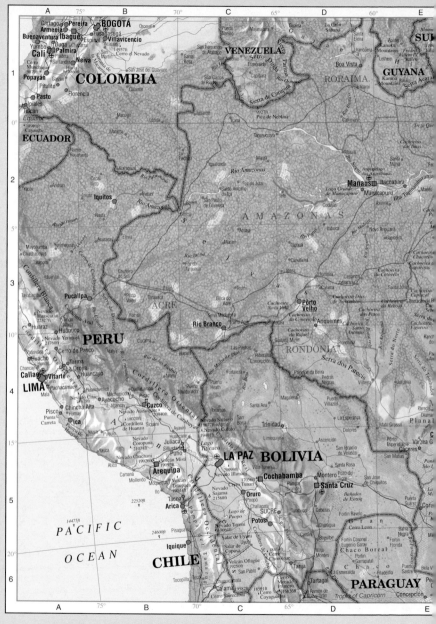

44 SOUTH AMERICA, central

Scale 1:20 000 000

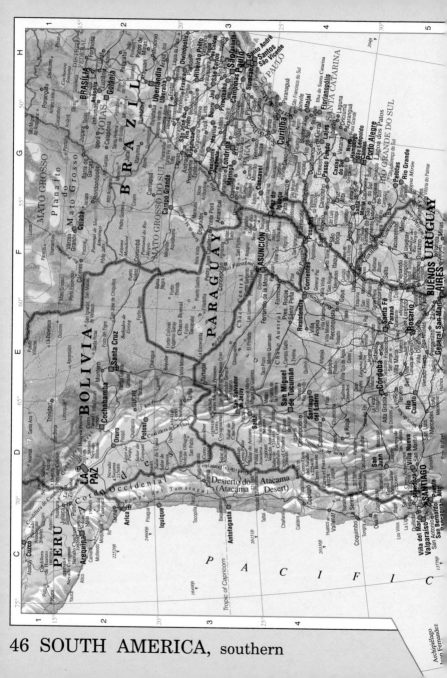

46 SOUTH AMERICA, southern

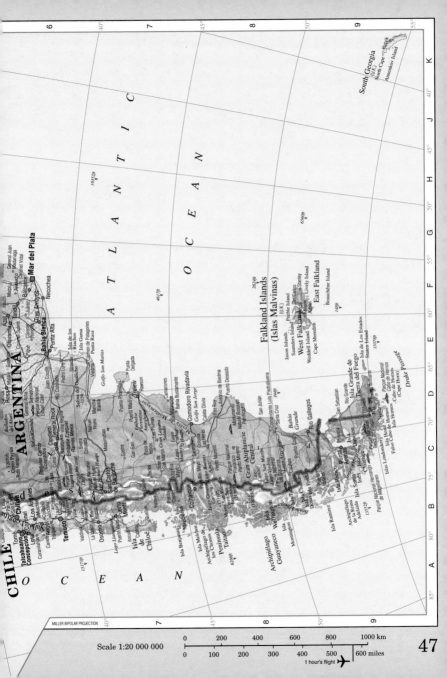

AFRICA : Facts & Figures

AREA:
11,70,000 mi² / 30,300,000 km²

SIZE IN COMPARISON:
2nd largest continent

COASTLINE:
14,244 mi / 36,888 km

NUMBER OF COUNTRIES: 50

BIGGEST COUNTRY: Sudan
Area : 967,500 mi² / 2,505,813 km²
Population: 28,527,000 (1998)

SMALLEST COUNTRY:
Seychelles
Area: 175 mi² / 455 km²
Population: 76,000 (1996)

BIGGEST CITY: Cairo
Area: 83 mi² / 215 km²
Population: 6,452,000 (1990)

HIGHEST MOUNTAIN:
Kilimanjaro, 19,319 ft / 5,890 m
First conquered by: Hans Mayer &
Ludwig Purtscheller 1889

LARGEST DESERT: Sahara
3,475,172 mi² / 9,000,000 km²

BIGGEST LAKE: Lake Victoria,
26,830 mi² / 69,484 km²

LONGEST RIVER:
Nile 4,145 mi / 6,671 km

HOTTEST TEMPERATURE:
57.7° C/136° F
Al Aziziyah, Libya, 1922

**GREATEST NIGHT/DAY
TEMP. RANGE:**
Sahara 50° C / 122° F

LENGTH OF ROAD NETWORK:
1,061,708 mi / 1,708,607 km

LENGTH OF RAIL NETWORK:
51,340 mi / 82,621 km

% WORLD OIL PRODUCTION:
10.4%

% WORLD GOLD PRODUCTION:
31.8%

NUMBER OF INHABITANTS:
728,000,000

POPULATION DENSITY:
108 per mi² / 42 per km²
Highest:
Mauritius 1,432 per mi² / 553 per km²
Lowest:
Mauritania 5 per mi² / 2 per km²

POP. GROWTH PER ANNUM: +2.7%
Highest: Liberia +8.6%
Lowest: Seychelles +1.0%

% MALE/FEMALE:
49.3% M, 50.7% F
Greatest difference: Uganda
46.7% M, 53.3% F
Least difference:
Madagascar 49.97% M, 50.03% F

LIFE EXPECTANCY AT BIRTH:
52.3yrs Male, 55.3yrs Female
Highest: Seychelles 69M, 78F
Lowest: Sierra Leone 40 M, 43 F

MARRIAGE RATE per 1000 annually: 7.6
Highest: Mauritius 9.5
Lowest: South Africa 3.3

DIVORCE RATE per 1000 annually: 1.1
Highest: Egypt 1.6
Lowest: Mauritius 0.7

AVERAGE SIZE OF HOUSEHOLD:
5.7
Highest: Algeria 7.0
Lowest: The Gambia 3.4

MAIN LANGUAGES:
Arabic, English, French,
Local, Portuguese

MAIN RELIGIONS (%):
38% Christian, 35% Muslim,
11% Traditional, 1% Hindu

OLDEST UNIVERSITY:
University of Karueein, Fez,
Morocco, AD 859

LARGEST UNIVERSITY:
Ain Shams University, Cairo
100,179 students

LITERACY: 51%
Highest: Equatorial Guinea 78%
Lowest: Eritrea 15%

SOME ENDANGERED ANIMALS:

Green Turtle   Golden Bamboo Lemur   Gorilla   Round Island Keel Scaled Boa

Mediterranean Monk Seal   Black Rhinoceros   African Elephant

Knysna Seahorse   Grevy's Zebra   Ethiopian Wolf

Sources: The Statesman's Yearbook 1998/99,
UN Statistical Yearbook 42nd edition

Scale 1:50 000 000

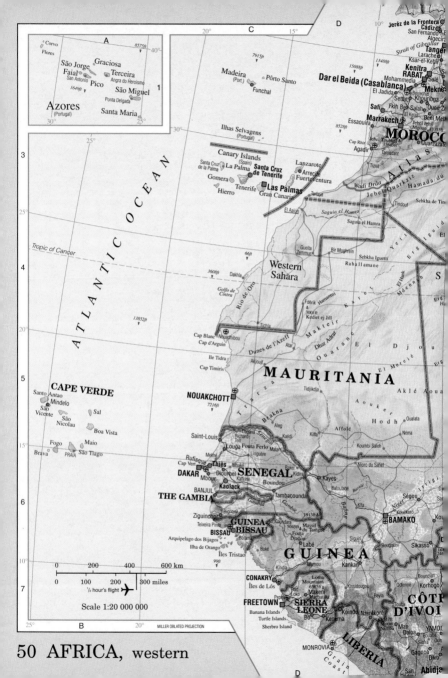

50 AFRICA, western

Azores (Portugal)

Corvo
Flores
8575ft
São Jorge
Faial
San Antonio
Graciosa
Terceira
Pico
1649ft
Angra do Heroismo
São Miguel
Ponta Delgada
Santa Maria

ATLANTIC OCEAN

Madeira (Port.)
Pôrto Santo
7915ft
Funchal

Ilhas Selvagens (Portugal)

Canary Islands (Spain)
Santa Cruz de la Palma
La Palma
Santa Cruz de Tenerife
Lanzarote
Arrecife
Fuerteventura
Gomera
Tenerife
Las Palmas
Hierro
Gran Canaria
Tarfaya

Tropic of Cancer

El Aaiún
Saguia el Hamra
Saguia el Hamra

Western Sahara

3608ft
Dakhla
Golfo de Cintra
Rio de Oro

13852ft

Cap Blanc
Nouadhibou
Cap d'Arguin
Ile Tidra
Cap Timiris

Dunes de l'Azefel
Akjoujt

MAURITANIA

NOUAKCHOTT
7216ft

Saint-Louis
Dagana
Richard Toll
Rosso
Louga
Fouta Ferlo
Linguère
Matam

CAPE VERDE
Santo Antao
Mindelo
São Vicente
São Nicolau
Sal
Boa Vista
Fogo
Maio
Brava
PRAIA
São Tiago

Rufisque
Cap Vert
DAKAR
Mbour
Thiès
Diourbel
Mbaké
Kaffrine
SENEGAL
Kaolack
BANJUL
THE GAMBIA
Tambacounda
Boundou

Ziguinchor
Teixeira Pinto
Bignona
Kolda
Gambie
BISSAU
GUINEA BISSAU
Arquipelago dos Bijagos
Ilha de Orango
Îles Tristao
990ft
Boké

GUINEA
Kindia
Labé
Manou
Kankan

CONAKRY
Îles de Lós
Loma Mountains
6391ft
Makeni
Marampa
FREETOWN
Banana Islands
Turtle Islands
SIERRA LEONE
Bo
Koindu
Nzerekoré
Kenema

MONROVIA
LIBERIA
Grain Coast

CÔTE D'IVOIRE

MOROCCO
Jerez de la Frontera
Cádiz
San Fernando
Algeciras
Strait of Gibraltar
Tanger
Larache
Ksar-el-Kebir
Kenitra
RABAT
Salé
Mohammedia
Dar el Beida (Casablanca)
El Jadida
Meknès
Khouribga
Oued Ze
Beni Mel
Safi
Fkih Bel Salah
El Kelaâ
Marrakech
Jebel Irhil
Essaouira
Cap Rhir
Jebel Sahro
Agadir
Taroudant
Ouarzazate
Tiznit
Atlas
Wadi Drâa
Jebel Ouarkziz
Hamada du

Tindouf
Sebkha de Tin

Bir Moghrein
Sebkha Iguereli
Rahallamane

Fdérik Hamammi
500ft
Kediet ej Jill
Zouérat

Atar
Dhur Adrar
Maéteir
Ouarane
El Djou
El Mereié

Tidjikdja
Aklé Aoua
Aouker
Hodh
Ualata
Néma
Koumbi Saleh

Aleg
Kaédi
Kiffa
Affolé

Bakel
Kidira
BAMAKO
Kayes
Baloubate
Kita
Ségou

Nioro du Sahel
Koulikoro
Kou

Massif du Tamgué
Fouta Djalon
Siguiri
Kankan
Bougouni
Sikasso

Kissidougou
Beyla
Odienê
Korhogo
Touba
Man
Daloa
YAMOU
Danané
Sinfra
Gagnoa
Duékoué
Abidjan

Scale 1:20 000 000

0   200   400   600 km

0   100   200   300 miles

⅓ hour's flight

MILLER OBLATED PROJECTION

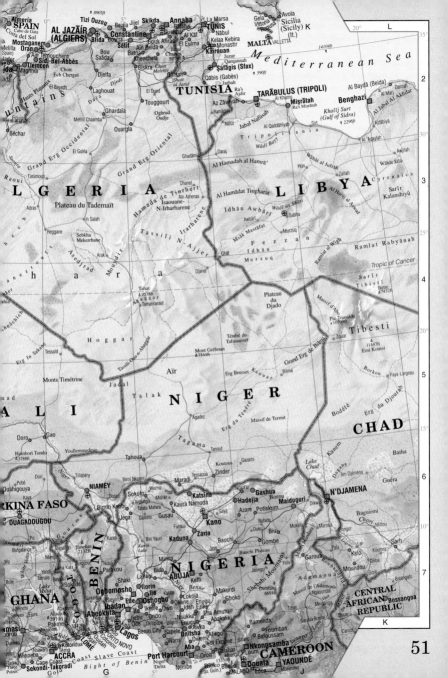

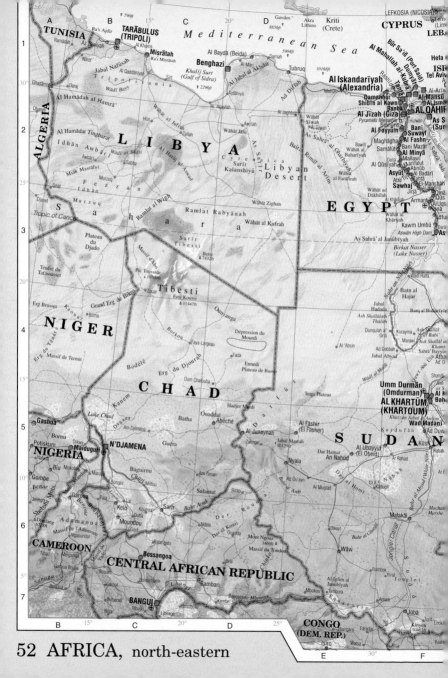

54 AFRICA, central

56 AFRICA, southern

F
G 40° 45° H 50° Saint Cerf K
Pierre
55°

TANZANIA
Lindi
Mtwara
6137ft
Masasi
Rio Rovuma
Mucojo
iassa
Marrupa
Anciuabe
Pemba
Ribaue
Nampula
Alto Molocue

BIQUE
Namacurra
Quelimane
3257ft

9840ft

COMOROS
Njazidja
(Grande Comore)
MORONI
Nzwani
(Anjouan)
Mwali
(Moheli)
17384ft
Mayotte
(France)

SEYCHELLES

Aldabra Islands

Tanjona Bobaomby
Antsirañana
Nosy Bé
Ambilobe
Massif
du
Tsaratanana
Analalava
Antsohihy
Antalaha
Mandritsara

Mahajanga
Marovoay
33ft
Tanjona Vilanandro
Tanjona Masoala
Maevatanana
Nosy Boraha
Juan de Nova
(France)

Heleodrano Antongila

Maintirano
MADAGASCAR
Ambatondrazaka
Tsiroanomandidy
Toamasina
ANTANANARIVO
Tsiafajavona
8668ft
Moramanga
Vatomandry
17456ft
Belo Tsiribihina
Miandrivazo
Antsirabe
Mahanoro

Morondava
Ambositra
Manja
Mongoky
Massif du Makay
Fianarantsoa
Mananjary
Ihosy
Andringitra
Manakara

Toliara
Betroka
Ivakoany
Farafangana

MAURITIUS
PORT LOUIS
Curepipe
7544ft
Saint-Denis
Saint-Pierre
Réunion
(France)
13851ft

Mascarene Islands

Tropic of Capricorn

Ampanihy
Tôlanaro
13245ft
Ambovombe
14104ft
Tanjona
Vohimena

INDIAN OCEAN

R OBLATED PROJECTION
40°
G
45°
H
50°
J
55°
K

Scale 1:20 000 000

0   200   400   600   800   1000 km
0 100   200   300   400   500 600 miles
1 hour's flight

57

ASIA : Facts & Figures

AREA:
17,350,000 mi² / 44,900,000 km²

SIZE IN COMPARISON:
Largest continent

COASTLINE:
78,341 mi / 126,074 km

NUMBER OF COUNTRIES: 49

BIGGEST COUNTRY:
Russia
Area : 4,928,798 mi² / 12,765,600 km²
Population: 147,231,000 (1998)

SMALLEST COUNTRY:
Maldives
Area: 115 mi² / 298 km²
Population: 284,000 (1998)

BIGGEST CITY:
Mumbai, India
Population: 15,700,000 (1996)

HIGHEST MOUNTAIN:
Mount Everest
29,181 ft / 8,848 m
First conquered by:
Edmund Hillary and
Tenzing Norgay, 1953

LOWEST LAND:
Dead Sea shore
1,309 ft / 399 m below sea level

BIGGEST LAKE:
Caspian Sea,
143,243 mi² / 371,000 km²

LONGEST RIVER:
Changjiang 3,714 mi / 5,980 km

HOTTEST TEMPERATURE:
54°C / 129°F Tirat Tsri, Israel

COLDEST TEMPERATURE:
-72°C / -162°F Oymyakon, Russia

LENGTH OF ROAD NETWORK:
3,931,273 mi / 6,326,598 km

LENGTH OF RAIL NETWORK:
198,850 mi / 320,000 km

% WORLD OIL PRODUCTION:
41.3%

% WORLD GOLD PRODUCTION:
21%

SOME ENDANGERED ANIMALS:

Tiger

Snow Leopard

Polar Bear

Indian Elephant

Siberian Musk Deer

Great Indian Rhinoceros

Chinese Alligator

Caspian Seal

Hawksbill Turtle

Horseshoe Crab

NUMBER OF INHABITANTS:
3,458,000,000

POPULATION DENSITY:
282 per mi² / 109 per km²
Highest:
Singapore 14,182 per mi² / 5,476 per km²
Lowest:
Mongolia 5 per mi² / 2 per km²

POP. GROWTH PER ANNUM: +1.9%
Highest: Afghanistan +5.3%
Lowest: Georgia -0.1%

% MALE/FEMALE:
52.1% M, 47.9% F
Greatest difference:
Qatar 67.1% M, 32.9% F
Least difference:
Mongolia, Thailand, Yemen
50% M, 50% F

LIFE EXPECTANCY AT BIRTH:
64.8yrs Male, 67.7yrs Female
Highest: Japan 77yrs M, 83yrs F
Lowest: Afghanistan 45yrs M, 46yrs F

MARRIAGE RATE per 1000 annually: 7.2
Highest: Bangladesh 10.9
Lowest: Qatar 2.5

DIVORCE RATE per 1000 annually: 1.8
Highest: China 4.6
Lowest: Iran 0.5

AVERAGE SIZE OF HOUSEHOLD:
5.2
Highest: Iraq 7.1
Lowest: Japan 3.0

MAIN LANGUAGES:
Arabic, Chinese, English, Russian

MAIN RELIGIONS (%):
43% Muslim, 14% Buddhist,
5% Hindu, 5% Christian, also
Animist, Jewish, Chinese religions
and Shinto

OLDEST UNIVERSITY:
Santo Tomàs, Manila, Philippines
1611

LARGEST UNIVERSITY:
University of Kolkata (Calcutta), India
300,000 students

LITERACY: 73%
Highest:
Japan, N. Korea, Georgia, Armenia 99%
Lowest: Nepal 31%

Sources: The Statesman's Yearbook 1998/99
UN Statistical Yearbook 42nd edition

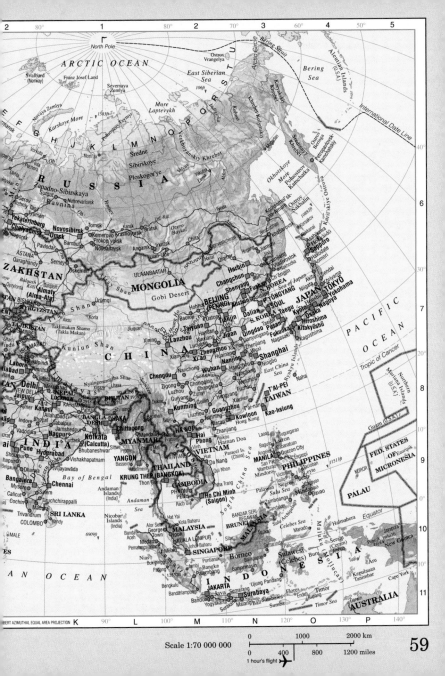

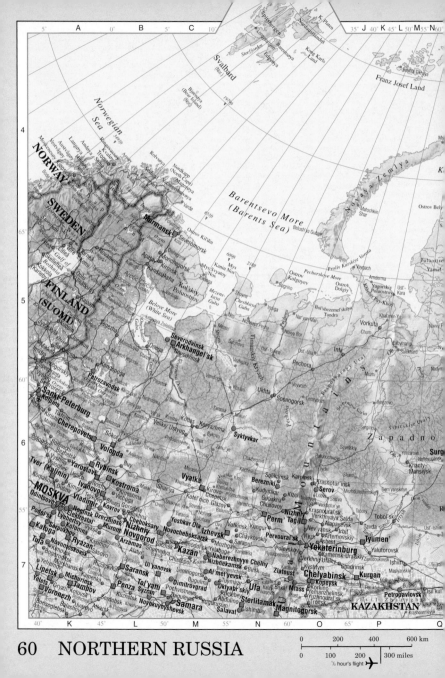

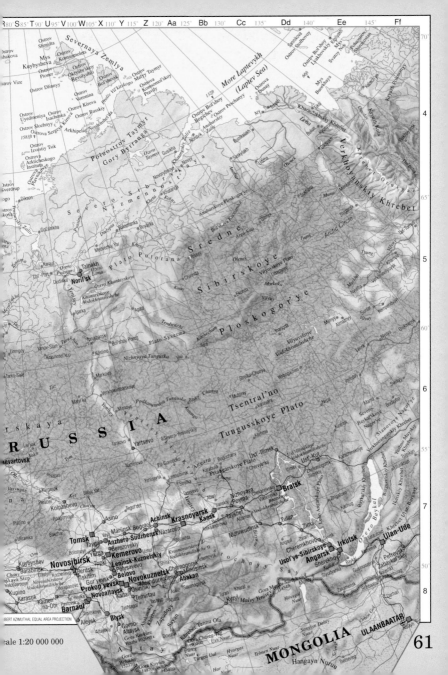

Scale 1:20 000 000

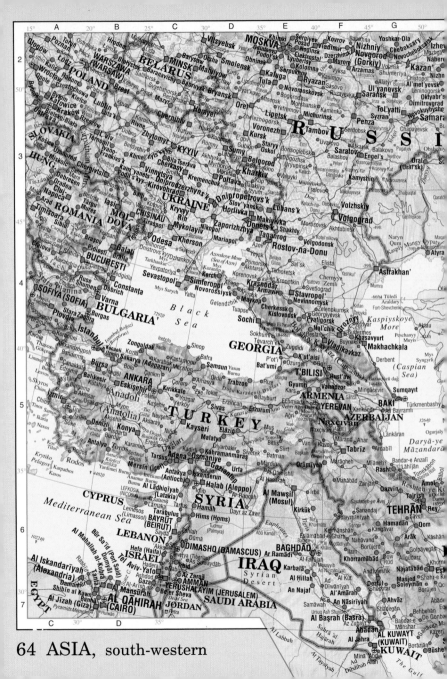

64 ASIA, south-western

Scale 1:20 000 000

| 0 | 200 | 400 | 600 | 800 | 1000 km |

| 0 | 100 | 200 | 300 | 400 | 500 | 600 miles |

1 hour's flight

BERTS CONFORMAL CONIC PROJECTION

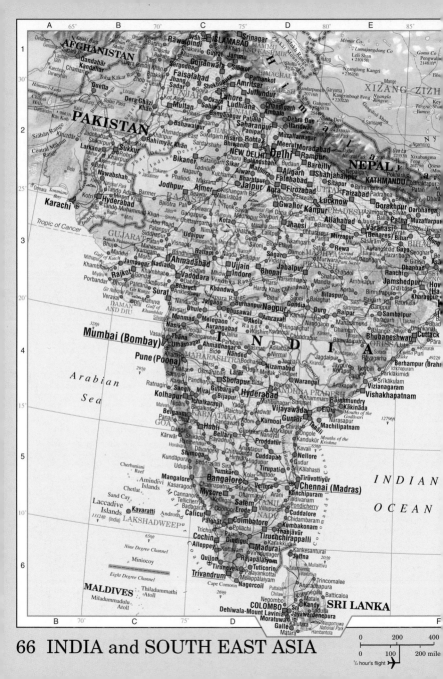

66 INDIA and SOUTH EAST ASIA

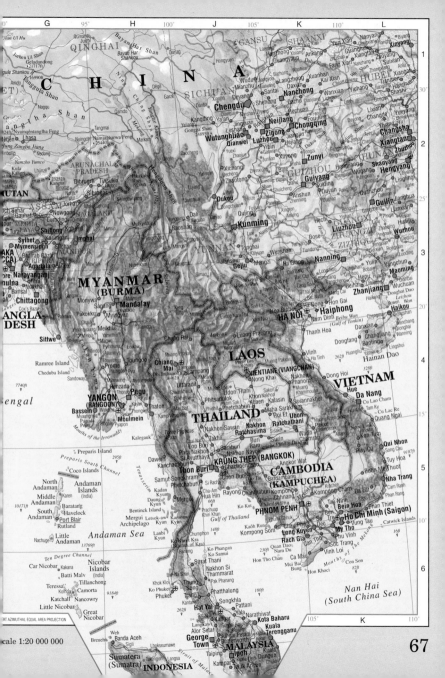

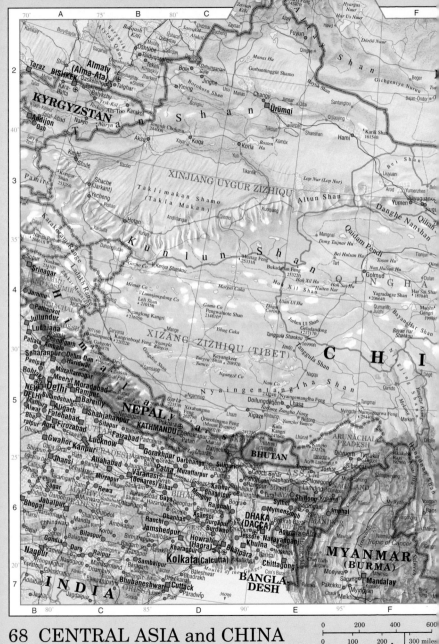

0	200	400	600
0	100	200	300 miles

½ hour's flight

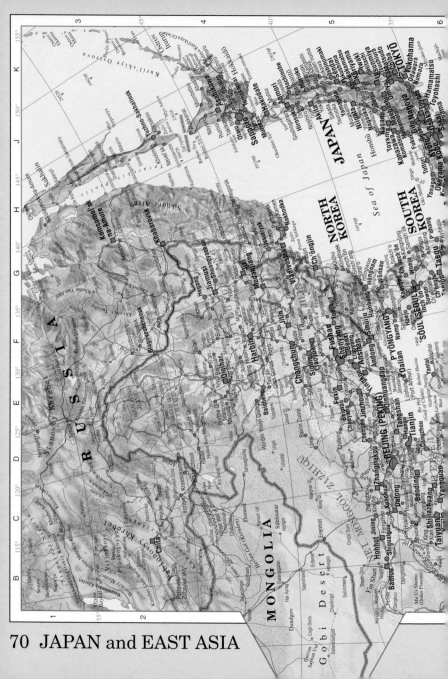

70 JAPAN and EAST ASIA

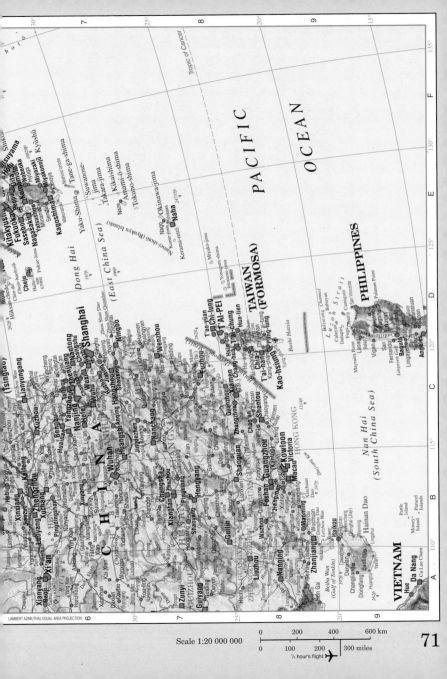

72 EAST INDIES

AUSTRALASIA : Facts & Figures

AREA:
3,397,946 mi² / 8,800,000 km²

SIZE IN COMPARISON:
Smallest continent

NUMBER OF COUNTRIES: 14

BIGGEST COUNTRY: Australia
Area : 2,966,368 mi² / 7,682,300 km²
Population: 18,490,000 (1998)

SMALLEST COUNTRY: Nauru
Area: 8 mi² / 21.3 km²
Population: 11,000 (1998)

BIGGEST CITY: Sydney
Population: 3,770,100 (1995)

HIGHEST MOUNTAIN:
Puncak Jaya, 16,503 ft / 5,030 m
First conquered by:
H. Harrer, A. Huizeng,
R. Kippax, P. Temple 1962

LONGEST REEF:
The Great Barrier Reef
1,180 mi / 1,900 km
The World's longest coral reef

DEEPEST DEPRESSION:
Lake Eyre, -38 ft / -12 m

LARGEST ISLAND:
New Guinea,
317,025 mi² / 821,030 km²
(World's 2nd largest)

LENGTH OF ROAD NETWORK:
580,428 mi / 934,083 km

LENGTH OF RAIL NETWORK:
26,013 mi / 41,863 km

% WORLD OIL PRODUCTION:
1%

% WORLD GOLD PRODUCTION:
15.4%

NUMBER OF INHABITANTS:
28,500,000

POPULATION DENSITY:
315 per mi² / 121.6 per km²
Highest:
Nauru 380 per mi² / 480 per km²
Lowest:
Australia 5 per mi² / 2 per km²

POP. GROWTH PER ANNUM: +2%
Highest:
Solomon Islands +3.2%
Lowest:
Tonga +0.4%

% MALE/FEMALE:
50.5% M, 49.5% F
Greatest difference:
Tuvalu 47.4% M, 52.6% F
Least difference:
Australia 49.9% M, 50.1% F

LIFE EXPECTANCY AT BIRTH:
71.5yrs Male, 76.4yrs Female
Highest:
Australia 75yrs M, 81yrs F
Lowest:
Papua New Guinea 59yrs M, 59yrs F

MARRIAGE RATE per 1000 annually: 5.9
Highest: New Zealand 6.3
Lowest: Kiribati 5.2

DIVORCE RATE per 1000 annually: 1.9
Highest: Australia 2.7
Lowest: Western Samoa 0.3

AVERAGE SIZE OF HOUSEHOLD:
3.8
Highest: Fiji 5.8
Lowest: Australia 2.6

MAIN LANGUAGES:
English, Local, some Japanese
and French

MAIN RELIGIONS (%):
72% Christian, 38% Hindu,
also Muslim, Buddhist, Jewish
and Traditional

OLDEST UNIVERSITY:
University of Sydney, Sydney,
Australia, 1850

LARGEST UNIVERSITY:
University of Sydney
30,990 students

LITERACY: 84%
Highest:
Australia, Nauru, New Zealand 99%
Lowest:
Vanuatu 53%

SOME ENDANGERED ANIMALS:

Long-beaked Echidna

Tusked Weta

Australian Freshwater Limpet

Northern hairy-nosed Wombat

Sea Lion

Queen Alexandra's Birdwing

Leadbeater's Possum

Dugong

White Headed Dolphin

Three-toed Snake-tooth Skink

Flatback

Ghost Bat

Black-striped Snake

Estuarine Crocodile

Western Swamp Turtle

Rock Lobster

Sources: The Statesman's Yearbook 1998/99
UN Statistical Yearbook 42nd edition

A LAMBERTS CONFORMAL CONIC PROJECTION

| 0 | 500 | 1000 |
| 0 | 250 | 500 | 750 miles |

1 hours flight ✈

76 AUSTRALIA and NEW ZEALAND

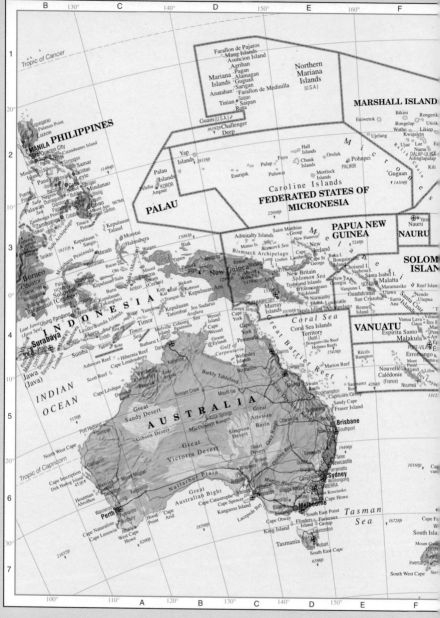

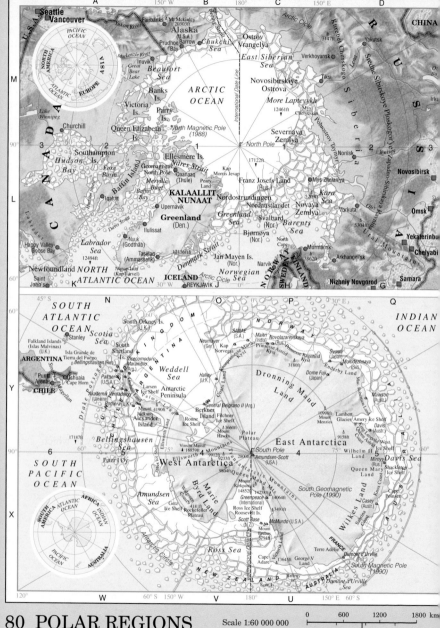

Scale 1:60 000 000

0	600	1200	1800 km

0	300	600	900 miles

1 hour's flight

⊛ **INDEX** ⊛

The index for the World Atlas was created digitally from a database and contains approximately 15,500 entries.

How to use the index: if you are looking for the town of Dublin, Ireland for example, simply find the entry in the alphabetical index listing and it will give you a page number (bold type) followed by a grid reference (letter and number). For example , Dublin **16** B3. Then go to the top or bottom of the page to find the index letter and to the left or right of the page to find the index number. Use these references to locate the required grid square and find Dublin.

Double entries: referring to different areas- Arlington **37** G5 and Arlington **37** L4. In this case the state name is added to distinguish between the two - Arlington (Texas, U.S.A) **37** G5 and Arlington (Washington, U.S.A) **37** L4. This could also occur with countries - Faro **18** A3, Faro **31** O3 and Faro **44** E2, so the country name is added. These entries will therefore appear as Faro (Brazil) **44** E2, Faro (Canada) **31** O3 and Faro (Portugal) **18** A3.

Double entries: referring to different features- Dagana **50** C5 and Dagana **52** C5. In this case the feature type is added to distinguish so these entries will appear as - Dagana **50** C5 and Dagana (River) **52** C5.

Local/English name forms: Entries such as Al Qāhirah (Cairo) will appear twice - under "A" for Al Qahirah and also under "C" for Cairo.

Former name forms: Country names which have changed recently or which appear on the map pages in their local language and in English will also be entrered twice - Myanmar **67** G3 and former name Burma **67** G3.

Map scales: All entries are referenced to the largest scale map it appears on.

A Coruña 18 A 2
Aachen 16 E 3
Aalen 17 F 4
Aare 19 D 1
Aasiaat 33 Aa 5
Aba 51 H 7
Ābādān 53 J 1
Ābādeh 64 H 6
Abaeté 45 G 5
Abaetetuba 45 G' 2
Abag Qi 70 B 4
Abagnar Qi 70 C 4
Abaiang 79 G 3
Abakaliki 51 H 7
Abakan 61 U 7
Abakanskiy Khrebet
  61 T 7
Aban 61 V 6
Abancay 44 B 4
Abariringa 79 H 4
Abashiri 70 H 4
Abay 65 M 3
Abaza 61 U 7
Abbeville (France)
  16 D 3
Abbeville (U.S.A.)
  37 H 6
Abd al Kūri 53 K 5
Abdulino 23 H 2
Abéché 52 D 5
Abel Tasman
  National Park 77 N 8
Abemama 79 G 3
Abengourou 51 F 7
Abeokuta 51 G 7
Aberdeen (U.K.) 16 C 2
Aberdeen (U.S.A.)
  36 G 2
Aberdeen Lake
  34 H 2
Abert, Lake 36 B 3
Aberystwyth 16 C 3
Abganerovo 23 F 3
Abha 53 H 4
Abidjan 50 F 7
Abilene 36 G 5
Abisko 26 J 2
Abnüb 52 F 2
Åbo 27 K 3
Abo, Massif d' 52 C 3
Abraham's Bay 39 J 3
Abrolhos, Arquipélago
  dos 45 J 5
Abruka Saar 27 K 4
Abū Arīsh 53 H 4
Abu Dhabi 53 K 3
Abū Kamāl 64 F 6
Abu Road 66 C 3
Abū Tīj 52 F 2
Abu Zaby 53 K 3
Abuna 44 C 3
Abyad, Jabal 52 E 4

Acacias 42 E 4
Acadia National Park
  37 N 3
Acámbaro 38 B 3
Acaponeta 38 A 3
Acapulco 38 C 4
Acarai, Serra 43 H 4
Acaraú 45 H 2
Acarigua 43 F 3
Acayucan 38 D 4
Accra 51 F 7
Acheng 70 E 3
Achill Head 16 A 3
Achinsk 61 U 6
Acireale 19 F 3
Acklins Island 39 H 3
Aconcagua, Cerro
  46 C 5
Acopiara 45 J 3
Acre 44 B 3
Acri 19 G 3
Actopan 38 D 3
Açude Araras 45 H 2
Acuracay 42 E 6
Ad Dabbah 52 F 4
Ad Dahnā 53 J 3
Ad' Dāmir 52 F 4
Ad Dammām 53 K 2
Ad Dawhah 53 K 2
Ad Dibdībah 53 J 2
Ad Diffah 52 D 1
Ad Dikākah 53 K 4
Ad Dīwānīyah 64 F 6
Ad Duwaym 52 F 5
Ad Ou'ayn 52 E 5
Ada 37 G 5
Adair, Cape 33 W 4
Adak Island 30 E 5
Adamantina 46 G 3
Adamaoua 54 B 2
Adamaoua, Massif de l'
  54 B 2
Adamstown 79 M 6
Adana 64 E 5
Adapazarı 64 D 4
Addis Abeba 53 G 6
Adelaide 77 F 6
Adele Island 76 C 3
Aden, Gulf of 53 J 5
Adi 73 J 6
Adi Kaie 53 G 5
Adi Ugri 53 G 5
Adigrat 53 G 5
Adilabad 66 D 4
Admiralty Island 31 O 4
Admiralty Islands 78 D 4
Ado 51 G 7
Ādoni 66 D 4
Adra 18 C 3
Adras 51 F 3
Adriatic Sea 19 F 2
Adwa 53 G 5
Adycha 62 L 3
Adzopé 51 F 7
Aegean Sea 21 D 5
Affolé 50 D 5
Afghanistan 65 K 6
Afikpo 51 H 7

Afognak Island 30 K 4
Afyon 64 D 5
Agadez 51 H 5
Agadir 50 E 2
Agartala 67 G 3
Agata 61 U 4
Agattu Island 30 C 5
Agawa Bay 34 L 5
Agboville 50 F 7
Agen 18 C 2
Agnibilékrou 51 F 7
Agra 66 D 2
Ağrı 64 F 5
Ağrı Dağı 64 F 5
Agrigento 19 E 3
Agrihan 78 D 2
Agrinio 21 D 5
Agua Branca 45 H 3
Agua Prieta 36 E 5
Agua Vermelha,
  Represa 46 H 3
Aguadulce 39 F 6
Aguascalientes 38 B 3
Águilas 18 C 3
Agulhas, Cape 56 C 6
Ahaggar 51 H 4
Ahar 64 G 5
Ahe 79 L 5
Ahlat 64 F 5
Ahmadābād 66 C 3
Ahmadnagar 66 C 4
Ahmadpur East 66 C 2
Ahmar, Erg el 50 F 4
Ahmar Mountains
  53 H 6
Ahunui 79 L 5
Ahvāz 53 J 1
Ahvenanmaa 27 J 3
Aihun 70 E 2
Aiken 37 K 5
Aileron 76 E 4
Ailinglapalap 78 F 3
Ailuk 78 F 2
Aim 62 K 5
Aimorés 45 H 5
Aïn Amenas 51 H 3
Aïn Beïda 51 H 1
Aïn Temouchent 51 F 1
Aina 27 K 4
Aïr 51 H 5
Air Force Island 33 W 5
Aitutaki Island 79 K 5
Aix-en-Provence 19 D 2
Āīzawl 67 G 3
Aizuwakamatsu 70 G 5
Ajaccio 19 D 2
Ajanta Range 66 D 3
Ajdābiyā 52 D 1
Ajdir, Ra's 52 B 1
Ajka 20 C 3
Ajmer 66 C 2
Akaki Beseka 53 G 6
Akashi 70 F 6
Akbaba Tepe 64 E 5
Akbulak 23 J 2
Ak-Dovurak 61 U 7
Akelamo 73 H 3
Aketi 54 D 3

Akhisar 64 C 5
Akhtubinsk 23 G 3
Akimiski Island 35 L 4
Akita 70 H 5
Akjoujt 50 D 5
'Akko 52 G 1
Aklé Aouana 50 E 5
Akola 66 D 3
Akordat 53 G 4
Akpatok Island 35 O 2
Akron 37 K 3
Aksaray 64 D 5
Akşehir 64 D 5
Aksha 62 F 6
Aksu 68 C 2
Aksum 53 G 5
Aktau 64 H 4
Aktobe 65 H 4
Akun Island 30 G 5
Akureyri 26 B 2
Akutan Island 30 G 5
Al' Amārah 64 G 6
Al-Arīsh 52 F 1
Al' Armah 53 J 2
Al' Atrun 52 E 4
Al-'Ayn 53 L 3
Al Badārī 52 F 2
Al-Balyanā 52 F 2
Al Başrah 64 G 6
Al Bayādh 53 J 3
Al Baydā 52 D 1
Al Fallūjah 64 F 6
Al Fāshir 52 E 5
Al Fashn 52 F 2
Al Fayyūm 52 F 2
Al Hamādah al
  Hamrā' 52 A 2
Al Hanish al Kabir
  53 H 5
Al Hanīyah 64 G 7
Al Harūjal Aswad 52 C 2
Al Hasakah 64 F 5
Al Hibāk 53 K 4
Al Hijāz 53 G 2
Al Hillah 64 F 6
Al-Hoceima 51 F 1
Al Hudaydah 53 H 5
Al Hufūf 53 J 2
Al Iglim al Janūbīyah
  52 E 6
Al Iskandarīyah 52 E 1
Al Ismā'īlīyah 52 F 1
Al Jafūrah 53 K 3
Al Jaghbūb 52 D 2
Al Jahra 64 G 7
Al Jawf 53 G 2
Al Jazā'ir 51 G 1
Al Jazīrah 64 F 6
Al Jiwā' 53 K 3
Al Jīzah 52 F 1
Al Jubayl 53 J 2
Al Junaynah 52 D 5
Al Kāf 51 H 1
Al Karak 53 G 1
Al Katham 53 L 3
Al Khālis 64 F 6
Al Khārijah 52 F 2
Al Kharṭūm 52 F 4

Al Khartūm Bahrī **52** F 4
Al Khubar **53** K 2
Al Khums **52** B 1
Al Khunfah **53** G 2
Al Kidn **53** K 3
Al Kūt **64** G 6
Al Kuwayt **64** G 7
Al Labbah **53** H 2
Al Lādhiqīyah **64** E 5
Al Lasā **53** J 2
Al Līth **53** H 4
Al Madīnah **53** G 3
Al Madōw **55** J 1
Al Mahallah al-Kubrā
 52 F 1
Al Mahrah **53** K 4
Al Manāmah **53** K 2
Al Mansūrah **52** F 1
Al Marij **52** D 1
Al Mawşil **64** F 5
Al Minyā **52** F 2
Al Miqdādīyah **64** F 6
Al Mubarraz **53** J 2
Al Muglad **52** E 5
Al Muharraq **53** K 2
Al Mukallā **53** J 5
Al Musayyib **64** F 6
Al Qāämīyāt **53** J 4
Al Qadārif **53** G 5
Al Qaddāhīyah **52** C 1
Al Qāhirah **52** F 1
Al Qāmishlī **64** F 5
Al Qūsīyah **52** F 2
Al Siwah **52** E 2
Al Tranallo **46** C 4
Al Ubayyid **52** F 5
Al Uqsur **52** F 2
Al Wajh **53** G 2
Al Widyān **53** H 1
Alabama **37** J 5
Alacrán **38** E 3
Alagoas **45** J 3
Alagoinhas **45** J 4
Alajuela **38** F 5
Alaköl **65** O 3
Alakurtti **24** D 1
Alamagan **78** D 2
Alamogordo **36** E 5
Åland **27** J 3
Ålands hav **27** J 4
Alapayevsk **25** K 3
Alaska **30** H 2
Alaska, Gulf of **30** L 4
Alaska Peninsula
 30 H 4
Alaska Range **30** K 3
Alatyr' **23** G 2
Alazeya **63** O 3
Alazeyskoye
 Ploskogor'ye **62** N 3
Alb **34** L 4
Alba **19** D 2
Alba-Iulia **20** D 3
Albacete **18** B 3
Albania **21** C 4
Albano Laziale **19** E 2
Albany (Australia)
 76 B 7

Albany (Georgia,
 U.S.A.) **37** K 5
Albany (New York,
 U.S.A.) **37** M 3
Albany (Oregon, U.S.A.)
 36 B 3
Albany River **35** L 5
Albatross Bay **77** G 2
Albert Nile **55** F 3
Alberta **31** R 4
Albi **18** C 2
Ålborg **27** G 4
Albstadt **17** E 4
Albuquerque **36** E 4
Albuquerque, Cayos de
 38 F 5
Albury **77** H 7
Alcalá de Guadaira
 18 A 3
Alcalá de Henares
 18 B 2
Alcamo **19** E 3
Alcázar de San Juan
 18 C 3
Alchevs'k **23** E 3
Alcolea del Pinar **18** C 2
Alcoy **18** B 3
Aldabra Islands **55** J 5
Aldan **62** J 5
Aldan (River) **62** K 4
Aldanskoye Nagor'ye
 62 J 5
Aleg **50** D 5
Alegrete **46** F 4
Alejandro Selkirk, Isla
 47 A 5
Aleksandrov **24** E 3
Aleksandrov Gay **23** G 2
Aleksandrovsk-
 Sakhalinskiy **62** M 6
Alekseyevka **23** E 2
Alençon **18** C 1
Alenquer **45** F 2
Aleppo **64** E 5
Aléria **19** E 2
Alert Point **32** T 2
Alès **18** C 2
Alessandria **19** D 2
Ålesund **26** G 3
Aleutian Islands **30** E 5
Aleutian Range **30** J 4
Alexander, Kap **33** W 3
Alexander Archipelago
 31 N 4
Alexander Island **80** Y 5
Alexandra **77** M 9
Alexandra Falls **32** N 6
Alexandria (Egypt)
 52 E 1
Alexandria (Louisiana,
 U.S.A.) **37** H 5
Alexandria (Romania)
 21 E 4
Alexandria (Washington,
 U.S.A.) **37** L 4
Alexandroupoli **21** E 4
Aleysk **61** S 7
Algarve **18** A 3

Algeciras **18** A 3
Algeria **51** F 2
Algha **65** J 3
Alghero **19** D 2
Algiers **51** G 1
Algoa Bay **56** D 6
Ali **51** F 5
Āli-Bayramlı **64** G 5
Alia **77** F 6
Alicante **18** B 3
Alice **36** G 6
Alice Springs **76** E 4
Aligarh **66** D 2
Alīgūdarz **64** G 6
Alim Island **78** D 4
Alitak, Cape **30** J 4
Aliwal North **56** D 6
Alkmaar **16** D 3
Allahabad **66** E 2
Allakaket **30** K 2
Allanmyo **67** H 4
Allegheny Plateau
 37 K 4
Allende **36** F 6
Allentown **37** L 3
Alleppey **66** D 6
Alliance **36** F 3
Alma **35** N 5
Alma-Ata **65** N 4
Almansa **18** C 3
Almaty **65** N 4
Almaznyy **61** Y 5
Almenara **45** H 5
Almería **18** B 3
Al'met'yevsk **23** H 2
Alnwick **16** C 2
Alofi, Île **79** H 5
Alor **73** G 7
Alor Setar **72** C 4
Alpena **37** K 2
Alpercatas, Serra das
 45 G 3
Alps, The **19** D 1
Alta **26** K 2
Alta Gracia **46** E 5
Altai Shan **68** D 1
Altamira **45** F 2
Altamura **19** F 2
Altanbulag **61** X 7
Altay **68** D 1
Altayskiy **61** T 7
Alto Araguaia **45** F 5
Alto Garças **45** F 5
Alto Molocue **57** F 2
Alto Rio Mayo **47** C 8
Alton **37** H 4
Altun Ha **38** E 4
Altun Shan **68** E 3
Altus **36** G 5
Alva **36** G 4
Alvarado **38** C 4
Alvord Valley **36** C 3
Alwar **66** D 2
Alxa Zuoqi **69** H 3
Alyaskitovyy **62** M 4
Alytus **27** K 5
Alzamay **61** V 6
Alzira **18** B 3

Am Djéména **52** C 5
Am Tīman **52** D 5
Amadeus, Lake **76** E 5
Amadi **52** F 6
Amadjuak Lake **35** N 2
Amahai **73** H 6
Amambai **45** E 6
Amami-ō-shima **71** E 7
Amanu **79** L 5
Amanu-Runga **79** L 6
Amanzimtoti **56** E 6
Amapá (Brazil) **45** F 1
Amapá (State, Brazil)
 45 F 1
Amapu-Raro **79** L 6
Amarillo **36** F 4
Amaro Leite **45** G 4
Amasya **64** E 4
Amazonas **44** C 2
Amazonas, Rio **42** E 5
Amba Farit **53** G 5
Ambala **66** D 1
Ambam **54** B 3
Ambarawa **72** E 7
Ambarchik **63** Q 3
Ambardakh **62** L 2
Ambato **42** D 5
Ambatondrazaka **57** H 3
Amberg **17** F 4
Ambikapur **66** E 3
Ambilobe **57** H 2
Ambon **73** H 6
Ambon (Island) **73** H 6
Ambositra **57** H 4
Ambovombe **57** H 5
Ambriz **54** B 5
Ambrym **78** F 1
Amderma **60** O 4
Amdo **68** E 4
Ameca **38** B 3
American Samoa **79** J 5
Americus **37** K 5
Amga **62** K 4
Amgun' **62** L 6
Amhara Welo **53** G 5
Amiens **16** D 4
Amīndīvi Islands **66** C 5
Amirante Islands **55** K 5
Amlia Island **30** F 5
Ammān **53** G 1
Ammassalik **33** Dd 5
Åmol **64** H 5
Amorgos **21** E 5
Amos **35** M 5
Åmot **27** G 4
Amoy **69** K 6
Ampanihy **57** G 4
Amravati **66** D 3
Amritsar **66** C 1
Amsterdam **16** D 3
Amund Ringnes Island
 32 R 3
Amundsen Gulf **32** L 4
Amur **62** J 6
An Nafūd **53** G 2
An Nahūd **52** E 5
An Najaf **64** F 6
An Nāsirīyah **64** G 6

Arezzo **19** E 2
Arga-Sala **61** Y 4
Argentina **47** D 6
Argentino, Lago **47** C 9
Argos **21** D 5
Arguin, Cap d' **50** C 4
Argun **70** C 2
Argungu **51** G 6
Argyle, Lake **76** D 3
Århus **27** H 4
Arica **46** C 2
Arid, Cape **76** C 6
Arima **39** K 5
Aripuanã, Rio **44** D 3
Ariquemes **44** D 3
Arismendi **43** F 3
Arizaro, Salar de **46** D 3
Arizgoit **18** B 2
Arizona **36** D 5
Arjeplog **26** J 2
Arjona **42** D 2
Arkadak **23** F 2
Arkadelphia **37** H 5
Arkansas **37** H 4
Arkansas City **37** G 4
Arkansas River **36** F 4
Arklow **16** B 3
Arkticheskogo Instituta, Ostrova **61** S 2
Arles **19** C 2
Arlington (Texas, U.S.A.) **37** G 5
Arlington (Washington, U.S.A.) **37** L 4
Armadale **76** B 6
Armagh **16** B 3
Armagnac **18** C 2
Armant **52** F 2
Armavir **23** F 4
Armenia **64** F 4
Armenia (Colombia) **42** D 4
Armeria **38** B 4
Armidale **77** J 6
Armstrong **34** K 4
Arnhem **16** E 3
Arnhem Land **76** E 2
Arno **79** G 3
Arnøy **26** K 1
Arod **68** F 2
Arorae **79** G 4
Arqalyq **65** L 2
Arrah **66** E 2
Arran **16** B 2
Arras **16** D 3
Arrecife **50** D 3
Arrecífe **38** E 3
Arrecifes **38** D 3
Arriaga **38** E 4
Arroio Grande **46** G 5
Arsen'yev **70** F 4
Arta **21** D 5
Artá **18** C 3
Artem **70** F 4
Artemisa **38** F 3
Artemivs'k **22** K 3
Artemovsk **61** U 7
Artemovskiy **25** K 3

Artesia **36** F 5
Artigas **46** F 5
Artillery Lake **34** F 2
Aru, Kepulauan **73** K 7
Arua **55** F 3
Aruaja **44** C 3
Aruanã **45** F 4
Aruba **39** J 5
Arun Qi **70** D 3
Arunāchal Pradesh **67** G 2
Arusha **55** G 4
Arviat **34** J 2
Arvidsjaur **26** J 2
Arvika **27** H 4
Arxan **70** C 3
Ary **62** H 2
Arys **65** L 4
Arzamas **23** F 1
Aş Şahrā' al Janūbīyah **52** E 3
Aş Şahrā' an Nūbiyah **53** G 3
Aş Şahrā' ash Sharqīyah **52** F 2
As Samāwah **64** G 6
As Sarīr **52** D 2
As Sulaymānīyah **64** G 5
As Sulayyil **53** J 3
As Summān **53** H 2
As Suwaydāh **64** E 6
As Suways **52** F 2
Asahikawa **70** H 4
Āsānsol **66** F 3
Asbest **25** K 3
Ascención **44** D 5
Ascoli Piceno **19** E 2
Asēanām **53** K 3
Asedjrad **51** G 3
Åsele **26** J 3
Aselle **53** G 6
Ash Shallāl al Khamis **52** F 4
Ash Shallāl ar Rabi' **52** F 4
Ash Shallāl as Sablūkah **52** F 4
Ash Shallālath Thālith **52** F 4
Ash Shaqrā' **53** J 2
Ash Shāriqah **53** L 2
Ash Shihr **53** J 5
Asha **25** J 4
Ashanti **51** F 7
Ashburton **77** N 8
Ashdod **52** F 1
Ashgabat **65** J 5
Ashkhabad **65** J 5
Ashland (Kentucky, U.S.A.) **37** K 4
Ashland (Oregon, U.S.A.) **36** B 3
Ashland (Wisconsin, U.S.A.) **37** H 2
Ashmore Reef **76** C 2
Ashton **36** D 3
Asino **61** T 6

Asipovichy **22** C 2
Askim **27** H 4
Askiz **61** U 7
Asmara **53** G 4
Aspiring, Mount **77** M 8
Assab **53** H 5
Assam **67** G 2
Assen **16** E 3
Assis **46** G 3
Astana **65** M 2
Asti **19** D 2
Astorga **18** B 2
Astrakhan' **23** G 3
Astrolabe, Récifs de **78** F 5
Astypalaia **21** E 5
Asunción **46** F 4
Asuncion Island **78** D 2
Aswān **52** F 3
Aswān High Dam **52** F 3
Asyūt **52** F 2
At Taff **53** K 3
At Tā'if **53** H 3
At Tawīl **53** G 2
At Taysīyah **53** H 2
Atacama Desert **46** D 4
Atacama, Desierto do **46** D 4
Atacama, Salar de **46** D 3
Atafu **79** H 4
Atakpamé **51** G 7
Atalya **44** B 4
Atar **50** D 4
Atascadero **36** B 4
Atasu **65** M 3
Atauro **73** H 7
Atbarah **52** F 4
Atbasar **65** L 2
Atchison **37** G 4
Athabasca **31** S 5
Athabasca, Lake **34** F 3
Athens (Georgia, U.S.A.) **37** K 5
Athens (Greece) **21** D 5
Athens (Tennessee, U.S.A.) **37** K 4
Athina **21** D 5
Athlone **16** B 3
Atico **44** B 5
Atiu **79** K 6
Atka **30** F 5
Atka Island **30** E 5
Atkarsk **23** F 2
Atlanta **37** K 5
Atlantic City **37** M 4
Atlantic Ocean **18** B 1
Atlasova, Ostrov **63** P 6
Atlin Lake **31** O 4
Atouila, Erg **50** E 4
Atqasuk **30** J 1
Ātran **27** H 4
Attapu **67** K 5
Attu Island **30** C 5
Atuel, Bañados del **47** D 6
Atyraū **64** H 3

Aubagne **19** D 2
Aubry Lake **32** L 5
Auburn **37** M 3
Auckland **77** N 7
Augsburg **17** F 4
Augusta (Australia) **76** B 6
Augusta (Georgia, U.S.A.) **37** K 5
Augusta (Maine, U.S.A.) **37** N 3
Augustów **17** H 3
Auld, Lake **76** C 4
Aur **79** G 3
Aurangabad **66** D 4
Aurangābād **66** E 3
Aurich **17** E 3
Aurillac **18** C 2
Aurora **36** F 4
Aust-Agder **27** G 4
Austin (Minnesota, U.S.A.) **37** H 3
Austin (Texas, U.S.A.) **37** G 5
Austin, Lake **76** B 5
Australia **76** D 4
Australian Alps **77** H 7
Australian Capital Territory **77** H 7
Austria **19** E 2
Austvågøy **26** H 2
Autlán **38** B 4
Auxerre **18** C 1
Auyuittuq National Park **33** X 5
Auzangate, Nevado **44** B 4
Avallon **18** C 1
Avan **65** K 3
Avaré **46** H 3
Aveiro **18** A 2
Avellaneda **46** F 5
Avellino **19** E 2
Averøya **26** G 3
Avesta **27** J 3
Avezzano **19** E 2
Avignon **19** C 2
Ávila **18** B 2
Avilés **18** A 2
Avola **19** F 3
Awara Plain **55** H 3
Awasa **53** G 6
Awka **51** H 7
Axel Heiberg Island **32** S 3
Axinim **44** E 2
Ayachi, Jbel **50** F 2
Ayacucho (Argentina) **47** F 6
Ayacucho (Peru) **44** B 4
Ayagoz **65** O 3
Ayamonte **18** B 3
Ayan **62** L 5
Ayaviri **44** B 4
Aydın **64** C 5
Ayers Rock-Mount Olga National Park **76** E 5
Aylmer Lake **34** F 2

Ayon, Ostrov **63** R 3
Ayr **16** C 2
Ayteke Bi **65** K 3
Az Zahrān **53** K 2
Az Zarqā **53** G 1
Az Zubayr **64** G 6
Azamgarh **66** E 2
Azaouad **51** F 5
Azare **51** J 6
Azeff, Dunes de l'
  50 C 4
Azerbaijan **64** G 4
Azogues **42** D 5
Azores **50** A 1
Azov **23** E 3
Azov, Sea of **22** E 3
Azovskoye More **22** E 3
Azrou **50** E 2
Azua **39** H 4
Azul **47** F 6
Azul, Cordillera **42** D 6

B

Baardheere **55** H 3
Bab al Māndab **53** H 5
Baba Burun **21** E 5
Babahoyo **42** D 5
Babar, Kepulauan
  73 H 7
Babayevo **24** E 3
Babi **72** B 5
Babine Lake **31** P 5
Bābol **64** H 5
Babruysk **22** C 2
Babuyan **69** L 7
Bac Can **67** K 3
Bac Ninh **67** K 3
Bacabai **44** E 3
Bacabal **45** H 2
Bacan **73** H 6
Bacău **20** E 3
Bachu **68** B 3
Bacolod **73** G 3
Badagara **66** D 5
Badajoz **18** A 3
Baden-Baden **17** E 4
Badin **66** B 3
Badjawa **73** G 7
Badland **36** F 2
Badulla **66** E 6
Bafang **54** B 2
Baffin Bay **33** W 4
Baffin Island **33** U 4
Bafing **50** D 6
Bafoulabé **50** D 6
Bafoussam **54** B 2
Bafra **64** E 4
Baga Bogd Uul **69** G 2
Bagalkot **66** D 4

Bagamoyo **55** G 5
Baganga **73** H 4
Bagansiapiapi **72** C 5
Bagé **46** G 5
Baghdād **64** F 6
Bagheria **19** E 3
Baghlan **65** L 5
Bagley **37** G 2
Baguirmi **52** C 5
Bagulo **73** G 2
Bahama Islands **37** M 6
Bahamas, The **37** L 6
Bahar Dar **53** G 5
Baharīyah, Wāhāt al
  52 E 2
Bahawalpur **66** C 2
Bahia **45** H 4
Bahía, Islas de la **38** E 4
Bahía Blanca **47** E 6
Bahía Bustamante
  47 D 8
Bahía Negra **46** F 3
Bahr al Abyad **52** E 6
Bahr al Azraq **53** G 5
Bahr Aouk **52** C 6
Bahrain **53** K 2
Baia Mare **20** D 3
Baicheng **70** D 3
Baie-Comeau **35** O 5
Baie-du-Poste **35** N 4
Baile Átha Cliath **16** B 3
Bailique, Ilha **45** G 1
Bailundo **56** B 2
Bainbridge **37** K 5
Baiquan **70** E 3
Baïrar Rimāl al 'Azīm
  52 D 2
Bairin Zuoqi **70** C 4
Bairnsdale **77** H 7
Baja **20** C 3
Baja California **36** D 6
Bājah **51** H 1
Bajan-Öndör **68** F 2
Bajandelger **70** A 3
Bakal **25** J 4
Bakchar **61** S 6
Bake **72** C 6
Bakel **50** D 6
Baker **36** C 3
Baker Lake (Australia)
  76 D 5
Baker Lake (Canada)
  34 H 2
Bakersfield **36** C 4
Bakhmach **22** D 2
Bakı **64** G 4
Bala Murghab **65** K 5
Balad **64** F 6
Baladiyat 'Adan **53** H 5
Balagannoye **63** N 5
Balaghat **66** E 3
Bālāghat Range **66** D 4
Balakhna **25** F 3
Balakhta **61** U 6
Balakliya **22** E 3
Balakovo **23** G 2
Balangan Islands **73** F 6

Balangan, Kepulauan
  73 F 6
Bālangīr **66** E 3
Balashov **23** F 2
Balcarce **47** F 6
Balchik **21** E 4
Bale **53** H 6
Baleares, Islas **18** C 3
Balearic Islands **18** C 3
Baleia, Ponta da
  45 J 5
Baler **73** G 2
Bāleshwar **66** F 3
Baley **62** G 6
Balezino **25** H 3
Bali **72** E 7
Balıkesir **64** C 5
Balıkpapan **73** F 6
Balintang Channel
  69 L 7
Balladonia **76** C 6
Ballarat **77** G 7
Ballard, Lake **76** C 5
Ballia **66** E 2
Ballinger **36** G 5
Ballymena **16** B 3
Balotra **66** C 2
Balqash **65** M 3
Balqash Köli **65** N 3
Balrampur **66** E 2
Balsas **45** G 3
Balsas, Rio das **45** G 3
Balta **22** E 3
Baltasar Brum **46** F 5
Bālţi **22** E 3
Baltic Sea **27** J 4
Baltimore **37** L 4
Baltiysk **17** G 3
Balurghat **67** F 2
Balykchy **65** N 4
Bam **53** L 2
Bamaga **77** G 2
Bamako **50** E 6
Bambari **54** D 2
Bamberg **17** F 4
Bamenda **54** B 2
Bampton, Récifs **78** E 5
Ban Ban **67** J 4
Ban Na Shan **67** H 6
Banaadir **55** H 3
Banana Islands **50** D 7
Bananal, Ilha do **45** F 4
Banās, Ra's **53** G 3
Banbury **16** C 3
Bancoran **73** F 4
Banda **66** E 2
Banda, Kepulauan
  73 H 6
Banda, Laut **73** H 7
Banda Aceh **72** B 4
Banda Sea **73** H 7
Bandar Abbas **53** L 2
Bandar Seri Begawan
  72 E 5
Bandar-e Anzalī **64** G 5
Bandar-e Māhshar
  64 G 6
Bandar-e Rīg **53** K 2

Bandar-e Torkaman
  64 H 5
Bandarlampung **72** D 7
Bandarpunch **68** B 3
Bandera **46** E 4
Bandırma **64** C 4
Bandundu **54** C 4
Bandung **72** D 7
Banes **39** G 3
Banff National Park
  31 R 5
Banfora **50** F 6
Bangalore **66** D 5
Bangar **72** F 5
Bangassou **54** D 3
Banggai, Kepulauan
  73 G 6
Banggi **73** F 4
Bangka **72** D 6
Bangkinang **72** C 5
Bangko **72** C 6
Bangkok **67** J 5
Bangladesh **67** F 3
Bangor (U.K.) **16** B 3
Bangor (U.S.A.) **37** N 3
Bangui **54** C 3
Bangweulu, Lake **56** D 2
Banhã **52** F 1
Banī Maārid **53** J 4
Bani Mazār **52** F 2
Banī Suwayf **52** F 2
Banihāl Pass **65** N 6
Banja Luka **21** C 4
Banjarmasin **72** E 6
Banjul **50** C 6
Banks, Îles **78** F 5
Banks Island (British
  Columbia, Canada)
  31 O 5
Banks Island (Northwest
  Territories, Canada)
  32 M 4
Banks Peninsula **77** N 8
Bannu **65** M 6
Banská Bystrica **17** G 4
Bantaeng **73** F 7
Bantry **16** B 3
Banyuwangi **72** E 7
Bao Ha **67** J 3
Bao Loc **67** K 5
Baoding **69** K 3
Baoji **69** H 4
Baoqing **70** F 3
Baoshan **68** F 5
Baoting **67** K 4
Baotou **69** H 2
Baoulé **50** E 6
Baoying **69** K 4
Baqanas **65** N 4
Baquedano **46** D 3
Barabinsk **61** R 6
Barabinskaya Step'
  61 Q 7
Baragarh **66** E 3
Barahona **39** H 4
Barakaldo **18** B 2
Baranagar **66** F 3
Baranavichy **20** E 2

Baranoa **42** D 2
Baranof Island **31** N 4
Barbacena **45** H 6
Barbados **39** L 5
Barbar **52** F 4
Barbaria, Cap de **18** C 3
Barbosa **42** E 3
Barbuda **39** K 4
Barca **38** B 3
Barcaldine **77** H 4
Barcelona (Spain)
 18 M 7
Barcelona (Venezuela)
 43 G 2
Bardeskan **65** J 5
Bareilly **66** D 2
Barents Sea **26** M 1
Barentsevo More **60** J 3
Bärez, Küh-e Jebal
 53 L 2
Barguzinskiy Khrebet
 62 E 6
Bari **19** F 2
Barinas **43** E 3
Barisal **67** G 3
Barisan, Pegunungan
 72 C 6
Barká' **53** L 3
Barkly Tableland **76** F 3
Bârlad **20** E 3
Barlee, Lake **76** B 5
Barlee Range **76** B 4
Barletta **19** F 2
Barmer **66** C 2
Barnaul **61** S 7
Barnes Icecap **33** W 4
Barnstaple **16** C 3
Barotseland **56** C 3
Barq al Bishārīyīn
 52 F 4
Barquisimeto **43** F 2
Barra (Brazil) **45** H 4
Barra (U.K.) **16** B 2
Barra do Garças **45** F 5
Barra Patuca **38** G 4
Barracão do Barreto
 44 E 3
Barrancabermeja **42** E 3
Barranquilla **42** E 2
Barre des Écrins **19** D 2
Barreiras **45** G 4
Barren Island, Cape
 76 H 8
Barren Islands **30** K 4
Barretos **46** H 3
Barrie **35** M 6
Barrow **30** J 1
Barrow, Point **30** J 1
Barrow Island **76** B 4
Barrow Range **76** D 5
Barsak, Poluo **65** J 3
Barshyn **65** L 3
Bārsi **66** D 4
Barstow **36** C 5
Bartin **64** D 4
Bartlesville **37** G 4
Bartow **37** K 6
Barú, Volcán **38** F 6

Baruun Urt **70** B 3
Barysaw **22** C 2
Basankusu **54** C 3
Basel **19** D 1
Bashi Haixia **69** L 6
Basilan **73** G 4
Basilan City **73** G 4
Başkale **64** F 5
Basmat **66** D 4
Baso **72** C 6
Basoko **54** D 3
Basra **64** G 6
Bass, Îlots de **79** L 6
Bass Strait **76** G 8
Bassari **51** G 7
Basse-Terre **39** K 4
Bassein **67** G 4
Basso, Plateau de
 52 D 4
Bastia **19** D 2
Basuo **67** K 4
Bata **54** A 3
Batac **73** G 2
Bataklik Gölü **64** D 5
Batam **72** C 5
Batang **72** D 7
Batangafo **54** C 2
Batangas **73** G 3
Batdambang **67** J 5
Bath (U.K.) **16** C 3
Bath (U.S.A.) **37** N 3
Batha **52** C 5
Bathurst (Australia)
 77 E 6
Bathurst (Canada)
 35 O 5
Bathurst, Cape **32** L 4
Bathurst Inlet **32** P 5
Bathurst Island
 (Australia) **76** E 2
Bathurst Island
 (Canada) **32** R 3
Batman **64** F 5
Batn al Hajar **52** F 3
Batna **51** H 1
Baton Rouge **37** H 5
Batti Malv **67** G 6
Batticaloa **66** E 6
Battle Harbour **35** Q 4
Batu **53** G 6
Batu Pahat **72** C 5
Batulicin **72** F 6
Bat'umi **64** F 4
Baturaja **72** C 6
Baubau **73** G 7
Bauchi **51** H 6
Bauchi Plateau **51** J 7
Baufarik **51** G 1
Bauld, Cape **35** Q 4
Bauru **46** H 3
Bavispe **36** E 5
Bawean **72** E 7
Bawītī **52** E 2
Bay Bulls **35** R 5
Bay City (Michigan,
 U.S.A.) **37** K 3
Bay City (Texas, U.S.A.)
 37 G 6

Bayamo **39** G 3
Bayanaūyl **65** N 2
Bayan **70** E 3
Bayan Har Shan **68** F 4
Bayan Har Shankou
 68 F 4
Bayan Mod **69** G 2
Bayan Obo **69** H 2
Bayburt **64** F 4
Baydhabo **55** H 3
Bayerischer Wald **17** F 4
Baykal **61** W 7
Baykal, Ozero **61** X 7
Baykal'skiy Khrebet
 61 X 7
Baykit **61** V 5
Baymak **65** J 2
Baynūnah **53** K 3
Bayo Nuevo **39** G 4
Bayombong **73** G 2
Bayonne **18** B 2
Bayramaly **65** K 5
Bayreuth **17** F 4
Bayrūt **53** G 1
Baysa **62** F 4
Baytik Shan **68** E 1
Baytown **37** H 6
Baza **18** C 3
Bazardüzü dağ **64** G4
Bazaruto, Ilha do **57** F 4
Bazhi **65** P 2
Bazhong **69** H 4
Beacon **76** B 6
Beal Range **77** G 5
Bearskin Lake **34** J 4
Beata, Cabo **39** G 4
Beatrice **37** G 3
Beatrice, Cape **76** F 2
Beatton River **31** Q 4
Beauchêne Island
 47 F 9
Beaufort Sea **32** G 4
Beaufort West **56** C 6
Beaumont **37** H 5
Beaune **19** C 1
Beaupré **35** N 5
Beauvais **18** C 1
Beaver Island **37** J 2
Beaverton **36** B 2
Beawar **66** C 2
Bebedouro **46** H 3
Becan **38** D 4
Bečej **21** D 3
Béchar **51** F 2
Becharof Lake **30** J 4
Beckley **37** K 4
Bedford **37** L 3
Be'er Sheva **52** F 1
Beeville **37** G 6
Beger **68** F 1
Béhagle **18** B 2
Behbehān **64** H 6
Behshahr **64** H 5
Bei Hulsan Hu **68** E 3
Bei Shan **68** F 2
Beian **70** E 3
Beibu Wan **67** K 3
Beida **52** D 1

Beihai **69** H 6
Beijing **69** K 3
Beiliu **69** J 6
Bein Hoa **67** K 5
Beipiao **70** D 4
Beira **56** E 3
Beirut **64** E 6
Beishan **68** F 2
Beitbridge **56** E 4
Beizhen **70** D 4
Beja **18** B 3
Bejaïa **51** H 1
Bekasi **72** D 7
Békéscsaba **20** D 3
Bekobod **65** L 4
Bela **66** B 2
Bela Vista (Brazil)
 44 E 6
Bela Vista
 (Mozambique) **56** E 5
Belaga **72** E 5
Belarus **22** B 2
Belaya **65** J 1
Belaya Glina **23** F 3
Belaya Kalitva **23** F 3
Belaya Kholunitsa
 25 H 3
Bełchatów **17** G 3
Belcher Islands **35** L 3
Belcheragh **65** L 5
Belebey **23** H 2
Beledweyne **55** J 3
Belém (Amazonas,
 Brazil) **44** C 2
Belém (Pará, Brazil)
 45 G 2
Belfast **16** B 3
Belfort **19** D 1
Belgaum **66** C 4
Belgium **18** D 3
Belgorod **22** E 2
Belinyu **72** D 6
Belitung **72** D 6
Belize **38** E 4
Belize City **38** E 4
Bell Ville **46** E 5
Bella Coola **31** P 5
Bella Vista **46** F 4
Bellary **66** D 4
Belle-Île **18** B 1
Belle Isle **35** Q 4
Belleville **35** M 6
Bellevue (Nebraska,
 U.S.A.) **37** G 3
Bellevue (Washington,
 U.S.A.) **36** B 2
Bellingham **36** B 2
Bello **42** D 3
Belluno **19** E 1
Belmonte **45** J 5
Belmopan **38** E 4
Belmullet **16** B 3
Belo Horizonte **45** H 5
Belo Jardim **45** J 3
Belo Tsiribihina **57** G 3
Belogorsk **62** J 6
Beloit **37** J 3
Belomorsk **24** D 2

Belorechensk 23 E 4
Belot, Lac 32 L 5
Belovo 61 T 7
Beloye, Ozero 24 E 2
Beloye More 24 E 1
Belozersk 24 E 2
Belsham 68 F 2
Belukha 65 P 2
Belush'ya Guba 60 M 3
Belyy, Ostrov 60 Q 3
Belyy Yar 61 T 6
Ben Nevis 16 B 2
Ben Tre 67 K 5
Benares 66 E 2
Benavente 18 B 2
Bend 36 B 3
Bendigo 77 G 7
Benevento 19 E 2
Bengal, Bay of 67 F 4
Bengbu 69 K 4
Benghazi 52 D 1
Bengkulu 72 C 6
Benguela 56 A 2
Beni 55 E 3
Beni, Rio 44 C 4
Beni Mellal 50 E 2
Benidorm 18 C 3
Benin 51 G 7
Benin, Bight of 51 G 8
Benin City 51 H 7
Benjamin, Isla 47 C 7
Benoue 54 B 2
Bentinck Island 77 F 3
Bento Gonçalves 46 G 4
Benton 37 H 5
Bentong 72 C 5
Benue 51 H 7
Benxi 70 D 4
Beograd 21 D 4
Beppu 71 F 6
Berat 21 C 4
Berbera 55 J 1
Berbérati 54 C 3
Berdigestyakh 62 J 4
Berdsk 61 S 7
Berdyans'k 22 E 3
Berdychiv 22 C 3
Berehove 22 B 3
Berekum 51 F 7
Berens River 34 H 4
Berezevo 25 L 2
Berezivka 22 D 3
Berezniki 25 J 3
Berezovo 60 O 5
Berezovskiy 61 T 6
Berezovyy, Ostrov 24 C 2
Berg 26 J 2
Berga 18 D 2
Bergama 64 C 5
Bergamo 19 D 1
Bergen 27 G 3
Bergerac 18 C 2
Bergö 26 K 3
Bergslagen 27 H 3
Berhampore 66 F 4
Berhampur 66 E 4
Bering Glacier 30 M 3

Bering Land Bridge National Reserve 30 H 2
Bering Sea 30 D 4
Beringa, Ostrov 63 R 6
Beringovskiy 63 T 4
Berkane 51 F 2
Berkeley 36 B 4
Berkner Island 80 N 4
Berlin (Germany) 17 F 3
Berlin (U.S.A.) 37 M 3
Bermuda Islands 29 O 6
Bern 19 D 1
Bernasconi 47 E 6
Berner Alpen 19 D 1
Berrechid 50 E 2
Bertoua 54 B 3
Besançon 19 D 1
Beskidy Zachodny 17 G 4
Beslan 23 F 4
Bestöbe 65 M 2
Bethel 30 H 3
Bethlehem 56 D 5
Béthune 16 D 3
Béticos, Sistemas 18 B 3
Betong 67 J 6
Betpak-Dala 65 M 3
Betroka 57 H 4
Bettiah 66 E 2
Bettles 30 K 2
Betul 66 D 3
Beveridge Reef 79 J 5
Beyla 50 E 7
Beyoneisu-retsugan 71 H 6
Beyra 55 J 2
Bezhetsk 24 E 3
Béziers 18 C 2
Bhadrakh 66 F 3
Bhadravāti 66 D 5
Bhagalpur 66 F 2
Bhairab Bāzār 67 G 3
Bhakkar 66 C 1
Bhaktapur 66 F 2
Bharatpur 66 D 2
Bharuch 66 C 3
Bhātpāra 66 F 3
Bhawanipatna 66 E 4
Bhilwara 66 C 2
Bhiwani 66 D 2
Bhongir 66 D 4
Bhopal 66 D 3
Bhubaneshwar 66 F 3
Bhuj 66 B 3
Bhusawal 66 D 3
Bhutan 67 F 2
Bīābān, Kūh-e 53 L 2
Biak 73 K 6
Biała Podlaska 17 H 3
Białogard 17 G 3
Białystok 17 H 3
Biaora 66 D 3
Biaro 73 H 5
Biarritz 18 B 2
Bibai 70 H 4
Bickerton Island 76 F 2

Bīd 66 D 4
Bida 51 H 7
Bīdar 66 D 4
Bidzhan 70 F 3
Biel 19 D 1
Bielefeld 17 E 3
Bielsk Podlaski 17 H 3
Bielsko-Biała 17 G 4
Bienville, Lac 35 N 3
Big Bend National Park 36 F 6
Big Island 35 N 2
Big Rapids 37 J 3
Big Smoky Valley 36 C 4
Big Spring 36 F 5
Big Trout Lake 34 K 4
Bighorn Basin 36 E 3
Bignona 50 C 6
Bihać 21 C 4
Bihar 66 F 3
Bīhār 66 F 2
Bijagos, Arquipélago dos 50 C 6
Bijapur 66 D 4
Bijeljina 21 C 4
Bijelo Polje 21 C 4
Bijie 69 H 5
Bikaner 66 C 2
Bikar 78 G 2
Bikin 70 F 3
Bikini 78 F 2
Bila Tserkva 22 D 3
Bilaspur 66 E 3
Bilauktaung Range 67 H 5
Bilbao 18 B 2
Bīldudalur 26 A 2
Bilhorod-Dnistrovs'kyy 22 D 3
Bilesha Plain 55 H 3
Billings 36 E 2
Bilma 51 J 5
Biloku 43 H 4
Bilopillya 22 D 2
Biloxi 37 J 5
Bin Xian 70 E 3
Bin Yauri 51 G 6
Bina-Etāwa 66 D 3
Binaiya, Gunung 73 H 6
Bindura 56 E 3
Binghampton 37 L 3
Binhai 69 K 4
Binjai (Indonesia) 72 B 5
Binjai (Indonesia) 72 D 5
Binongko 73 G 7
Bintan 72 C 5
Bintuhan 72 C 6
Bintulu 72 E 5
Binyang 69 H 6
Bioko 54 A 3
Bir Moghrein 50 D 3
Bira 70 G 3
Birakan 70 F 3
Birao 54 D 1
Biratnagar 66 F 2
Bird 34 J 3
Birdsville 77 F 5

Birikchul' 61 T 7
Birkat Nasser 52 F 3
Birksgate Range 76 D 5
Birmingham (U.K.) 16 C 3
Birmingham (U.S.A.) 37 J 5
Birmitrapur 66 E 3
Birni Nkonni 51 H 6
Birnie Island 79 H 4
Birnin Kebbi 51 G 6
Birobidzhan 70 F 3
Birsk 25 J 3
Biryusa 61 V 7
Biscay, Bay of 18 B 2
Bishkek 65 M 4
Bishop 36 C 4
Biskra 51 H 2
Bislig 73 H 4
Bismarck 36 F 2
Bismarck, Kap 33 Hh 3
Bismarck Archipelago 78 D 4
Bismarck Range 78 D 4
Bismarck Sea 78 D 4
Bissau 50 C 6
Bistriţa 20 D 3
Bitlis 64 F 5
Bitola 21 D 4
Bitterfontein 56 B 6
Biu 51 J 6
Biya 61 T 7
Biysk 61 T 7
Björkön 26 K 3
Björneborg 27 K 3
Black Rock Desert 36 C 3
Black Sea 22 D 4
Blackall 77 H 4
Blackburn 16 C 3
Blackburn, Mount 30 M 3
Blackfoot 36 D 3
Blackpool 16 C 3
Blagodatnyy 70 G 3
Blagoevgrad 21 D 4
Blagoveshchensk (Russia) 23 J 1
Blagoveshchensk (Russia) 62 J 6
Blaine 37 H 2
Blanc, Cap 50 C 4
Blanc, Mont 19 D 1
Blanc-Sablon 35 Q 4
Blanca, Cordillera 42 D 6
Blanche, Lake 77 F 5
Blantyre 56 E 3
Blekinge 27 H 4
Blenheim 77 N 8
Blida 51 G 1
Blitar 72 E 7
Bloemfontein 56 D 5
Blois 18 C 1
Bloomington (Illinois, U.S.A.) 37 J 3
Bloomington (Indiana, U.S.A.) 37 J 4

Bloomington
  (Minnesota, U.S.A.)
  37 H 3
Blora **72** E 7
Blosseville Kyst **33** Ff 5
Blossom, Mys **63** T 2
Blue Mountain Peak
  39 G 4
Blue Mountains **77** H 6
Blue Nile **52** F 5
Blue Ridge **37** K 4
Bluefields **38** F 5
Bluenose Lake **32** M 5
Bluff **77** M 9
Blumenau **46** H 4
Blytheville **37** J 4
Bo **50** D 7
Bø **27** G 4
Bo Hai **69** K 3
Bo Xian **69** K 4
Boa Esperança,
  Represa **45** H 3
Boa Vista (Brazil) **44** D 1
Boa Vista (Cape Verde)
  50 B 5
Boac **73** G 3
Boaco **38** F 5
Boano **73** H 6
Bobai **69** H 6
Bobaomby, Tanjona
  57 H 2
Bobbili **66** E 4
Bobo Dioulasso **50** F 6
Bobrov **23** F 2
Bobrynets' **22** D 3
Boca, Cachoeira de
  45 F 3
Bôca do Acre **44** C 3
Boca Grande **43** G 3
Boca Raton **37** K 6
Bocaiúva **45** H 5
Bochum **17** E 3
Boconó **42** E 3
Bocşa **21** D 3
Bodaybo **62** F 5
Bodélé **52** C 4
Boden **26** K 2
Bodhan **66** D 4
Bodjonegoro **72** E 7
Bodø **26** H 2
Boende **54** D 4
Boeng Tonle Chhma
  67 J 5
Bogale **67** H 4
Bogalusa **37** J 5
Bogatá **42** E 4
Boghra Dam **65** K 6
Bogo **73** G 3
Bogor **72** D 7
Bogoroditsk **22** E 2
Bogotol **61** T 6
Bogra **67** F 3
Boguchany **61** V 6
Bohai Haixia **69** L 3
Böhmerwald **17** F 4
Bohodukhiv **22** E 2
Bohol **73** G 4
Bohuslän **27** H 4

Bois, Lac des **32** L 5
Boise **36** C 3
Bojnürd **65** J 5
Boké **50** D 6
Bolivar, Pico **42** E 3
Bol'shaya Chernigovka
  23 H 2
Bol'shaya Glushitsa
  23 H 2
Bol'shaya Kuonamka
  61 X 4
Bol'sheretsk **63** P 6
Bol'shevik, Ostrov
  61 W 2
Bol'shezemel'skaya
  Tundra **25** J 1
Bol'shoy Begichev,
  Ostrov **61** Y 3
Bol'shoy Kamen **70** F 4
Bol'shoy Kavkaz **23** F 4
Bol'shoy Lyakhovskiy,
  Ostrov **62** M 2
Bol'shoy Porog **61** U 4
Bol'shoy Shantar **62** L 6
Bolama **50** C 6
Bolan Pass **66** B 2
Bole (China) **68** C 2
Bole (Ghana) **51** F 7
Bolesławiec **17** G 3
Bolgatanga **51** F 6
Boli **70** F 3
Bolívar **47** E 6
Bolivia **44** D 5
Bolkhov **22** E 2
Bollnäs **27** J 3
Bolobo **54** C 4
Bologna **19** E 2
Bologoye **24** D 3
Bolon' **70** G 3
Bolotnoye **61** S 6
Bolsón de Mapimi
  36 F 6
Bolu **64** D 4
Bolzano **19** E 1
Bom Jesus da
  Gurguéia, Serra
  45 H 3
Bom Jesus da Lapa
  45 H 4
Boma **54** B 5
Bombala **77** H 7
Bombay **66** C 4
Bømlo **27** F 4
Bon, Cap **51** J 1
Bona, Mount **30** M 3
Bonaire **39** J 5
Bonampak **38** D 4
Bonanza **38** G 5
Bonaparte Archipelago
  76 C 2
Bondo **54** D 4
Bondoukou **51** F 7
Bondowoso **72** E 7
Bonete, Cerro **46** D 4
Bongka **73** G 6
Bongor **52** C 5
Bonifacio, Strait of
  19 D 2

Bonn **17** E 3
Bonneville Saltflats
  36 D 3
Böön Tsagaan Nuur
  68 F 1
Boosaaso **55** J 1
Boothia, Gulf of **32** S 4
Booué **54** B 4
Boquillas del Carmen
  36 F 6
Bor (Russia) **25** F 3
Bor (Yugoslavia) **21** D 4
Bora-Bora **79** K 5
Borås **27** H 4
Borāzjān **53** K 2
Borborema, Planalto da
  45 J 3
Borçka **64** F 4
Bordeaux **18** B 2
Borden Island **32** O 3
Borden Peninsula
  33 U 4
Bordertown **77** G 7
Borgholm **27** J 4
Borisoglebsk **23** F 2
Borkou **52** C 4
Borlänge **27** J 3
Borneo **72** E 6
Bornholm **17** G 3
Bornu **51** J 6
Borogontsy **62** K 4
Borohoro Shan
  68 C 2
Boroko **73** G 5
Borovichi **24** D 3
Borovskoye **60** O 7
Borroloola **76** F 3
Borşa **20** D 3
Borüjen **53** K 1
Borüjerd **53** J 1
Boryslav **22** B 3
Boryspil' **22** D 2
Borzya **62** G 6
Bosca **21** D 3
Bose **69** H 6
Boshan **69** K 3
Bosnia-Herzegovina
  21 C 4
Bosnian-Croat
  Federation **21** C 4
Bosobolo **54** C 3
Bosporus **64** C 4
Bossangoa **54** C 2
Bossembele **54** C 2
Bossier City **37** H 5
Bosten Hu **68** D 2
Boston **37** M 3
Bothnia, Gulf of **27** J 3
Botoşani **20** E 3
Botswana **56** C 4
Bottineau **36** F 2
Botucatu **46** H 3
Bou Saâda **51** G 1
Bouaflé **50** E 7
Bouaké **50** E 7
Bouar **54** C 2
Boubandjida **54** B 2
Boufarik **18** C 3

Bougainville Island
  78 E 4
Bougainville Strait
  78 E 4
Bougouni **50** E 6
Bouïra **51** G 1
Boulder **36** E 3
Boulia **77** F 4
Boulogne-sur-Mer
  16 D 3
Bouna **51** F 7
Boundiali **50** E 7
Boundou **50** D 6
Bountiful **36** D 3
Bourg-en-Bresse **19** D 1
Bourges **18** C 1
Bourgogne **19** C 1
Bourke **77** H 6
Bournemouth **16** C 3
Bowen **77** H 3
Bowling Green **37** J 4
Bowling Green, Cape
  77 H 3
Bowman **36** F 2
Boxing **69** K 3
Boyang **69** K 5
Boyarka **61** V 3
Boyuibe **44** D 6
Bozashchy Tübegi
  23 H 3
Brač **21** C 4
Bräcke **26** J 3
Bradenton **37** K 6
Bradford (U.K.) **16** C 3
Bradford (U.S.A.) **37** L 3
Bradley Reefs **78** F 4
Braemar **16** C 2
Braga **18** A 2
Bragado **46** E 6
Bragança (Brazil)
  45 G 2
Bragança (Portugal)
  18 A 2
Brahmapur **66** E 4
Brahmaputra **68** E 5
Brăila **21** E 3
Brainerd **37** H 2
Brakna **50** D 5
Brampton **35** M 6
Brandberg **56** A 4
Brandenburg **17** F 3
Brandon **34** H 5
Braniewo **17** G 3
Brantford **35** L 6
Bras d'Or, Lake **35** P 5
Brasília **45** G 5
Braşov **20** E 3
Bratislava **17** G 4
Bratsk **61** W 6
Bratskoye
  Vodokhranilishche
  61 W 6
Braunschweig **17** F 3
Brava **50** A 6
Bravo, Cerro **42** D 6
Bravo, Rio **36** E 5
Brawley **36** C 5
Bray Island **33** V 5

Calamian Group **73** F 3
Calapan **73** G 3
Cǎlǎraşi **21** E 4
Calatat **21** D 4
Calatayud **18** C 2
Calayan **71** D 9
Calbayog **73** G 3
Calcutta **66** F 3
Caldas da Rainha **18** B 3
Caldera **46** C 4
Caldwell **36** C 3
Caleta Olivia **47** D 8
Calgary **31** S 5
Cali **42** D 4
Calicut **66** D 5
California **36** B 4
California, Golfo de **36** D 6
Callao **44** A 4
Caltanissetta **19** E 3
Caluula **55** K 1
Calvi **19** E 2
Calvinia **56** B 6
Cam Ranh **67** K 5
Camaçari **45** J 4
Camacupa **56** B 2
Camagüey **39** G 3
Camaná **44** B 5
Camapuã **45** F 5
Camaqua **46** G 5
Camarat, Cap **19** D 2
Camarón, Cabo **38** D 4
Camarones **47** D 7
Cambodia **67** J 5
Cambrai **16** D 3
Cambridge (U.K.) **16** D 3
Cambridge (U.S.A.) **36** C 3
Cambridge Bay **32** P 5
Camden **37** H 5
Cameroon **54** B 2
Cameroun Mountain **54** A 3
Cametá **45** G 2
Camiguin **73** G 2
Camiri **44** D 6
Camocim **45** H 2
Camooweal **77** F 3
Camorta **67** G 6
Campana **46** F 5
Campbell, Cape **77** N 8
Campbell River **31** P 5
Campbell Town **76** H 8
Campbelltown **77** J 6
Campbeltown **16** B 2
Campeche **38** D 4
Campeche, Bahía de **38** D 4
Campina Grande **45** J 3
Campina Verde **45** G 5
Campinas **46** H 3
Campo de Diauarum **45** F 4
Campo Formoso **45** H 4
Campo Gallo **46** E 4
Campo Grande **45** F 6

Campo Maior **45** H 2
Campo Mourão **46** G 3
Campobasso **19** E 2
Campos **45** H 6
Camrose **31** S 5
Can Tho **67** K 5
Canada **34** F 3
Canada de Gómez **46** E 5
Çanakkale **64** C 4
Çanakkale Boğazi **21** E 5
Cananea **36** D 5
Canar **42** D 5
Canarreos, Archipiélago de los **38** F 3
Canary Islands **50** C 3
Canavieiras **45** J 5
Canberra **77** H 7
Canchyuaya, Cerros de **42** E 6
Cancún **38** E 3
Canelones **46** F 5
Canete **47** C 6
Canguçu **46** G 5
Cangzhou **69** K 3
Canindé **45** J 2
Çankırı **64** D 4
Cannanore **66** D 5
Cannes **19** D 2
Canoas **46** G 4
Canoinhas **46** G 4
Canon City **36** E 4
Canora **34** G 4
Cantábrica, Cordillera **18** A 2
Cantagalo, Cachoeira **45** F 3
Cantaura **43** G 3
Canterbury **16** D 3
Canterbury Bight **77** N 8
Canterbury Plains **77** N 8
Canton (China) **69** J 6
Canton (U.S.A.) **37** K 3
Canutama **44** D 3
Canyon **36** F 1
Cao Bang **67** K 3
Cao Xian **69** K 4
Cap-Haïtien **39** H 4
Capanema **45** G 2
Capão Bonito **46** H 3
Cape Arid National Park **76** C 6
Cape Breton Highlands National Park **35** P 5
Cape Breton Island **35** P 5
Cape Coast **51** F 7
Cape Dorset **35** M 2
Cape Girardeau **37** J 4
Cape Krusenstern National Monument **30** H 2
Cape Smith **35** M 2
Cape Town **56** B 6
Cape Verde **50** B 5
Cape Yakataga **30** M 3

Cape York Peninsula **77** G 2
Capelinha **45** H 5
Capibara **43** F 4
Capinzal, Cachoeira **44** E 3
Capitan Bado **46** F 3
Capivari, Represa de **46** G 3
Capoeira **44** E 3
Capoeiras, Cachoeira das **44** E 3
Capricorn Channel **77** J 4
Capricorn Group **77** J 4
Car Nicobar **67** G 6
Carabaya, Cordillera **44** B 4
Caracal **21** D 4
Caracarai **44** D 1
Caracas **43** F 2
Carajás, Serra dos **45** F 3
Caratinga **45** H 5
Carazinho **46** G 4
Carbonara, Capo **19** D 3
Carbonia **19** D 3
Carcassonne **18** C 2
Carcross **31** O 3
Cárdenas **38** C 3
Cardiel, Lago **47** C 8
Cardiff **16** C 3
Carei **20** D 3
Carey, Lake **76** C 5
Carey Øer **33** W 3
Caribbean Sea **39** F 5
Carletonville **56** D 5
Carlisle **16** C 3
Carlos Casares **47** E 6
Carlos Chagas **45** H 5
Carlow **16** B 3
Carlsbad (California, U.S.A.) **36** C 5
Carlsbad (New Mexico, U.S.A.) **36** F 5
Carlyle **34** G 5
Carmacks **31** N 3
Carmel Head **16** B 3
Carmelo **46** F 5
Carmen, Isla **36** D 6
Carmen de Patagones **47** E 7
Carnarvon (Australia) **76** A 4
Carnarvon (South Africa) **56** C 6
Carnegie, Lake **76** C 5
Carnot **54** C 3
Carnot, Cape **75** C 7
Carolina **45** G 3
Caroline Islands **78** D 3
Carondelet **79** H 4
Carora **43** E 2
Carozal **42** D 3
Carpathian Mountains **20** D 3
Carpaţii Meridionali **21** D 3

Carpentaria, Gulf of **77** F 2
Carpina **45** J 3
Carrara **19** E 2
Carrauntoohil **16** B 3
Carreta, Punta **44** A 4
Carson City **36** C 4
Cartagena (Colombia) **42** D 2
Cartagena (Spain) **18** B 3
Caruaru **45** J 3
Carupano **43** G 2
Carutapera **45** G 2
Casa Grande **36** D 5
Casablanca **50** E 2
Casamance **50** C 6
Cascavel **46** G 3
Caserta **19** E 2
Caseyr, Raas **53** K 5
Casilda **46** E 5
Casino **77** J 5
Casper **36** E 3
Caspian Sea **64** H 4
Cassai, Rio **56** C 2
Cassiar **31** P 4
Castanhal **45** G 2
Castanho **44** D 3
Castelló de la Plana **18** B 2
Castelo Branco **18** B 3
Castelvetrano **19** E 3
Castilla **42** C 6
Castilla La Mancha **18** B 2
Castilla y León **18** B 2
Castlebar **16** B 3
Castres **18** C 2
Castries **39** K 5
Castro (Brazil) **46** G 3
Castro (Chile) **47** C 7
Cat Island **37** L 7
Cataguases **45** H 6
Cataluña **18** C 2
Catamarca **46** D 4
Catanduanes **73** G 3
Catanduva **46** H 3
Catania **19** F 3
Catanzaro **19** F 3
Catastrophe, Cape **76** F 6
Catbalogan **73** G 3
Catete **54** B 5
Catrimani **44** D 1
Catwick Islands **67** K 5
Caucasia **42** D 3
Caucasus **64** F 4
Caucete **46** D 5
Cauchari, Salar de **46** D 3
Cauquenes **47** C 6
Cavalcante **45** G 4
Caviana, Ilha **45** G 1
Cavili **73** F 4
Caxias **45** H 2
Caxias do Sul **46** G 4
Caxito **54** B 5
Cayambe **42** D 4

Cayambe (Mountain) 42 D 5
Cayenne 43 J 4
Cayman Brac 39 G 4
Cayman Islands 39 F 4
Cazombo 56 C 2
Ceará 45 H 2
Ceará Mirim 45 J 3
Cebaco, Isla 39 F 6
Cebu 73 G 3
Cedar City 36 D 4
Cedros, Isla 36 C 6
Ceduna 76 E 6
Cefalù 19 F 3
Celaya 38 B 3
Celebes 73 F 6
Celebes Sea 73 F5
Celestún 38 E 3
Celje 20 C 3
Celle 17 F 3
Celtic Sea 16 B 3
Cendrawasih, Teluk 73 K 6
Central, Cordillera (Ecuador) 42 D 6
Central, Cordillera (Philippines) 73 G 2
Central African Republic 54 C 2
Central Brahui Range 66 B 2
Central Makrän Range 66 A 2
Central Range 78 D 4
Centralia 36 B 2
Cepu 72 E 7
Ceram 73 H 6
Cereal 31 S 5
Ceres (Argentina) 46 E 4
Ceres (Brazil) 45 G 5
Cereté 42 D 3
Cerf 55 K 5
Cerralvo, Isla 36 E 7
Cerritos 38 B 3
Cerro de Pasco 44 A 4
Cerros Colorados, Embalse 47 D 6
České Budějovice 17 F 4
Çeşme 21 E 5
Cessnock 77 J 6
Ceuta 50 E 1
Cevennes 18 C 2
Ch'eönan 70 E 5
Ch'öngjin 70 E 4
Cha-Am 67 H 5
Chachani, Nevado 44 B 5
Chachapoyas 42 D 6
Chachoengsao 67 J 5
Chaco Austral 46 E 4
Chaco Boreal 46 E 3
Chaco Central 46 E 3
Chacorão, Cachoeira do 44 E 3
Chad 52 C 5

Chad, Lake 52 B 5
Chägai Hills 66 A 2
Chagda 62 K 5
Chagyl 65 J 4
Chai Nat 67 J 4
Chäïbäsa 66 F 3
Chajari 46 F 5
Chalkida 21 D 5
Chañaral 46 C 4
Chakwal 66 C 1
Chalbi Desert 55 G 3
Challapata 44 C 5
Challenger Deep 78 D 2
Challis 36 D 3
Châlons-en-Champagne 19 C 1
Chalon-sur-Saône 19 C 1
Chaman 65 L 6
Chambéry 19 D 1
Champagne 18 C 1
Champasak 67 K 5
Chanbogd 69 H 2
Chancay 44 A 4
Chandalar 30 L 2
Chandeleur Islands 37 J 6
Chandigarh 66 D 1
Chandrapur 66 D 4
Chang Cheng 70 C 4
Chang Rai 67 H 4
Changane, Rio 56 E 4
Changara 56 E 3
Changbai Shan 70 E 4
Changchun 70 E 4
Changde 69 J 5
Chang-hua 69 L 6
Changji 68 D 2
Changjiang 67 K 4
Changjiang (River) 69 H 4
Changli 69 K 3
Changling 70 D 4
Changsha 69 J 5
Changshu 69 L 4
Changting 69 K 5
Changwu 69 H 3
Changzhi 69 J 3
Changzhou 69 K 4
Chania 21 D 5
Channapatna 66 D 5
Channel Islands 16 C 4
Chanthaburi 67 J 5
Chany, Ozero 65 N 1
Chao Hu 69 K 4
Chao'an 69 K 6
Chaoyang 70 D 4
Chapadinha 45 H 2
Chapaev 23 H 2
Chapala 38 B 3
Chapala, Laguna de 38 B 3
Chaparral 42 D 4
Chapayevsk 23 G 2
Chapecó 46 E 4
Chapleau 35 L 5
Chaplygin 23 E 2

Chara 62 G 4
Charagua 44 D 5
Charcas 38 B 3
Chari 52 C 5
Chärjew 65 K 5
Charleroi 16 D 3
Charles Island 35 N 2
Charles Louis, Pegunungan 73 K 6
Charles Point 76 D 2
Charlesbourg 35 N 5
Charleston (South Carolina, U.S.A.) 37 L 5
Charleston (West Virginia, U.S.A.) 37 K 4
Charleville 77 H 5
Charleville-Mézières 16 D 4
Charlotte 37 K 4
Charlottesville 37 L 4
Charlottetown 35 P 5
Charlton Island 35 L 4
Charsadda 65 M 6
Charters Towers 77 H 4
Chartres 18 C 1
Chascomús 47 F 6
Chasma Barrage 66 C 1
Châteauroux 18 C 1
Châtellerault 18 D 1
Chatham 35 L 6
Chatham, Isla 47 C 9
Chattanooga 37 J 4
Chau Phu 67 K 5
Chauk 67 G 3
Chaumont 19 D 1
Chaves 18 B 2
Chaykovskiy 25 H 3
Chazhegovo 25 H 2
Cheb 17 F 3
Chebarkul' 25 K 4
Cheboksary 25 G 3
Chech, Erg 50 F 4
Chech'on 70 E 5
Cheduba Island 67 G 4
Chegdomyn 62 K 6
Cheju 71 E 6
Cheju-do 71 E 6
Cheju-haehyöb 71 E 6
Chekanovskij 61 W 6
Chela, Serra da 56 A 2
Chelyabinsk 25 K 3
Chelyuskin, Mys 80 E 1
Chemnitz 17 F 3
Chemult 36 B 3
Cheng'an 69 J 3
Chengde 70 C 4
Chengdu 69 G 4
Chengmai 67 L 4
Chennai 66 E 5
Chenxi 69 J 5
Chenzhou 69 J 5
Cherangany Mountains 55 G 3
Cherbaniani Reef 66 C 5
Cherbourg 16 C 4
Cheremkhovo 61 W 7

Cherepanovo 61 S 7
Cherepovets 24 E 3
Chergui, Chott ech 51 G 2
Cherkasy 22 D 3
Cherkessk 23 F 4
Chermoz 25 J 3
Chernihiv 22 D 2
Chernivtsi 22 C 3
Chernogorsk 61 U 7
Chernyakhiv 22 C 2
Chernyakhovsk 27 K 5
Chernyye Zemli 23 F 3
Chernyy Yar 23 G 3
Cherskiy 63 Q 3
Cherskogo, Khrebet 62 F 6
Chervonohrad 22 B 2
Chervyanka 61 V 6
Chervyen' 22 C 2
Cheshkaya Guba 25 G 1
Chester 16 C 3
Chesterfield Inlet 34 J 2
Chetlat 66 C 5
Chetm 22 B 2
Chetumal 38 E 4
Chew Bahir 53 G 6
Cheyenne 36 F 3
Cheyne Bay 76 B 6
Chhatarpur 66 D 3
Chhindwara 66 D 3
Chia-i 69 L 6
Chiang Mai 67 H 4
Chiange 56 A 3
Chiapas, Meseta de 38 D 4
Chiavari 19 D 2
Chiba 70 H 5
Chibougamau 35 N 5
Chibuto 56 E 4
Chicago 37 J 3
Chichas, Cordillera de 44 C 5
Chichagof Island 31 N 4
Chichén Itzá 38 E 3
Chichester Range National Park 76 B 4
Chickasha 36 G 4
Chiclayo 42 D 7
Chico 36 B 4
Chicoutimi 35 N 5
Chicualacuala 56 E 4
Chidambaram 66 D 5
Chieti 19 E 2
Chifeng 70 C 4
Chigorodó 42 D 3
Chihli, Gulf of 69 K 3
Chihuahua 36 E 6
Chihumba 56 E 2
Chikhacheva 62 N 2
Chilaw 66 D 6
Chile 47 C 8
Chilecito 46 D 4
Chilik 23 H 2
Chililabombwe 56 D 2
Chilka Lake 66 F 4
Chillán 47 C 6

Chiloé, Isla de **47** B 7
Chilpancingo **38** C 4
Chi-lung **69** L 5
Chimaltenango **38** D 5
Chimborazo, Cerro
  42 D 5
Chimbote **42** D 6
Chimolo **56** E 3
Chin Hills **67** G 3
China **69** G 4
Chinandega **38** E 5
Chincha Alta **44** A 4
Chinchilla **77** J 5
Chinchorro, Banco
  38 E 4
Chin-do **71** E 6
Chingola **56** D 2
Chinhoyi **56** D 3
Chinju **70** E 5
Chioggia **19** E 1
Chios **21** E 5
Chios (Island) **21** E 5
Chiquinquirá **42** E 3
Chirala **66** E 4
Chirchiq **65** L 4
Chiriguanos **46** E 3
Chirikof Island **30** J 4
Chirinda **61** W 4
Chiriqui, Golfo de **38** F 6
Chirripo, Cerro **38** F 6
Chisamba **56** D 2
Ch'i-shan **69** L 6
Chişinău **22** C 3
Chistoozernoye **61** R 7
Chistopol' **23** H 1
Chita **62** F 6
Chitose **70** H 4
Chitradurga **66** D 5
Chitré **39** F 6
Chittagong **67** G 3
Chittaurgarh **66** C 3
Chittoor **66** D 5
Chitungwiza **56** E 3
Chivilcoy **46** E 5
Ch'ŏngju **70** E 5
Chocope **42** D 6
Choiseul Island **78** E 4
Chojnice **17** G 3
Choke Mountains
  53 G 5
Chokwe **56** E 4
Cholet **18** B 1
Choluteca **38** E 5
Choma **56** D 3
Chomutov **17** F 3
Chon Buri **67** J 5
Chone **42** C 5
Chong'an **69** K 5
Ch'ŏngju **70** E 5
Chongqing **69** H 5
Chornobyl' **22** D 2
Chorog **65** M 5
Choroique, Cerro **44** C 6
Chōshi **70** H 5
Chotanagpur Plateau
  66 E 3

Choybalsan **70** B 3
Christchurch **77** N 8
Christian IV Gletscher
  33 Ff 5
Christianshåb **33** Aa 5
Christmas Island
  (Australia) **72** D 8
Christmas Island
  (Kiribati) **79** K 3
Chudskoye Ozero
  24 C 3
Chuginadak Island
  30 F 5
Chukai **72** C 5
Chukotskiy Poluostrov
  63 U 3
Chula Vista **36** C 5
Chulym **61** S 6
Chum **25** K 1
Chumbicha **46** D 4
Chumikan **62** L 6
Chumphon **67** H 5
Chuna **61** V 6
Ch'unch'ŏn **70** E 5
Chunya (Russia) **61** V 5
Chunya (Tanzania)
  55 F 5
Chuor Phnum Dangrek
  67 J 5
Chupa **24** D 1
Chuquicamata **46** D 3
Chur **19** D 1
Churapcha **62** K 4
Churchill **34** J 3
Churchill Falls **35** P 4
Churchill Lake **34** F 3
Chureg **65** Q 2
Chureg-Tag, Gora
  61 U 7
Churu **66** C 2
Chusovoy **25** J 3
Chust **65** M 4
Chuuk Islands **78** E 3
Chuxian **69** K 4
Chuxiong **69** G 5
Chybalsan **70** B 3
Cianjur **72** D 7
Cianorte **46** G 3
Ciego de Avila **39** G 3
Ciénaga **42** E 2
Cienfuegos **39** F 3
Cieza **18** C 3
Cikobia **79** H 5
Cilacap **72** D 7
Cincinnati **37** K 4
Cintra, Golfo de **50** C 4
Cipolletti **47** D 6
Circle (Alaska, U.S.A.)
  30 M 2
Circle (Montana, U.S.A.)
  36 E 2
Cirebon **72** D 7
Ciskei **56** D 6
Citac, Nevado **44** A 4
Ciudad Acuna **36** F 6
Ciudad Bolívar **43** G 3
Ciudad Camargo
  36 E 6

Ciudad Cuauhtémoc
  38 D 4
Ciudad del Carmen
  38 D 4
Ciudad Guayana **43** G 3
Ciudad Guzman **38** B 4
Ciudad Hidalgo **38** B 4
Ciudad Juárez **36** E 5
Ciudad Madero **38** C 3
Ciudad Obregón **36** E 6
Ciudad Ojeda **42** E 2
Ciudad Real **18** B 3
Ciudad Rodrigo **18** B 2
Ciudad Valles **38** C 3
Ciudad Victoria **36** G 7
Ciudada Mante **38** C 3
Civitanova Marche
  19 E 2
Civitavecchia **19** E 2
Clacton-on-Sea **16** D 3
Claire, Lake **31** S 4
Clarence, Isla **47** C 9
Clarence Town **39** H 3
Clarke Island **76** H 8
Clarke Range **77** H 4
Clarksdale **37** H 5
Clarksville **37** J 4
Claveria **73** G 2
Clavering Ø **33** Gg 4
Clearwater **37** K 6
Clermont **77** H 4
Clermont-Ferrand
  18 C 1
Cleveland (Mississippi,
  U.S.A.) **37** H 5
Cleveland (Ohio, U.S.A.)
  37 K 3
Clifden **16** B 3
Clinton (Iowa, U.S.A.)
  37 H 3
Clinton (Oklahoma,
  U.S.A.) **36** G 4
Cloncurry **77** G 4
Clonmel **16** B 3
Clorinda **46** F 4
Clovis **36** F 5
Cluj-Napoca **20** D 3
Clyde Inlet **33** X 4
Clyde River **33** X 4
Coan, Cerro **42** D 6
Coaraci **45** J 4
Coast Mountains **31** O 4
Coast Range **77** J 5
Coatepec **38** C 4
Coats Island **35** L 2
Coatzacoalcos **38** D 4
Coba **38** E 3
Coban **38** D 4
Cobar **77** H 6
Cobourg Peninsula
  76 E 2
Coburg **17** F 3
Coburg Island **33** V 3
Cocalinho **45** F 4
Cocamá **44** B 4
Cochabamba **44** C 5
Cochin **66** D 5
Cochrane **35** L 5

Coco, Isla del **38** D 6
Coco Islands **67** G 5
Cocos **45** H 4
Cocula **38** B 3
Codajás **44** D 2
Codó **45** H 2
Coesfeld **17** E 3
Coeur d'Alene **36** C 2
Coffs Harbour **77** J 6
Cogt-Ovoo **69** H 2
Coiba, Isla de **38** F 6
Coihaique **47** C 8
Coihaique, Paso **47** C 8
Coimbatore **66** D 5
Coimbra **18** A 2
Coipasa, Salar de
  44 C 5
Cojutepeque **38** E 5
Colalao del Valle **46** D 4
Colatina **45** H 5
Colchester **16** D 3
Coleman **36** G 5
Colesberg **56** D 6
Colfax **36** C 2
Colhué Huapi, Lago
  47 D 8
Colima **38** B 4
Coll **16** B 2
College Station **37** G 5
Collier Ranges National
  Park **76** B 4
Collipulli **47** C 6
Colmar **19** D 1
Cololo, Nevado **44** C 4
Colombia **42** E 4
Colombo (Brazil) **46** H 4
Colombo (Sri Lanka)
  66 D 6
Colón (Cuba) **39** F 3
Colón (Panama) **39** G 6
Colón (Uruguay) **46** F 5
Colonia Las Heras
  47 D 8
Colonna, Capo **19** F 3
Colonsay **16** B 2
Colorado **36** E 4
Colorado Plateau
  36 D 4
Colorado River **36** D 4
Colorado Springs **36** F 4
Columbia (Montana,
  U.S.A.) **37** H 4
Columbia (South
  Carolina, U.S.A.)
  37 K 5
Columbia (Tennessee,
  U.S.A.) **37** J 4
Columbia Plateau
  36 C 3
Columbia River **31** R 5
Columbine, Cape **56** B 6
Columbus (Georgia,
  U.S.A.) **37** K 5
Columbus (Mississippi,
  U.S.A.) **37** J 5
Columbus (Ohio,
  U.S.A.) **37** K 3
Colville Lake **32** L 5

Colville Lake (Lake) **32** L 5
Colwyn Bay **16** C 3
Comalcalco **38** D 4
Comandante Luis Piedrabuena **47** D 8
Combarabala **46** C 5
Comino, Capo **19** D 2
Comitán **38** D 4
Como **19** D 1
Comodoro Rivadavia **47** D 8
Comorin, Cape **66** D 6
Comoros **57** G 2
Compiégne **18** C 1
Comrat **22** C 3
Con Son **67** K 6
Conakry **50** D 7
Conceição, Cachoeira da **44** D 3
Conceição da Araguaia **45** G 3
Concepción (Argentina) **46** D 4
Concepción (Bolivia) **44** C 4
Concepción (Chile) **47** C 6
Concepción (Paraguay) **46** F 3
Concepción, Estrecho de **47** B 9
Concepción del Uruguay **46** F 5
Conception Bay **56** A 4
Concord **37** M 3
Concordia (U.S.A.) **37** G 4
Concordia (Uruguay) **46** F 5
Condobolin **77** H 6
Condon **36** B 2
Cóndor, Cerro el **46** D 4
Condor, Cordillera del **42** D 5
Conghua **69** J 6
Congo **54** C 4
Connecticut **37** M 3
Conselheiro Lafaiete **45** H 6
Conselheiro Pena **45** H 5
Constanţa **21** E 4
Constantine **51** H 1
Constantine, Cape **30** J 4
Constitución **47** C 6
Contwoyto Lake **32** O 5
Conway (Arkansas, U.S.A.) **37** H 4
Conway (South Carolina,U.S.A.) **37** L 5
Coober Pedy **76** E 5
Cooch Behär **67** F 2
Cook, Mount **77** N 8
Cook Inlet **30** K 3

Cook Islands **79** J 5
Cook Strait **77** N 8
Cooktown **77** H 3
Coolgardie **76** C 6
Cooma **77** H 7
Coonoor **66** D 5
Cooray **77** J 5
Coos Bay **36** B 3
Cootamundra **77** H 6
Copal Urco **42** E 5
Copán **38** E 5
Copenhagen **27** H 4
Copiapó **46** C 4
Coposa, Salar de **44** C 6
Copper Cliff **35** L 5
Copper Harbor **37** J 2
Coquimbo **46** C 4
Coral Harbour **35** L 2
Coral Sea **77** J 2
Coral Sea Islands Territory **77** H 2
Corato **19** F 2
Corbeil-Essonnes **18** C 1
Corbett National Park **66** D 2
Corcaigh **16** B 3
Cordele **37** K 5
Cordilheiras, Serra das **45** G 3
Cordoba **38** C 4
Córdoba (Argentina) **46** E 5
Córdoba (Spain) **18** B 3
Cordova **30** L 3
Corigliano Calabro **19** F 3
Corinth **37** J 5
Corinto **45** H 5
Corisco Bay **54** A 3
Cork **16** B 3
Cornélio Procópio **46** G 3
Corner Brook **35** Q 5
Cornwall Island **32** R 3
Cornwallis Island **32** R 3
Coro **43** F 2
Coroatá **45** H 2
Coromandel Coast **66** E 5
Coronation Gulf **32** O 5
Coronel **47** C 6
Coronel Fabriciano **45** H 5
Coronel Oviedo **46** F 4
Coronel Pringles **47** E 6
Coronel Suárez **47** E 6
Coronel Vidal **47** F 6
Coronel Vivida **46** G 4
Coropuna, Nevado **44** B 5
Corpus Christi **37** G 6
Correntina **45** H 4
Corrientes **46** F 4
Corrientes, Cabo **42** D 3
Corrigin **76** B 6
Corse **19** D 2
Corse, Cap **19** D 2

Corsica **19** D 2
Corsicana **37** G 5
Cortegana **18** B 3
Çorum **64** D 4
Corumbá **44** E 5
Corvallis **36** B 3
Cosamaloapan **38** C 4
Cosenza **19** F 3
Cosquín **46** E 5
Costa, Cordillera de la **43** F 3
Costa Brava **18** C 2
Costa de Mosquites **38** F 5
Costa del Sol **18** B 3
Costa Rica **38** E 5
Coswig **17** F 3
Cotabato **73** G 4
Côte d'Argent **18** B 2
Côte d'Ivoire **50** E 8
Cotonou **51** G 7
Cotopaxi **42** D 5
Cotovélo, Cachoeira do **44** E 3
Cottbus **17** F 3
Coubre, Pointe de la **18** B 1
Council Bluffs **37** G 3
Coventry **16** C 3
Cowan, Lake **76** C 6
Cowell **76** F 6
Coxilha de Santana **46** F 5
Coxim **45** F 5
Cox's Bazar **67** G 3
Coyaguaima, Cerro **46** D 3
Coyotitlán **36** E 7
Cozumel, Isla de **38** E 3
Cradock **56** D 6
Craig **36** E 3
Craigs Range **77** J 5
Cranbrook **31** R 6
Cratéus **45** H 3
Crato **45** J 3
Crawford **36** F 3
Crawley **16** C 3
Cree Lake **34** F 3
Creil **18** C 1
Cremona **19** E 1
Crescent City **36** B 3
Crete **21** E 5
Creus, Cap de **18** C 2
Crianlarich **16** C 2
Criciúma **46** H 4
Crimea **64** D 3
Cristóbal Colón, Picó **42** E 2
Cristal, Montes de **54** A 3
Cristalina **45** G 5
Croatia **20** C 3
Croker, Cape **76** E 2
Croker Island **76** E 2
Cromer **16** D 3
Crooked Creek **30** J 3
Crooked Island **39** H 3

Crooked Island Passage **39** G 3
Crookston **37** G 2
Crotone **19** F 3
Crown Prince Frederik Island **32** T 5
Crowsnest Pass **31** S 6
Croydon **77** G 3
Cruz, Cabo **39** G 3
Cruz Alta **46** G 4
Cruz del Eje **46** E 5
Cruzeiro do Oeste **46** G 3
Cruzeiro do Sul **44** B 3
Cu Lao Cham **67** K 4
Cu Lao Re **67** K 4
Cuahtémoc **36** E 6
Cuamba **57** F 2
Cuando Cubango **56** B 3
Cuango, Rio **54** C 5
Cuanza, Rio **56** B 2
Cuanza Norte **54** B 5
Cuanza Sul **56** A 2
Cuba **38** E 3
Cubango **56** B 3
Cuchi **56** B 2
Cuchilla Grande **46** F 5
Cúcuta **42** E 3
Cuddalore **66** D 5
Cuddapah **66** D 5
Cue **76** B 5
Cuéllar **18** C 2
Cuenca (Ecuador) **42** D 5
Cuenca (Spain) **18** B 2
Cuernavaca **38** C 4
Cuiabá **44** E 5
Culiacan **36** E 7
Cumaná **43** G 2
Cumbal **42** D 4
Cumberland Lake **34** G 4
Cumberland Sound **35** O 1
Cunene **56** A 3
Cuneo **19** D 2
Cunnamulla **77** H 5
Curaçao **39** J 4
Curacautín **47** C 6
Curanilahue **47** C 6
Curepipe **57** K 4
Curicó **46** C 6
Curitiba **46** H 4
Curitibanos **46** G 4
Curtis Island **77** J 4
Curuá, Ilha **45** F 1
Curupira, Sierra de **43** F 4
Curuzú Cuatiá **46** F 4
Curvelo **45** H 5
Custer **36** F 3
Cutral-Có **47** D 6
Cuttack **66** F 3
Cuxhaven **17** E 3
Cuzco **44** B 4
Cyprus **64** D 6
Cyrenaica **52** C 2

Czech Republic **17** F 4
Częstochowa **17** G 3
Człuchów **17** G 3

D

Da Lat **67** K 5
Da Nang **67** K 4
Da Yunhe **69** K 3
Daba Shan **69** H 4
Dabat **53** G 5
Dabhoi **66** C 3
Dacca **67** G 3
Dadiangas **73** H 4
Dadu **66** B 2
Daet **73** G 3
Dafang **69** H 5
Dafeng **69** L 4
Dafni **21** D 5
Dagana **50** C 5
Dagana (River) **52** C 5
Dagu **69** K 3
Dagupan **73** G 2
Dahlak Archipelago **53** H 4
Dahongliutan **68** B 3
Dahy, Nafūd ad **53** J 3
Dai **78** F 4
Daïa **51** G 2
Daintree River National Park **77** H 3
Dajarra **77** F 4
Dakar **50** C 6
Dākhīlah, Wāhāt ad **52** E 2
Dakhla **50** C 4
Dalälven **27** J 3
Dalandzadgad **69** G 2
Dalanjagalan **70** A 3
Dalarna **27** H 3
Dalbandin **66** A 2
Dalby **77** J 5
Dali **68** G 5
Dalí **69** H 4
Dalian **70** D 5
Daljā **52** F 2
Dall **31** O 5
Dall Lake **30** H 3
Dallas **37** G 5
Dal'negorsk **70** G 4
Dal'nerechensk **70** F 3
Dal'nyaya **70** H 3
Daloa **50** E 7
Dalou Shan **69** H 5
Dalstand **27** H 4
Dāltonganj **66** E 3
Dalupiri **73** G 2
Daly Waters **76** E 3
Damān **66** C 3
Daman and Diu **66** C 3
Damanhūr **52** F 1

Damar (Indonesia) **73** H 6
Damar (Indonesia) **73** H 7
Damaraland **56** B 4
Damascus **64** E 6
Damavand, Qolleh-ye **64** H 5
Damba **54** C 5
Dāmghān **65** H 5
Damoh **66** D 3
Dampier **76** B 4
Dampier Land **76** C 3
Danakil Plain **53** H 5
Danau Toba **72** B 5
Danba **69** G 4
Dandeli **66** C 4
Dangara **65** L 5
Danghe Nanshan **68** F 3
Dangshan **69** K 4
Danilov **24** F 3
Danilovka **23** F 2
Danmarkshavn **33** Hh 3
Danube **20** C 3
Danville (Illinois, U.S.A.) **37** J 3
Danville (Kentucky, U.S.A.) **37** K 4
Danville (Virginia, U.S.A.) **37** L 4
Danxian **67** K 4
Danzig, Gulf of **17** G 3
Dao Phu Quoc **67** J 5
Daocheng **68** G 5
Daoxian **69** J 5
Dapango **51** G 6
Dar Hamar **52** E 5
Dar Nūbah **52** E 5
Dar Rounga **54** D 2
Dar al Homr **52** E 5
Dar el Beida **50** E 2
Dar el Kouti **54** D 2
Dar es Salaam **55** G 5
Dar'a **64** E 6
Dārāb **53** K 2
Darāw **52** F 3
Darbhanga **66** F 2
Darbod **70** D 3
Dardanelles **21** E 5
Darfūr **52** D 5
Darganata **65** K 4
Dargaville **77** N 7
Darhan **61** X 8
Darien, Serranía del **39** G 6
Darīya **65** M 3
Darjeeling **66** F 2
Darlag **68** F 4
Darling **77** G 6
Darling Downs **77** J 5
Darling Range **76** B 6
Darlington **16** C 3
Darlot, Lake **76** C 5
Darmstadt **17** E 4
Darnah **52** D 1
Darreh Gaz **65** J 5
Dartmouth **35** P 6
Darvaza **65** J 4

Darwin **76** E 2
Daryācheh-ye Orūmīyeh **64** F 5
Daryā-ye Māzandarān **64** H 5
Dashhowuz **65** J 4
Dasht-e Kavīr **65** H 5
Date **70** H 4
Datia **66** D 2
Datong (Qinghai, China) **69** G 3
Datong (Shanxi, China) **70** B 5
Datong Shan **68** F 3
Daugaard-Jensen Land **33** Y 2
Daugava **27** K 4
Daugavpils **27** L 5
Daung Kyun **67** H 5
Dāvangere **66** D 5
Davao **73** H 4
Davenport **37** H 3
David **38** F 6
Davis Inlet **35** P 3
Davis Strait **33** Z 5
Dawei **67** H 5
Dawson **30** N 3
Dawson, Isla **47** C 9
Dawson Creek **31** Q 4
Dax **18** C 2
Daxian **69** H 4
Daxing **69** K 3
Dayangshu **70** D 3
Dayao **69** G 5
Dayong **69** J 5
Dayr az Zawr **64** F 5
Dayton **37** K 4
Daytona Beach **37** K 6
Dayu **69** J 5
Dazhu **69** H 4
De Aar **56** C 6
De Kastri **62** M 6
De Ridder **37** H 5
Dead Sea **53** G 1
Deadhorse **30** L 1
Deán Funes **46** E 5
Dease Lake **31** O 4
Death Valley **36** C 4
Death Valley National Monument **36** C 4
Dęblin **20** D 2
Deborah East, Lake **76** B 6
Deborah West, Lake **76** B 6
Debra Birhan **53** G 6
Debra Tabor **53** G 5
Debre Markos **53** G 5
Debrecen **20** D 3
Decatur (Alabama, U.S.A.) **37** J 5
Decatur (Illinois, U.S.A.) **37** J 4
Deccan **66** D 5
Decheng **69** G 5
Děčín **17** F 3
Deda **20** D 3
Dêgê **68** F 4

Dehiwala-Mount Lavinia **66** D 6
Dehra Dun **66** D 1
Dehui **70** E 4
Dej **20** D 3
Dekese **54** D 4
Del Rio **36** F 6
Del Verme Falls **53** H 6
Delaram **65** K 6
Delaware **37** M 4
Delhi **66** D 2
Delicias **36** E 6
Déline **32** M 5
Delmenhorst **17** E 3
Delta Junction **30** L 3
Dem'yanka **60** Q 6
Dem'yanskoye **60** P 6
Dembidollo **52** F 6
Den Helder **16** D 3
Denali **30** L 3
Denali National Park **30** K 3
Dengkou **69** H 2
Dengxian **69** J 4
Denham Sound **76** A 5
Denia **18** D 3
Deniliquin **77** G 7
Denison **37** G 5
Denizli **64** C 5
Denmark **27** G 4
Denmark (Australia) **76** B 6
Denow **65** L 5
Denpasar **72** F 7
Denton **37** G 5
D'Entrecasteaux Islands **78** E 4
Denver **36** E 4
Deoghar **66** F 3
Deolāli **66** C 4
Deprésion del Balsas **38** B 4
Dêqên **68** F 5
Deqing **69** J 6
Dera Ghāzi Khān **66** C 1
Dera Ismāïl Khān **66** C 1
Derbent **64** G 4
Derby (Australia) **76** C 3
Derby (U.K.) **16** C 3
Derdap **21** D 4
Dergachi **23** D 2
Derzhavīnsk **65** L 2
Des Moines **37** H 3
Désappointement, Îles du **79** L 5
Deschambault Lake **34** G 4
Dese **53** G 5
Desna **22** D 2
Dessau **17** F 3
Destruction Bay **31** N 3
Detmold **17** E 3
Detroit **37** K 3
Deva **20** D 3
Devon Island **32** S 3
Devonport **76** H 8

Dunedin **77** N 9
Dunfermline **16** C 2
Dunhua **70** E 4
Dunkerque **16** D 3
Dunkwa **51** F 7
Duolun **70** C 4
Durack Ranges **76** D 3
Durand, Récifs **78** F 6
Durango (Colorado, U.S.A.) **36** E 4
Durango (Mexico) **36** F 7
Durango (Spain) **18** B 2
Durant **37** G 5
Durazno **46** F 5
Durban **56** E 5
Durg **66** E 3
Durgāpur **66** F 3
Durham **37** L 4
Durmitor **21** C 4
Durrës **21** C 4
Durville Island **77** N 8
Dushan **69** H 5
Dushanbe **65** L 5
Düsseldorf **16** E 3
Dutch Harbor **30** G 5
Duyun **69** H 5
Dyat'kovo **22** D 2
Dyer, Cape **33** Y 5
Dzerzhinsk **25** F 3
Dzhagdy, Khrebet **62** J 6
Dzhalinda **62** H 6
Dzhaltyr **65** L 2
Dzhankoy **22** D 3
Dzhugdzhur, Khrebet **62** L 5
Dzhungarian Gate **68** C 1
Dzyarzhynsk **22** C 2

E

Eagle **30** M 3
Eagle Lake **36** B 3
Eagle Pass **36** F 6
Eagle Summit **30** L 2
Ear Falls **34** J 4
East Cape **79** G 7
East China Sea **71** D 6
East Coast Bays **77** N 7
East Falkland **47** F 9
East London **56** D 6
East Point **37** K 5
East Siberian Sea **63** P 2
Eastbourne **16** D 3
Eastern Ghāts **66** E 5
Eastmain **35** M 4
Eau Claire **37** H 3
Eauripik **78** D 3

Ebano **38** C 3
Ebe **62** M 4
Eboli **19** G 2
Ebro, Rio **18** B 2
Echeng **69** J 4
Echmiadzin **64** F 4
Echo Bay **32** N 5
Echuca **77** G 7
Écija **18** A 3
Eckerö **27** J 3
Ecuador **42** D 5
Ede **51** G 7
Edéa **54** B 3
Eder **17** E 3
Edgar Range **76** C 3
Edgell Island **35** P 2
Edgemont **36** F 3
Edinburgh **16** C 2
Edineţ **22** C 3
Edmonds **36** B 2
Edmonton **31** S 5
Edmundston **35** O 5
Edremit **64** C 5
Edso **32** N 6
Eduardo Castex **47** E 6
Edward, Lake **54** E 4
Edwards Plateau **36** F 5
Eek **30** H 3
Éfaté **78** F 5
Effingham **37** J 4
Egedesminde **33** Aa 5
Egegik **30** J 4
Egersund **27** G 4
Eglinton Island **32** N 3
Egvekinot **63** U 3
Egypt **52** E 2
Eha Amufu **51** H 7
Eiao **79** L 4
Eifel **16** E 3
Eigg **16** B 2
Eight Degree Channel **66** C 6
Eighty Mile Beach **76** B 3
Eiler Rasmussen, Kap **33** Gg 2
Eindhoven **16** E 3
Eire **16** B 3
Eisenach **17** F 3
Eisleben **17** F 3
Eivissa **18** C 3
Ejura **51** F 7
Ekarma, Ostrov **70** K 3
Ekibastuz **65** N 2
Ekimchan **62** K 6
Ekonda **61** X 4
El Aaiún **50** D 3
El Banco **42** E 3
El Bayadh **51** G 2
El Cajon **36** C 5
El Carmen de Bolivar **42** D 3
El Centro **36** C 5
El Djouf **50** E 4
El Dorado (Arkansas, U.S.A.) **37** H 5
El Dorado (Kansas, U.S.A.) **37** G 4

El Espinal **42** E 4
El Eulma **51** H 1
El Fasher **52** E 5
El Ferrol **18** A 2
El Goléa **51** G 2
El Hank **50** E 4
El Jadida **50** E 2
El Kelaa **50** E 2
El Khnâchîch **51** F 4
El Mahia **51** F 4
El-Manshāh **52** F 2
El Mereié **50** E 5
El Mirador **38** D 4
El Obeid **52** F 5
El Oued **51** H 2
El Paso **36** E 5
El Pintado **46** E 3
El Progreso **38** E 4
El Reno **37** G 4
El Salto **36** E 7
El Salvador **38** D 5
El Sueco **36** E 6
El Tajin **38** C 3
El Tigre **43** G 3
El Triunto **36** D 7
Elat **53** G 2
Elâziğ **64** E 5
Elba **19** E 2
Elbasan **21** D 4
Elbe **17** F 3
Elblag **17** G 3
El'brus, gora **23** F 4
Elche **18** B 3
Elcho Island **76** F 2
Elda **18** B 3
El'dikan **62** L 4
Eldorado **46** G 4
Eldoret **55** G 3
Elektrostal' **23** E 1
Eleuthera Island **37** L 6
Elgin **16** C 2
El'ginskoye Ploskogor'ye **62** L 3
Elgon, Mount **55** F 3
Elim **30** H 3
Elista **23** F 3
Elizabeth **77** F 6
Elizabeth City **37** L 4
Elizabeth Falls **34** F 3
Elizavety, Mys **62** M 6
Elk **22** B 2
Elkhart **37** J 3
Elkhovo **21** E 4
Ellef Ringnes Island **32** Q 3
Ellendale **36** G 2
Ellensburg **36** B 2
Ellesmere Island **33** U 3
Ellice Islands **79** G 4
Elliston **76** E 6
Elmira **37** L 3
Elmshorn **17** E 3
Elūru **66** E 4
Elvas **18** B 3
Elverum **27** H 3
Elvira **44** B 3
Ely **37** H 2
Embi **65** J 3

Emden **17** E 3
Emei **69** G 5
Emerald **77** H 4
Emerald Isle **32** O 3
Emi Koussi **52** C 4
eMijindini **56** E 5
Emmaboda **27** J 4
Emmen **17** E 3
Empalme **36** D 6
Empangeni **56** E 5
Emporia **37** G 4
Enarotali **73** K 6
Encarnación **46** F 4
Endeh **73** G 7
Enderbury Island **79** H 4
Engel's **23** G 2
Engershatu **53** G 4
Enggano **72** C 7
England **16** C 3
Englee **35** Q 4
English Channel **16** C 4
Enid **37** G 4
Eniwa **70** H 4
Eniwetok **78** F 2
Enköping **27** J 4
Enna **19** E 3
Ennadai **34** G 2
Ennadai Lake **34** G 2
Ennedi **52** D 4
Ennis **16** B 3
Enschede **16** E 3
Ensenada **36** C 5
Enshi **69** H 4
Entebbe **55** F 3
Enterprise (Canada) **32** N 6
Enterprise (U.S.A.) **36** C 2
Entre Ríos **45** F 3
Entroncamento **18** B 3
Enugu **51** H 7
Enugu Ezike **51** H 7
Envigado **42** D 3
Épernay **18** C 1
Épi **78** F 5
Épinal **19** D 1
Eqlīd **66** H 6
Equatoria **52** E 6
Equatorial Guinea **54** A 3
Érd **20** C 3
Erdene **70** B 4
Ereğli **64** D 5
Erenhot **70** B 4
Erepecu, Lago do **45** E 2
Erexim **46** G 4
Ereymentaü **65** M 2
Erfoud **50** F 2
Erfurt **17** F 3
Ergun Zuoqi **70** D 2
Erichsen Lake **33** U 4
Erie **37** K 3
Erie, Lake **35** L 6
Erikub **78** F 3
Erimo-misaki **70** H 4
Eritrea **53** G 5
Erlangen **17** F 4

Flint (Michigan, U.S.A.) **37** K 3
Flisa **27** H 3
Florence (Alabama, U.S.A.) **37** J 5
Florence (South Carolina,U.S.A.) **37** L 5
Florencia **42** D 4
Florentino Ameghino, Embalse **47** D 7
Flores (Guatemala) **38** F 4
Flores (Indonesia) **73** G 7
Flores, Laut **73** F 7
Flores Sea **73** F 7
Floriano **45** H 3
Florianopólis **46** H 4
Florida (U.S.A.) **37** K 6
Florida (Uruguay) **46** F 5
Florida, Straits of **37** K 7
Floridablanca **42** E 3
Florina **21** D 4
Florø **26** F 3
Flowers Cove **35** Q 4
Fluk **73** H 6
Focşani **20** E 3
Foggia **19** F 2
Fogo **50** B 5
Fogo Island **35** R 5
Foley Island **33** V 5
Foleyer **35** L 5
Fond du Lac **34** F 3
Fontas **31** Q 4
Fontur **26** C 2
Fonualei **79** H 6
Foraker, Mount **30** K 3
Førde **26** G 3
Forlì **19** E 2
Formatina, Sierra de **46** D 4
Formentera **18** C 3
Formentor, Cap de **18** C 2
Formia **19** E 2
Formiga **45** G 6
Formosa **69** L 6
Formosa (Argentina) **46** F 4
Formosa (Brazil) **45** G 5
Formosa, Serra **45** E 4
Formosa do Rio Prêto **45** G 4
Formosa Strait **69** L 6
Forrest **76** D 6
Forrest City **37** H 4
Forsayth **77** G 3
Forst **17** F 3
Fort Albany **35** L 4
Fort Beaufort **56** D 6
Fort Black **34** F 3
Fort Chimo **35** O3
Fort Chipewyan **31** S 4
Fort Collins **36** E 3
Fort Collinson **32** N 4
Fort Dodge **37** H 4
Fort George **35** M 4

Fort Good Hope **32** L 5
Fort Kent **35** O 5
Fort Lauderdale **37** K 6
Fort Liard **32** M 6
Fort Mackay **31** S 4
Fort McMurray **31** S 4
Fort McPherson **32** K 5
Fort Myers **37** K 6
Fort Nelson **31** Q 4
Fort Peck Dam **36** E 2
Fort Peck Lake **36** E 2
Fort Pierce **37** K 6
Fort Portal **55** F 3
Fort Providence **32** N 6
Fort Rupert **35** M 4
Fort Saint James **31** Q 5
Fort Saint John **31** Q 4
Fort Saskatchewan **31** S 5
Fort Severn **34** K 3
Fort-Shevchenko **23** H 4
Fort Simpson **32** M 6
Fort Smith (Canada) **32** O 6
Fort Smith (U.S.A.) **37** H 4
Fort Stockton **36** F 5
Fort Vermillion **31** R 4
Fort Wayne **37** J 3
Fort Worth **37** G 5
Fort Yukon **30** M 2
Fort-de-France **39** K 5
Fortaleza (Bolivia) **44** C 4
Fortaleza (Brazil) **45** J 2
Fortín Coronel Eugenia Garay **46** E 3
Fortín Florida **46** F 3
Fortín Garrapatal **46** E 3
Fortín Ravelo **44** D 5
Fortín Sargento Primero Leyes **46** F 3
Foshan **69** J 6
Fosna **26** H 3
Fou-ling **69** H 5
Foula **16** C 1
Foumban **54** B 2
Fouta Djallon **50** D 6
Fouta Ferlo **50** C 5
Foveaux Strait **77** M 9
Fox Islands **30** G 5
Foxe Basin **33** V 5
Foxe Channel **35** L 1
Foz do Jutaí **44** C 2
Foz do Tarauacá **44** C 3
Franca **46** H 3
France **18** B 1
France, Île de **33** Hh 3
Franceville **54** B 4
Francis Case, Lake **36** G 3
Francistown **56** D 4
Frankfort **37** K 4
Frankfurt **17** F 3
Frankfurt am Main **17** E 3
Franklin Lake **32** R 5

Fransisco Perito Moreno, Parçue Nacional **47** C 8
Franz Josefs Land **60** N 2
Franzz **34** L 5
Fraser Island **77** J 5
Fraser Plateau **31** Q 5
Fraser River **31** Q 5
Fraserburgh **16** C 2
Fray Bentos **46** F 5
Fredericia **27** G 4
Frederick Hills **76** E 2
Fredericksburg **37** L 4
Fredericton **35** O 5
Frederikshåb **33** Bb 6
Frederikshåb Isblink **33** Aa 6
Frederikshavn **27** H 4
Fredricksburg **36** G 5
Fredrik Willem IV Vallen **43** H 4
Fredrikstad **27** H 4
Freetown **50** D 7
Freiburg **17** E 4
Freising **17** F 4
Fréjus **19** D 2
Fremantle **76** B 6
French Guiana **43** J 4
French Polynesia **79** L 6
Fresnillo **38** B 3
Fresno **36** C 4
Freuchen Land **33** Cc 2
Freycinet Peninsula **76** H 8
Frías **46** D 4
Frisian Islands **16** E 3
Frodden, Isla **47** C 9
Frolovo **23** F 3
Frontera **38** D 4
Frosione **19** E 2
Frøya **26** G 3
Frutal **45** G 6
Frýdek-Místek **17** G 4
Fu'an **69** K 5
Fuding **69** L 5
Fuerteventura **50** D 3
Fuga **73** G 2
Fugloy **16** B 5
Fuji-san **70** G 5
Fujian **69** K 5
Fujin **70** F 3
Fukue-Jima **71** E 6
Fukui **70** G 5
Fukuoka **71** F 6
Fukushima **70** H 5
Fukuyama **70** F 6
Fulaga **79** H 5
Fulda **17** E 3
Funchal **50** C 2
Fundación **42** E 2
Fundo, Passo **46** G 4
Funing **69** K 4
Funtua **51** H 6
Fuqing **69** K 5
Furano **70** H 4
Furmanov **24** F 3
Furneaux Group **76** H 8

Fürth **17** F 4
Furukawa **70** H 5
Fushan **70** D 4
Fusong **70** E 4
Futuna, Île **79** H 5
Fuxian **70** D 5
Fuxin **70** D 4
Fuyang **69** K 4
Fuyu **70** D 3
Fuyuan **69** G 5
Fuyun **68** D 1
Fuzhou (Fujian, China) **69** K 5
Fuzhou (Jiangxi, China) **69** K 5
Fyn **27** H 4

G

Gabela **56** A 2
Gabès **51** H 2
Gabon **54** B 4
Gaborone **56** D 4
Gäddede **26** H 3
Gadsden **37** J 5
Gadwäl **66** D 4
Gag **73** H 6
Gagarin **22** D 1
Gagnoa **50** E 7
Gagnon **35** O 4
Gaillimh **16** B 3
Gainesville **37** K 6
Gainsville **37** K 5
Gairdner, Lake **76** F 6
Gaixian **70** D 4
Gaizinkalns **27** L 4
Gakona **30** L 3
Galán, Cerro **46** D 4
Galápagos Islands **42** A 5
Galaţi **21** E 3
Galatina **19** F 2
Galdhøpiggen **26** G 3
Galela **73** H 5
Galena **30** J 3
Galesburg **37** H 3
Galich **24** F 3
Galicia **18** A 2
Galle **66** E 6
Gallinas, Punta **42** E 2
Gallup **36** E 4
Galveston **37** H 6
Gálvez **46** E 5
Galway **16** B 3
Gama, Isla **47** E 7
Gambia, The **50** C 6
Gambier, Îles **79** M 6
Gamboma **54** B 4
Gamo Gofa **53** G 6
Gan Gan **47** D 7
Ganäveh **64** H 7

Gäncă **64** G 4
Gandajika **54** D 5
Gāndhi Sāgar **66** D 3
Gándhinagar **66** C 3
Gandía **18** B 3
Gandu **45** J 4
Ganga **66** D 2
Gangānagar **66** C 2
Gangapur **66** C 2
Gangaw **67** G 3
Gangawati **66** D 4
Gangdisê Shan **68** C 4
Ganges **66** F 2
Ganges, Mouths of the
  67 F 3
Gangotri **68** B 4
Gangtok **66** F 2
Gangu **69** H 4
Gannan **70** D 3
Ganquan **69** H 3
Gansu **69** G 3
Ganzhou **69** J 5
Gao **51** F 5
Gao'an **69** K 5
Gaoping **69** J 3
Gaotang **69** K 3
Gaoxian **69** G 5
Gaoyou **69** K 4
Gaozhou **69** J 6
Gap **19** E 2
Gapan **73** G 2
Garabogazköl Aylagy
  64 H 4
Garagum Kanaly **65** K 5
Garanhuns **45** J 3
Gardaneh-ye Ävej
  64 G 5
Garden City **36** F 4
Garden Reach **66** F 3
Gardez **65** L 6
Garissa **55** G 4
Garmisch-Partenkirchen
  17 F 4
Garonne **18** B 2
Garoua **54** B 2
Garoua Boulai **54** B 2
Garry Lake **34** G 1
Garut **72** D 7
Gary **37** J 3
Garyarsa **68** C 4
Garzê **68** F 4
Gascogne **18** B 2
Gascoyne Junction
  76 B 5
Gashua **51** J 6
Gaspé **35** P 5
Gaspé, Cap de **35** P 5
Gastonia **37** K 4
Gastre **47** D 7
Gästrikland **27** J 3
Gata, Cabo de **18** B 3
Gatchina **24** D 3
Gates of the Arctic
  National Park **30** K 2
Gateshead Island
  32 R 4
Gatineau, Parc de la
  35 M 5

Gaua **78** F 5
Gauhati **67** G 2
Gäuwän **66** E 3
Gavdos **52** D 1
Gävle **27** J 3
Gawler Ranges **76** F 6
Gaya (India) **66** E 3
Gaya (Nigeria) **51** H 6
Gayndah **77** J 5
Gaza **64** D 6
Gazami **51** J 6
Gaziantep **64** E 5
Gboko **51** H 7
Gdańsk **17** G 3
Gdynia **17** G 3
Gealdton **78** A 6
Gebe **73** H 6
Gedser **17** F 3
Geelong **77** G 7
Geelvink Channel
  76 A 5
Geilo **27** G 3
Gejiu **69** G 6
Gela **19** E 3
Geladandong **68** E 4
Gelendzhik **22** E 4
Gemena **54** C 3
General Acha **47** E 6
General Alvear **46** D 6
General Carrera, Lago
  47 C 8
General Juan
  Madariaga **47** F 6
General Martín Miguel
  De Güemes **46** D 3
General Paz **46** F 4
General Pico **47** E 6
General Roca **47** D 6
General San Martín
  46 F 5
General Santos **73** H 4
General Villegas **46** E 5
Geneva, Lake **19** D 1
Genève **19** D 1
Gengma **68** F 6
Genova **19** D 2
Gent **16** D 3
Geographical Society Ø
  33 Gg 4
George **56** C 6
George V Land **80** U 5
George, Lake **76** C 4
George Town (Malaysia)
  72 C 4
Georgetown (Bahamas)
  39 H 3
Georgetown (Guyana)
  43 H 3
Georgetown (South
  Carolina, U.S.A.)
  37 L 5
Georgia **64** F 4
Georgia (U.S.A.) **37** K 5
Georgian Bay **35** L 5
Georgīevka **65** O 3
Georgiyevsk **23** F 4
Gera **17** F 3
Geral, Serra **46** G 4

Geraldton **76** A 5
Gerba **63** O 4
Gereshk **65** K 6
Germania Land **33** Gg 3
Germany **17** E 3
Getafe **18** B 2
Geysir **26** A 3
Ghadāmis **51** H 2
Ghana **51** F 7
Ghanzi **56** C 4
Ghardaïa **51** G 2
Ghazni **65** L 6
Ghazzah **52** F 1
Gheorghieni **20** E 3
Ghurian **65** K 6
Giannitsa **21** D 4
Gibara **39** G 3
Gibraltar **18** A 3
Gibraltar, Estrecho de
  18 A 3
Gibraltar, Strait of
  18 A 3
Gibson Desert **76** C 4
Gichgeniyn Nuruu
  68 E 1
Gideälven **26** J 3
Gidgi, Lake **76** D 5
Gifu **70** G 5
Gijón **18** A 2
Gilbert Islands **79** G 3
Gilgit **65** M 5
Gillen, Lake **76** D 5
Gillette **36** E 3
Gingoog **73** H 4
Gir National Park **66** C 3
Gir Range **66** C 3
Giridih **66** F 3
Girona **18** C 2
Girvan **16** C 2
Gisborne **77** O 7
Giurgiu **21** E 4
Giza **52** F 1
Gizjiga **63** Q 4
Gizycho **22** B 2
Gjirokastër **21** D 4
Gjoa Haven **32** R 5
Gjøvik **27** H 3
Glaciares, Parçue
  Nacional los **47** C 9
Glacier Bay National
  Park and Reserve
  31 N 4
Glacier National Park
  36 D 2
Gladstone **77** J 4
Glasgow **16** C 2
Glazov **25** H 3
Glen Canyon National
  Recreation Area
  36 D 4
Glen Innes **77** J 5
Glendale **36** D 5
Glennallen **30** L 3
Glens Falls **37** M 3
Gliwice **17** G 3
Głogów **17** G 3
Glomfjord **26** H 2
Glomma **27** H 4

Glommersträsk **26** J 2
Gloucester (U.K.)
  16 C 3
Gloucester (U.S.A.)
  37 M 3
Glübokoe **65** O 2
Gniezno **17** G 3
Goa **66** C 4
Gobi Desert **69** G 2
Godavari **66** E 4
Godavari, Mouths of the
  66 E 4
Godby **27** J 3
Godhavn **33** Aa 5
Godhra **66** C 3
Gödöllő **20** D 3
Gods Lake **34** J 4
Godthåb **33** Aa 6
Gogland, Ostrov **27** L 3
Goianesia **45** G 5
Goiânia **45** G 5
Goiás **45** F 5
Goiás (State) **45** F 5
Goio-Erê **46** G 3
Gojam **53** G 5
Gojra **66** C 1
Gökçeada **64** B 4
Gol **27** G 3
Gol'chikha **61** S 3
Gold Coast **51** F 8
Golden **31** R 5
Goldsboro **37** L 4
Golmud **68** E 3
Golpäyegän **64** H 6
Goma **54** E 4
Gombe **51** J 6
Gomera **50** C 3
Gómez Palacio **36** F 6
Gomo Co **68** D 4
Gonaïves **39** H 4
Gonáve, Île de la **39** H 4
Gonbad-e Qābūs
  65 J 5
Gondal **66** C 3
Gondar **53** G 5
Gondia **66** E 3
Gongan **69** J 4
Gongcheng **69** J 6
Gongga Shan **69** G 5
Gonghe **68** G 3
Gongliu **68** C 2
Gonzalés **38** C 3
Good Hope, Cape of
  56 B 6
Goodnews Bay **30** H 4
Goondiwindi **77** J 5
Goose Lake **36** B 3
Gorakhpur **66** E 2
Goražde **21** C 4
Gore (Ethiopia) **53** G 6
Gore (New Zealand)
  77 M 9
Goré **52** C 6
Gorgan **65** H 5
Gorgona, Isla **42** D 4
Gori **64** F 4
Gorizia **20** B 3
Gorkiy **23** F 1

Gorna Oryakhovitsa
21 E 4
Gorno-Altaysk 61 T 7
Gornozavodsk 70 H 3
Gornyak 65 O 2
Gorodets 25 F 3
Goroka 78 D 4
Gorong 73 J 6
Gorontalo 73 G 5
Gorzów Wielkopolski
17 G 3
Goshogahara 70 H 4
Gosnells 76 B 6
Götaland 27 H 4
Göteborg 27 H 4
Gotland 27 J 4
Goto-Retto 71 E 6
Gotse Delchev 21 D 4
Gotska Sandön 27 J 4
Göttingen 17 E 3
Gottwaldov 17 G 4
Gouda 16 D 3
Goulburn 77 H 6
Goulburn Island
76 E 2
Goundam 50 F 5
Gourma 51 G 6
Gourounsi 51 F 6
Governador Valadares
45 H 5
Govind Ballabah Pant
Sagar 66 E 3
Goya 46 F 4
Gozho Co 68 C 3
Graaff-Reinet 56 C 6
Grace, Lake 76 B 6
Gracias a Dios, Cabo de
38 E 5
Graciosa 50 A 1
Gradaús 45 F 3
Gradaús, Serra dos
45 F 3
Grafton 77 J 5
Graham Island (British
Columbia, Canada)
31 O 5
Graham Island
(Nunavut, Canada)
32 S 3
Grahamstown 56 D 6
Grain Coast 50 D 7
Grajaú 45 G 3
Grajewo 22 B 2
Grampian Mountains
16 B 2
Gran Altiplanicie Central
47 D 8
Gran Canaria 50 C 3
Gran Chaco 46 E 4
Gran Laguna Salada
47 D 7
Granada (Nicaragua)
38 E 5
Granada (Spain) 18 B 3
Granby 35 N 5
Grand Bassam 51 F 7
Grand Canal 69 K 3
Grand Canyon 36 D 4

Grand Canyon National
Park 36 D 4
Grand Cayman 39 F 4
Grand Coulee Dam
36 C 2
Grand Erg de Bilma
51 J 5
Grand Forks 37 G 2
Grand Island 36 G 3
Grand Junction 36 E 4
Grand Manan Island
35 O 6
Grand Rapids
(Michigan, U.S.A.)
37 J 3
Grand Rapids
(Minnesota, U.S.A.)
37 H 2
Grand Turk 39 J 3
Grande, Bahía 47 D 9
Grande, Rio 36 E 5
Grande, Sierra 45 J 3
Grande Comore 57 G 2
Grande de Manacapuru,
Lago 44 D 2
Grande de Tierra del
Fuego, Isla 47 D 9
Grande Prairie 31 R 4
Grandin, Lac 32 N 6
Grane 26 H 2
Granite City 37 H 4
Granite Dam 35 Q 5
Granollers 18 C 2
Grantham 16 C 3
Grants 36 E 4
Grants Pass 36 B 3
Granville 18 C 1
Gras, Lac de 32 O 6
Gravatá 45 J 3
Graz 19 F 1
Great Abaco Island
37 L 6
Great Artesian Basin
77 G 4
Great Australian Bight
76 D 6
Great Barrier Island
77 O 7
Great Barrier Reef
77 G 2
Great Basin 36 C 3
Great Bear Lake
32 M 5
Great Bear River 32 L 5
Great Dividing Range
77 G 3
Great Exuma Island
37 L 7
Great Falls 36 D 2
Great Himalaya Range
66 D 1
Great Inagua Island
39 H 3
Great Indian Desert
66 B 2
Great Karns Mount
56 B 5
Great Karoo 56 C 6

Great Nefud, The
53 G 2
Great Nicobar Island
67 G 6
Great North East
Channel 77 G 2
Great Plain of the
Koukdjuak 35 N 1
Great Plains (Canada)
31 R 4
Great Plains (U.S.A.)
36 F 3
Great Salt Lake 36 D 3
Great Salt Lake Desert
36 D 4
Great Sandy Desert
76 C 4
Great Sitkin Island
30 E 5
Great Slave Lake 32 N 6
Great Victoria Desert
76 D 5
Great Victoria Desert
Nature Reserve 76 D 5
Great Wall of China
70 B 5
Great Yarmouth 16 D 3
Greater Antilles 39 H 4
Gréboun, Mont 51 H 4
Gredos, Sierra de
18 A 3
Greece 21 C 5
Greeley 36 F 3
Green Bay 37 J 3
Green Islands 78 E 4
Green River 36 D 4
Green River (River)
36 E 4
Greenland 33 Aa 3
Greenland Sea 33 Ll 3
Greensboro 37 L 4
Greenville (Mississippi,
U.S.A.) 37 H 5
Greenville (North
Carolina, U.S.A.)
37 L 4
Greenwood 37 K 5
Gregory, Lake (South
Australia) 77 F 5
Gregory, Lake (Western
Australia) 76 B 5
Gregory, Lake (Western
Australia) 76 D 4
Gregory Range 77 G 3
Greifswald 17 F 3
Grená 27 H 4
Grenada 39 K 5
Grenadine Islands
39 K 5
Grenoble 19 D 1
Grenville (Grenada) 77 G 2
Gresik 72 E 7
Gretna 16 C 2
Grey Islands 35 Q 4
Grey Range 77 G 5
Greymouth 77 N 8
Griffin 37 K 5
Griffith 77 H 6

Grimsby 16 C 3
Grimshaw 31 R 4
Grimstad 27 G 4
Grise Fjord 33 U 3
Groix, Île de 18 B 1
Groningen 16 E 3
Grong 26 H 3
Groot Winter Berg
56 D 6
Groote Eylandt 76 F 2
Grootfontein 56 B 3
Grosseto 19 E 2
Großglockner 19 E 1
Grotte de Lascaux
18 C 1
Groznyy 23 G 4
Grudziądz 17 G 3
Gryada Chernysheva
25 J 1
Gryazi 23 E 2
Grytice 17 G 3
Guacara 43 F 2
Guadalajara (Mexico)
38 B 3
Guadalajara (Spain)
18 B 2
Guadalcanal 78 E 5
Guadalquivir, Río 18 A 3
Guadalupe, Isla 36 C 6
Guadeloupe 39 K 4
Guadiana, Río 18 A 3
Guadix 18 C 3
Guaini, Rio 43 F 4
Guaíra 46 G 3
Guajará-Mirim 44 C 4
Guañape, Islas de
42 D 6
Guale guaychú 46 F 5
Guam 78 D 2
Guamíchil 36 E 6
Guamini 47 E 6
Guan Xian 69 G 4
Guanajuato 38 B 3
Guanambi 45 H 4
Guanare 43 F 3
Guandacol 46 D 4
Guane 38 G 3
Guangdong 69 J 6
Guanghua 69 J 4
Guangji 69 K 5
Guangxi Zhuangzu
Zizhiqu 69 H 6
Guangyaun 69 H 4
Guangzhou 69 J 6
Guantanamo 39 G 3
Guanyun 69 K 4
Guarabira 45 J 3
Guarapari 45 H 6
Guarapuava 46 G 4
Guarda 18 B 2
Guardafui, Cape 53 K 5
Guarenas 43 F 2
Guárico, Embalse del
43 F 2
Guasave 36 E 6
Guasdualito 42 E 3
Guatemala 38 D 5
Guayaoul 42 C 5

Hattiesburg **37** J 5
Hatutu **79** L 4
Haud **53** J 6
Haugesund **27** G 4
Haukeligrend **17** E 2
Haut Atlas **50** E 2
Havana **38** F 3
Havelock Island **67** G 5
Havlíčkuv Brod **17** G 4
Havre **36** E 2
Hawaii **79** K 2
Hawaiian Islands
  79 K 1
Hawera **77** N 7
Hawke Bay **77** O 7
Hawrā **53** J 4
Hay **77** G 6
Hay River **32** N 6
Hayes, Mount **30** L 3
Hays **36** G 4
Haysyn **22** C 3
Hazaradjat **65** K 6
Hazaribagh **66** F 3
Hazelton **31** P 4
Hazen, Lake **33** W 2
Hazen Strait **32** O 3
Hazlett, Lake **76** D 4
Hearst **35** L 5
Hebei **69** J 3
Hebi **69** J 3
Hebrides **16** B 2
Hebron **35** P 3
Hechi **69** H 6
Hechuan **69** H 4
Hecla, Cape **33** Y 2
Hede **26** H 3
Hedmark **27** H 3
Hefa **52** G 1
Hefei **69** K 4
Hegang **70** F 3
Heidelberg **17** E 4
Heidenheim **17** F 4
Heilbronn **17** E 4
Heilongjiang **70** E 3
Heilprin Land **33** Hh 2
Heilprin Ø **33** Y 3
Heimaey **26** A 3
Heishan **70** D 4
Hejiang **69** H 5
Hejlong-Jiang **70** D 2
Helena **36** D 2
Helgoländer Bucht
  17 E 3
Helgøy **26** J 1
Heli **70** F 3
Hellín **18** C 3
Helsingborg **27** H 4
Helsingfors **27** K 3
Helsingør **27** H 4
Helsinki **27** K 3
Hemsön **26** J 3
Henan **69** J 4
Henderson **36** D 4
Henderson Island
  79 N 6
Hendersonville **37** J 4
Hendrik Verwoerd Dam
  56 D 6

Hengdnan Shan **68** F 5
Hengshan **69** J 5
Hengshui **69** K 3
Hengxian **69** H 6
Hengyang **69** J 5
Heniches'k **22** D 3
Henrietta Maria, Cape
  35 L 3
Henryetta **37** G 4
Henzada **67** H 4
Hepu **69** H 6
Herat **65** K 6
Heredia **38** F 5
Hereford (U.K.) **16** C 3
Hereford (U.S.A.) **36** F 5
Herlen Gol **70** B 3
Hermit Islands **78** D 4
Hermosillo **36** D 6
Hernandarias **46** G 4
Hernando de
  Magellanes, Parçue
  Nacional **47** C 9
Herning **27** G 4
Heroica Zitacuaro
  38 B 4
Herschel Island **30** N 2
Hertungen af Orléans
  Land **33** Gg 3
Hestur **16** B 1
Hexian **69** J 6
Heyuan **69** J 6
Heze **69** K 3
Hialeah **37** K 6
Hibernia Reef **76** C 2
Hidalgo del Parral
  36 E 6
Hierro **50** C 3
High Level **31** R 4
High Prairie **31** R 4
Highrock Lake **34** G 3
Hiiumaa **27** K 4
Hikueru **79** L 5
Hildesheim **17** E 3
Hilo **79** K 2
Himachal **66** D 1
Himi **70** G 5
Hims **64** E 6
Hinchinbrook Island
  (Australia) **77** H 3
Hinchinbrook Island
  (U.S.A.) **30** L 3
Hindukush **65** L 6
Hindupur **66** D 5
Hinganghat **66** D 3
Hinnøya **26** J 2
Hinton **31** R 5
Hirado **71** E 6
Hiriyūr **66** D 5
Hirosaki **70** H 4
Hiroshima **70** F 6
Hirtshals **27** G 4
Hisār **66** D 2
Hispaniola **39** H 4
Hitachi **70** H 5
Hiti **79** L 5
Hitra **26** G 3
Hjälmaren **27** H 4
Hjukhiv **22** D 2

Ho Chi Minh **67** K 5
Hoa Binh **67** K 3
Hobart **76** H 8
Hobbs **36** F 5
Hoburgen **27** J 4
Hobyo **55** J 2
Hochstetter Forland
  33 Gg 3
Hodeida **53** H 5
Hodh **50** E 5
Hódmezővásárhely
  20 D 3
Hodna, Chott el
  51 G 1
Hodonin **17** G 4
Hofsjökull **26** B 3
Höfu **71** F 6
Hoggar **51** G 4
Hoh Sai Hu **68** E 3
Hoh Xil Hu **68** E 3
Hoh Xil Shan **68** D 3
Hohhot **70** B 4
Hoi An **67** K 4
Hokkaidō **70** H 4
Hola Prystan **22** D 3
Holbox, Isla **38** D 3
Holbrook **36** D 5
Holguín **39** G 3
Holland **37** J 3
Hollywood **37** K 6
Holm Land **33** Hh 2
Holm Ø **33** Z 4
Holman **32** N 4
Holmön **26** K 3
Holovanivs'k **22** D 3
Holstebro **27** G 4
Holsteinsborg **33** Aa 5
Holycross **30** J 3
Hombori Tondo **51** F 5
Hombre Muerto, Salar
  del **46** D 4
Homer **30** K 4
Homewood **37** J 5
Homs **64** E 6
Homyel' **22** D 2
Hon Gai **67** K 3
Hon Khoci **67** J 6
Hon Tho Chau **67** J 6
Honãvar **66** C 5
Honduras **38** E 5
Honduras, Golfo de
  38 D 4
Hönefoss **27** H 3
Hong Kong **69** J 6
Hongjiang **69** H 5
Hongor **70** B 3
Hongshui He **69** H 6
Hongwon **70** E 4
Hongyuan **69** G 4
Hongze **69** K 4
Hongze Hu **69** K 4
Honiara **78** E 4
Honningsvåg **26** L 1
Honolulu **79** K 1
Honshū **70** H 5
Hood Point **76** B 6
Hoorn **16** E 3

Hoover Dam **36** D 4
Hopedale **35** P 3
Hopes Advance, Cap
  35 O 2
Hopewell, Isles **35** M 3
Hoquiam **36** B 2
Hora Dzyarzhynskaya
  20 E 2
Hordaland **27** G 3
Horlivka **22** E 3
Hormuz Strait of **53** L 2
Horn **26** A 2
Horn, Cape **47** D 10
Horn Plateau **32** M 6
Hornavan **26** J 2
Hörnefors **26** J 3
Hornos, Cabo de
  47 D 10
Hornos, Isla **47** D 10
Horodenka **22** C 3
Horqin Youyi Qiahqi
  70 D 3
Horqin Zuoyi Zhongqi
  70 D 4
Horqueta **46** F 3
Horsens **27** G 4
Horsham **77** G 7
Horten **27** H 4
Hose Mountains **72** E 5
Hosseina **53** G 6
Hoste, Isla **47** D 10
Hot Springs **37** H 5
Hotan **68** B 3
Hotazel **56** C 5
Hoting **26** J 3
Hottah Lake **32** N 5
Houlton **37** N 2
Houma (China) **69** J 3
Houma (U.S.A.) **37** H 6
Houston **37** G 6
Houterive **35** O 5
Houtman Abrolhos
  76 A 5
Hovd **61** U 8
Hovgaard Ø **33** Hh 2
Hövsgöl **70** A 4
Hövsgöl Nuur **61** V 7
Howe, Cape **77** J 7
Howrah **68** D 6
Hoy **16** C 2
Hradec Králové **17** G 3
Hrebinka **22** D 2
Hrodna **22** B 2
Hsi-lo **69** L 6
Hsin-chu **69** L 6
Hu Men **69** J 6
Hua Hin **67** H 5
Huacho **44** A 4
Huadian **70** E 4
Huahine **79** K 5
Huai'an **70** B 4
Huaide **70** D 4
Huaiji **69** J 6
Huailai **70** C 4
Huainan **69** K 4
Huairen **69** J 3
Huajuapan de Léon
  38 C 4

Inuvik 32 K 5
Invercargill 77 M 9
Inverness 16 C 2
Inya 62 M 4
Inza 23 G 2
Ioannina 21 D 5
Iokanga 24 E 1
Ionian Sea 19 F 3
Ionioi Nisoi 21 C 5
Iony, Ostrov 62 M 5
Ios 21 E 5
Iossar 25 H 2
Iowa 37 G 3
Iowa City 37 H 3
Ipameri 45 G 5
Ipatinga 45 H 5
Ipatovo 23 F 3
Ipeiros 21 D 5
Ipiales 42 D 4
Ipiaú 45 J 4
Ipoh 72 C 5
Iporá 45 F 5
Ipswich (Australia)
    77 J 5
Ipswich (U.K.) 16 D 3
Ipu 45 H 2
Iqaluit 35 O 2
Iquique 46 C 3
Iquitos 42 E 5
Irakleio 21 E 5
Iran 64 H 6
Iran, Pegunungan
    72 E 5
Irapuato 38 B 3
Iraq 64 F 5
Irbid 53 G 1
Irbil 64 F 5
Irbit 25 K 3
Irecê 45 H 4
Ireland 16 B 3
Iringa 55 G 5
Iriomote-jima 69 L 6
Iriona 38 F 4
Irish Sea 16 B 3
Irkutsk 61 W 7
Ironwood 37 J 2
Irrawaddy 67 H 3
Irrawaddy, Mouths of
    the 67 G 4
Irrigi 50 E 6
Irtysh 60 Q 6
Irún 18 B 2
Irving 37 G 5
Isa 51 H 6
Isabel 54 A 3
Isachenka, Ostrov
    61 T 2
Isachsen 32 Q 3
Isachsen, Cape 32 P 3
Isafjörður 26 A 2
Isa-haya 71 F 6
Isaouane-N-Irharharene
    51 H 3
Isernia 19 E 2
Ise-wan 70 G 6
Iseyin 51 G 7
Isfara 65 M 4
Ishikari-wan 70 H 4

Ishikawa 71 E 7
Ishikotrau 6 N 2
Ishim 60 P 6
Ishim (River) 60 Q 6
Ishimbay 23 J 2
Ishinomaki 70 H 5
Isil'kul' 60 Q 7
Isiolo 55 G 3
Isipingo beach 56 E 6
Isiro 54 E 3
Isjichly 64 G 5
Iskenderun 64 E 5
Iskitim 61 S 7
Islamabad 65 M 6
Island Lake 34 H 4
Islay 16 B 2
Isnä 52 F 2
Isoka 56 E 2
Isparta 64 D 5
Israel 52 F 1
Istanbul 64 C 4
Istanbul Boğazi 64 C 4
Istra 21 B 3
Isua 33 Bb 6
Itabaiana (Paraíba,
    Brazil) 45 J 3
Itabaiana (Sergipe,
    Brazil) 45 J 4
Itaberaba 45 H 4
Itabira 45 H 5
Itaboca 44 D 2
Itabuna 45 J 4
Itacoatiara 44 E 2
Itagüí 42 D 3
Itaituba 44 E 2
Itajaí 46 H 4
Itajuipe 45 J 4
Italy 19 E 2
Itamaraju 45 J 5
Itambé 45 H 5
Itanagar 67 G 2
Itaobim 45 H 5
Itapecuru Mirim 45 H 2
Itaperuna 45 H 6
Itapetinga 45 H 5
Itapetininga 46 H 3
Itapipoca 45 J 2
Itaquari 45 H 6
Itaqui 46 F 4
Itaquyry 46 F 4
Itarsi 66 D 3
Itaruma 45 F 5
Itaúna 45 H 6
Itbay 53 G 3
Ithaca 37 L 3
Ithaki 21 D 5
Ithnayn, Harrat 53 H 2
Itoigawa 70 G 5
Ittoqqortoormiit 33 Gg 4
Ituiutaba 45 G 5
Itumbiara 45 G 5
Iturup, Ostrov 70 J 4
Ituverava 46 H 3
Itzehoe 17 E 3
Iul'tin 63 U 3
Ivakoany 57 H 4
Ivalo 26 L 2
Ivanava 22 C 2

Ivanhoe 77 G 6
Ivano-Frankivs'k 22 B 3
Ivanovka 23 H 2
Ivanovo 24 F 3
Ivao, Gora 70 J 3
Ivdel' 25 K 2
Ivittuut 33 Bb 6
Ivory Coast 50 E 8
Ivrea 19 D 1
Ivujivik 35 M 2
Iwaki 70 H 5
Iwakuni 71 F 6
Iwanai 70 H 4
Iwôn 70 E 4
Ixiamas 44 C 4
Izhevsk 25 H 3
İzmir 64 C 5
İzmit 64 C 4
Izozog, Bañados de
    44 D 5
Izu-shotō 71 G 6
Izvestiy Tsik, Ostrov
    61 S 2
Izyum 22 E 3

J

Jabalpur 66 D 3
Jaboticabal 46 H 3
Jacarézinho 46 G 3
Jaciara 45 E 5
Jackson (Tennessee,
    U.S.A.) 37 J 4
Jackson (Wyoming,
    U.S.A.) 36 D 3
Jacksonville (Florida,
    U.S.A.) 37 K 5
Jacksonville (Illinois,
    U.S.A.) 37 H 4
Jacksonville (North
    Carolina, U.S.A.)
    37 L 5
Jacksonville (Texas,
    U.S.A.) 37 G 5
Jacksonville Beach
    37 K 5
Jäckvik 26 J 2
Jacobabad 66 B 2
Jacobina 45 H 4
Jacona de Plancarte
    38 B 4
Jacundá 45 G 2
Jadal 51 G 5
Jaén (Peru) 42 D 6
Jaén (Spain) 18 B 3
Jaffa, Cape 77 F 7
Jaffna 66 E 6
Jagdalpur 66 E 4
Jagdaqi 70 D 2
Jagtiäl 66 D 4
Jaguarão 46 G 5

Jaguaribe 45 J 3
Jagüé 46 D 4
Jahrom 53 K 2
Jaipur 66 D 2
Jaisalmer 66 C 2
Jakarta 72 D 7
Jakobshavn 33 Aa 5
Jalalabad 65 M 6
Jalal-Abad 68 A 2
Jalapa Enríquez 38 C 4
Jalgaon 66 D 3
Jalingo 51 J 7
Jalna 66 D 4
Jälor 66 C 2
Jalostotitlán 38 B 3
Jalpáiguri 67 F 2
Jälü, Wähät 52 D 2
Jamaica 39 G 4
Jamaica Channel
    39 G 4
Jamãme 55 H 3
Jambi 72 C 6
Jambusar 66 C 3
James Bay 35 L 4
Jameson Land 33 Gg 4
Jamestown 37 L 3
Jamiltepec 38 D 4
Jammu 66 C 1
Jammu and Kashmir
    65 N 6
Jamnagar 66 C 3
Jampur 66 C 2
Jamshedpur 66 F 3
Jämtland 26 H 3
Jamuna 67 F 2
Jan Mayen 33 Kk 4
Janaúba 45 H 5
Janauca, Ilha 45 F 5
Janchuan 68 F 5
Janos 38 E 3
Januária 45 H 5
Jaora 66 D 3
Japan 70 G 6
Japan, Sea of 70 F 5
Jaraguá 45 G 5
Jarbah 51 J 2
Jardines de la Reina,
    Archipiélago de los
    39 F 3
Jarid, Shatt al 51 H 2
Jarkant 68 B 3
Jarosław 22 B 2
Järpen 26 H 3
Jarud Qi 70 D 4
Järvenpää 27 L 3
Jarvis 79 J 4
Jäsk 53 L 2
Jasło 17 H 4
Jason Islands 47 E 9
Jasper 31 R 5
Jasper National Park
    31 R 5
Jászberény 20 C 3
Jataí 45 F 5
Jatni 66 F 3
Jatuarana 44 D 3
Jaú 46 H 3
Jauareté 44 C 1

K

Kalibo **73** G 3
Kalima **54** E 4
Kalimantan **72** E 6
Kalinin **24** E 3
Kaliningrad **17** H 3
Kalinkavichy **22** C 2
Kalispell **36** D 2
Kalisz **17** G 3
Kaliua **55** F 5
Kalix **26** K 2
Kalixälven **26** K 2
Kalmar **27** J 4
Kalsong **73** G 4
Kalsoy **16** B 1
Kaltag **30** J 3
Kaltan **61** T 7
Kaluga **22** E 2
Kalukalukuang **73** F 7
Kalulushi **56** D 2
Kalush **22** B 3
Kalutara **66** E 6
Kalyazin **24** E 3
Kalymnos **21** E 5
Kama **25** H 3
Kamaishi **70** H 5
Kamarān **53** H 4
Kambarka **25** H 3
Kamchatka, Poluostrov
 63 P 5
Kamchatskiy Poluostrov
 63 Q 5
Kamen'-na-Obi **61** S 7
Kamenjak, Rt **21** B 4
Kamenka **23** F 2
Kamensk **61** X 7
Kamensk-Shakhtinskiy
 23 F 3
Kamensk-Ural'skiy
 25 K 3
Kamenskoye **63** R 4
Kamet **66** D 1
Kamina **54** D 5
Kaminak Lake **34** H 2
Kaminuriak Lake **34** H 2
Kamkaly **65** M 4
Kamloops **31** Q 5
Kamoa Mountains
 43 H 4
Kampala **55** F 3
Kampar **72** C 5
Kampen **16** E 3
Kamphaeng Phet **67** H 4
Kampuchea **67** J 5
Kāmthī **66** D 3
Kam"yanets'-Podil's'kyy
 22 C 3
Kamyshin **23** G 2
Kamyshlov **25** K 3
Kanaga Island **30** E 5
Kananga **54** D 5
Kanangra Boyd
 National Park **77** J 6
Kanazawa **70** G 5
Kanchana-buri **67** H 5
Kanchenjunga **68** D 5
Kānchipuram **66** D 5
Kandahar **66** B 1
Kandalaksha **24** D 1

Kandavu Island **79** G 5
Kandhkot **66** B 2
Kandi **51** G 6
Kandi, Tanjung **73** G 5
Kandukūr **66** D 4
Kandy **66** E 6
Kane Basin **33** X 3
Kanem **52** C 5
Kang **56** C 4
Kangaarsussuaq **33** W 3
Kangan **53** K 2
Kangar **72** C 4
Kangaroo Island **76** F 7
Kangāvar **64** G 6
Kangbao **70** B 4
Kangding **69** G 4
Kangean **72** F 7
Kangerlussuaq **33** Aa 5
Kangersuatsiaq **33** Z 4
Kanggye **70** E 4
Kangikajik **33** Gg 4
Kangiqsualujjuaq
 35 O 3
Kangirsuk **35** N 2
Kangnüng **70** E 5
Kango **54** B 3
Kangping **70** D 4
Kangrinboqê Feng
 68 C 4
Kang-shan **69** L 6
Kangto **67** G 2
Kaniet Islands **78** D 4
Kanin Nos **24** F 1
Kanin Nos, Mys **24** F 1
Kankakee **37** J 3
Kankan **50** E 6
Känker **66** E 3
Kankesanturai **66** E 6
Kanmaw Kyun **67** H 5
Kannapolis **37** K 4
Kano **51** H 6
Kanona **56** E 2
Kanowit **72** E 5
Kanoya **71** F 6
Kanpur **66** E 2
Kansas **36** F 4
Kansas City **37** H 4
Kansk **61** V 6
Kantama **54** D 5
Kantang **67** H 6
Kanton **69** J 6
Kanuku Mountains
 43 H 4
Kanye **56** D 4
Kao-hsiung **69** L 6
Kaolack **50** C 6
Kaouar **51** J 5
Kapfenberg **19** F 1
Kaposvár **20** C 3
Kapuskasing **35** L 5
Kara-Balta **65** M 4
Kara Sea **60** R 2
Karabash **25** K 3
Karabük **64** D 4
Karabula **61** V 6
Karachev **22** D 2
Karachi **66** B 3
Karad **66** C 4

Karaginskiy, Ostrov
 63 Q 5
Karaikkudi **66** D 5
Karakelong **73** H 5
Karakol **65** N 4
Karakoram Range
 65 N 5
Karaman **64** D 5
Karaqoyyn Köli **65** L 3
Karasburg **56** B 5
Karasjok **26** L 2
Karaskoye More **60** R 2
Karasu **64** F 5
Karasuk **61** R 7
Karaul **61** S 3
Karawang **72** D 7
Karbalā' **64** F 6
Karditsa **21** D 5
Karen **67** G 5
Karesuando **26** K 2
Karet **50** D 4
Kargasok **61** S 6
Kargopol' **24** E 2
Kariba **56** D 3
Kariba, Lake **56** D 3
Karigasniemi **26** L 2
Karik Shan **68** E 2
Karimata **72** D 6
Karimata, Selat
 72 D 6
Karimganj **67** G 3
Karisimbi **55** E 4
Karkār **55** J 2
Karkar Island **78** D 4
Karleby **26** K 3
Karlovac **20** C 3
Karlovy Vary **17** F 3
Karlshamn **27** J 4
Karlskoga **27** H4
Karlskrona **27** J 4
Karlsruhe **17** E 4
Karlstad **27** H 4
Karluk **30** K 4
Karmøy **27** F 4
Karnātaka **66** D 5
Karnobat **21** E 4
Karonga **56** E 1
Karossa, Tanjung
 76 B 1
Karpathos **21** E 5
Karpinsk **25** J 3
Kars **64** F 4
Kärsava **27** L 4
Karskiye Vorota, Proliv
 60 N 3
Kartaly **65** K 2
Karür **66** D 5
Karviná **17** G 4
Kärwär **66** C 5
Karymskoye **62** F 6
Kas Rong **67** J 5
Kasai **54** C 4
Kasai Occidental **54** D 5
Kasai Oriental **54** D 4
Kasaji **54** D 6
Kasama **56** E 2
Kasane **56** D 3
Kasaragod **66** D 5

Kasba Lake **34** G 2
Käshän **64** H 6
Kashi **68** B 3
Kashin **24** E 3
Kashiwazaki **70** G 5
Kashmor **66** B 2
Kasimov **23** F 2
Kasiruta **73** H 6
Kaskinen **26** K 3
Kaskö **26** K 3
Kasongo **54** E 4
Kasos **21** E 5
Kaspïy Mangy Oypaty
 23 G 3
Kaspiyskoye More
 23 G 3
Kasr, Ra's **53** G 4
Kassala **53** G 4
Kassel **17** E 3
Kastamonu **64** D 4
Kastoria **21** D 4
Kasungan **72** E 6
Kataba **56** D 3
Katanga **61** V 5
Katangli **62** M 6
Katanning **76** B 6
Katav-Ivanovsk **25** J 4
Katchall Island **67** G 6
Katende, Chutes de
 54 D 5
Katende Falls **54** D 5
Katerini **21** D 4
Katete **56** E 2
Katherine **76** E 2
Kathīri **53** J 4
Kathmandu **66** F 2
Katihar **66** F 2
Katiu **79** L 5
Katmai National Park
 and Reserve **30** K 4
Katowice **17** G 3
Kätrīna, Jabal **52** F 2
Katrineholm **27** J 4
Katsina **51** H 6
Kattaqürghon **65** L 5
Kattegatt **27** H 4
Kauai **79** J 1
Kaufbeuren **17** F 4
Kaukura **79** L 5
Kaunas **27** K 5
Kaura Namoda **51** H 6
Kautokeino **26** K 2
Kavajë **21** C 4
Kavala **21** D 4
Kavali **66** D 5
Kavaratti **66** C 5
Kavïr-e Namak **65** J 6
Kawalusu **73** H 5
Kawio, Kepulauan
 73 H 5
Kawm Umbū **52** F 3
Kaya **51** F 6
Kayak Island **30** M 4
Kayan **67** H 4
Kayangel Islands **78** C 3
Kayes **50** D 6
Kayseri **64** E 5
Kayuagung **72** C 6

Kirkwall **16** C 2
Kirkwood **37** H 4
Kirov **22** D 2
Kirova, Ostrov **61** U 2
Kirovabad **64** G 4
Kirovo-Chepetsk **25** H 3
Kirovohrad **22** D 3
Kirovsk **24** D 1
Kirovskiy (Russia)
  62 J 6
Kirovskiy (Russia)
  63 P 6
Kīrovskīy **65** N 4
Kirs **25** H 3
Kirsanov **23** F 2
Kırşehir **64** D 5
Kirthar National Park
  66 B 2
Kirthar Range **66** B 2
Kiruna **26** K 2
Kisangani **54** E 3
Kisar **73** H 7
Kisaran **72** B 5
Kishangarh Bäs **66** C 2
Kishoreganj **67** F 2
Kisii **55** F 4
Kiska Island **30** D 5
Kiskunhalas **20** C 3
Kislovodsk **23** F 4
Kismaayo **55** H 4
Kissidougou **50** D 7
Kisumu **55** F 4
Kita **50** E 6
Kitakyūshū **71** F 6
Kitale **55** F 3
Kitami **70** H 4
Kitchener **35** L 6
Kitimat **31** P 5
Kitsissut **33** W 3
Kitwe **56** D 2
Kivalina **30** H 2
Kiviöli **27** L 4
Kivu **54** E 4
Kizel **25** J 3
Kizema **25** F 2
Kızılırmak **64** D 4
Kizlyar **23** G 4
Kjöpsvik **26** J 2
Kladno **17** F 3
Klagenfurt **19** E 1
Klamath Falls **36** B 3
Klarälven **27** C 3
Klerksdorp **56** D 5
Klimpfjäll **26** H 2
Klin **24** E 3
Klintsy **22** D 2
Klodzko **17** G 3
Klondike Plateau **30** M 3
Kluczbork **17** G 3
Klyuchevskaya Sopka
  63 Q 5
Knezha **21** D 4
Knjaževac **21** D 4
Knoxville **37** K 4
Knud Rasmussen Land
  33 Z 2
Ko Khrot Kra **67** H 5
Ko Kut **67** J 5

Ko Phangan **67** J 6
Ko Phuket **67** H 6
Ko Samui **67** J 6
Ko Tao **67** H 5
Koba **72** D 6
Köbe **70** G 6
København **27** H 4
Koblenz **17** E 3
Kobroor **73** J 7
Kobryn **22** B 2
Kobuk Valley National
  Park **30** J 2
Kocaeli **64** C 4
Koch Island **33** V 5
Kochenevo **61** S 7
Kochi **71** F 6
Kochubey **23** G 4
Kodar, Khrebet **62** G 5
Kodiak **30** K 4
Kodiak Island **30** K 4
Koechechum **61** V 5
Koforidua **51** G 7
Kogon **65** K 5
Koh-i-Mazar **65** L 6
Kohat **65** M 6
Kohīma **67** G 2
Kohtla-Järve **27** L 4
Kohunlich **38** E 4
Koindu **50** D 7
Kokkola **26** K 3
Kokomo **37** J 3
Kökpekti **65** O 3
Kokshetaü **65** L 2
Kokstad **56** D 6
Kola **24** D 1
Kola Peninsula **24** E 1
Kolaka **73** G 6
Kolar **66** D 5
Kolari **26** K 2
Kolding **27** G 4
Kolhapur **66** C 4
Kolhoa **67** G 6
Kolka **27** K 4
Kolkata **66** F 3
Kolky **22** C 2
Kollegal **66** D 5
Kolmården **27** J 4
Köln **17** E 3
Kołobrzeg **17** G 3
Kolombangara Island
  78 E 4
Kolomna **23** E 1
Kolomyya **22** C 3
Kolpashevo **61** S 6
Kolpino **24** D 3
Kol'skiy Poluostrov
  24 E 1
Koltur **16** B 1
Kolwezi **54** E 6
Kolyma **63** O 3
Kolymskaya **63** P 3
Kolymskaya
  Nizmennost' **63** O 3
Kolymskiy, Khrebet
  63 P 4
Komandorskiye Ostrova
  63 R 5
Komárno **20** C 3

Komatsu **70** G 5
Kome Island **55** F 4
Komfane **73** J 7
Komló **20** C 3
Komodo **73** F 7
Kompong Cham
  67 K 5
Kompong Chhnang
  67 J 5
Kompong Som **67** J 5
Komotini **21** E 4
Komsomolets, Ostrov
  61 U 1
Komsomol'sk-na-Amure
  62 L 6
Komsomol'skoy Pravdy,
  Ostrova **61** X 2
Kon Tum **67** K 5
Konakovo **24** E 3
Konarak **66** F 4
Kondagaon **66** E 4
Kondoa **55** G 4
Kondopoga **24** D 2
Kong Christian X Land
  33 Ee 4
Kong Frederik IX Land
  33 Aa 5
Kong Frederik VI-Kyst
  33 Cc 6
Kong Frederik VIII's
  Land **33** Ff 3
Kong Wilhelm Land
  33 Gg 3
Konginskiye Gory
  63 P 3
Kongolo **54** E 5
Kongsberg **27** G 4
Kongsvinger **27** H 3
Kongur Shan **68** B 3
Koni, Poluostrov **63** O 5
Konin **17** G 3
Konitsa **21** D 4
Konosha **24** F 2
Konotop **22** D 2
Konstanz **19** D 1
Konya **64** D 5
Konya Ovası **64** D 5
Koolivoo, Lake **77** F 4
Kootenay National Park
  31 R 5
Kópavagur **26** A 3
Kopeysk **25** K 3
Köping **27** J 4
Koppang **26** H 3
Kopychyntsi **22** C 3
Korab **21** D 4
Koräput **66** E 4
Korba **66** E 3
Korçë **21** D 4
Korčula **21** C 4
Kordestan **64** G 5
Korea Strait **71** E 6
Korenovsk **23** E 3
Korf **63** R 4
Korhogo **50** E 7
Korinthos **21** D 5
Koriolei **55** H 3
Kōriyama **70** H 5

Korkino **25** K 4
Korkodon **63** O 4
Korla **68** D 2
Kornat **21** C 4
Koro **79** G 5
Koro Sea **79** G 5
Koronadal **73** G 4
Korosten' **22** C 2
Korostyshiv **22** C 2
Korsakov **70** H 3
Koryakskaya Sopka
  63 P 6
Koryakskiy Khrebet
  63 R 4
Koryazhma **25** G 2
Kos **21** E 5
Kosava **22** C 2
Kosciusko, Mount
  77 H 7
Kosiče **17** H 4
Koslan **25** G 2
Kosöng **70** E 5
Kosovo **21** D 4
Kosovska Mitrovica
  21 D 4
Kostino **61** T 4
Kostopil' **22** C 2
Kostroma **24** F 3
Kostyantynivka **22** E 3
Koszalin **17** G 3
Kot Addu **66** C 1
Kota **66** D 2
Kota Baharu **72** C 4
Kota Kinabalu **73** F 4
Kotaagung **72** C 7
Kotabumi **72** C 6
Kotchevo **25** H 3
Kotel'nich **25** G 3
Kotel'nikovo **23** F 3
Kotel'nyy, Ostrov **62** L 1
Kotka **27** L 3
Kotlas **25** G 2
Kotlik **30** H 3
Kotovsk **23** F 2
Kotovs'k **22** C 3
Kotri **66** B 2
Kottayam **66** D 6
Kotuy **61** W 3
Kotzebue **30** H 2
Kotzebue Sound **30** H 2
Koudougou **51** F 6
Kougaberge **56** C 6
Koukdjuak River **33** W 5
Koulikoro **50** E 6
Koumbi Saleh **50** E 5
Koumra **52** C 6
Koundara **50** D 6
Koutiala **50** E 6
Koutous **51** H 6
Kouvola **27** L 3
Kovel' **22** B 2
Kovrov **24** F 3
Kowloon **69** J 6
Koyuk **30** H 3
Koyukuk **30** J 3
Kozani **21** D 4
Kozel'sk **22** E 2
Kozlu **64** D 4

Loop Head **16** A 3
Lop Buri **67** J 5
Lop Nor **68** E 2
Lop Nur **68** E 2
Lopatin **23** G 4
Lopatka **63** P 6
Lopatka, Mys **63** P 3
Lopez, Cap **54** A 4
Loralai **66** B 1
Lorca **18** B 3
Lorica **42** D 3
Lorient **18** B 1
Lorraine **19** D 1
Lós, Îles de **50** D 7
Los Alamos **36** E 4
Los Angeles **36** C 5
Los Angeles **47** C 6
Los Estados, Isla de
 47 E 10
Lošinj **19** E 2
Los Mochis **36** E 6
Los Teques **43** F 2
Los Testigos **43** G 2
Los Vilos **46** C 5
Lota **47** C 6
Loubomo **54** B 4
Louga **50** C 5
Lougheed Island **32** P 3
Louis Trichardt **56** D 4
Louisiade Archipelago
 78 E 5
Louisiana **37** H 5
Louisville **37** J 4
Loukhi **24** D 1
Loum **54** A 3
Louny **17** F 3
Lourdes **18** C 2
Loushan **69** J 4
Lovech **21** D 4
Lovozero **24** E 1
Low, Cape **34** K 2
Lowell **37** M 3
Lower California **36** D 6
Lower Hutt **77** N 8
Lowestoft **16** D 3
Loyauté, Îles **78** F 6
Lualaba **54** E 4
Lu'an **69** K 4
Luanda **54** B 5
Luang Prabang **67** J 4
Luangue, Rio **54** C 5
Luanshya **56** D 2
Luba **54** A 3
Lubang Islands **73** F 3
Lubango **56** A 2
Lubao **54** E 5
Lubbock **36** F 5
Lübeck **17** F 3
Lubeflu **54** D 4
Lubilash **54** D 5
Lubin **17** G 3
Lublin **17** H 3
Lubny **22** D 2
Lubudi **54** D 6
Lubuklinggau **72** C 6
Lubumbashi **54** E 6
Lubutu **54** E 4
Lucania, Mount **31** M 3

Lucas **44** E 4
Lucas, Lake **76** D 4
Lucca **19** E 2
Lucea **39** H 4
Lucena (Philippines)
 73 G 3
Lucena (Spain) **18** C 3
Lučenec **17** G 4
Lucera **19** F 2
Lucero **36** E 5
Lucknow **66** E 2
Luçon **18** C 1
Lüderitz **56** B 5
Ludhiana **66** D 1
Ludwigshafen **17** E 4
Luebo **54** D 5
Luena **56** B 2
Lüeyang **69** H 4
Lufeng **69** K 6
Lufira, Chutes de la
 54 E 5
Lufira Falls **54** E 5
Luga **24** C 3
Lugano **19** D 1
Lugards Falls **55** G 4
Lugo **18** A 2
Lugoj **21** D 3
Luhans'k **23** E 3
Luilaka **54** D 4
Luimeach **16** B 3
Lukenie **54** C 4
Lukoyanov **23** F 1
Lukuga **54** E 5
Luleå **26** K 2
Luleälven **26** K 2
Lultin **63** U 3
Lumajangdong Co
 68 C 4
Lumberton **37** L 5
Lumding **67** G 2
Lund **27** H 4
Lunda Norte **54** C 5
Lunda Sul **56** B 2
Lundu **72** D 5
Lüneburg **17** F 3
Lüneburger Heide
 17 E 3
Luninyets **22** C 2
Luoding **69** J 6
Luohe **69** J 4
Luong Nam Tha
 67 J 3
Luoxiao Shan **69** J 5
Luoyang **69** J 4
Luoyuan **69** K 5
Lupeni **21** D 3
Luqu **69** G 4
Lurín **44** A 4
Lusaka **56** D 3
Lusambo **54** D 4
Lüshun **70** D 5
Lusk **36** F 3
Luton **16** C 3
Łutselk'e **32** O 6
Luts'k **22** C 2
Luvua **54** E 5
Luwuk **73** G 6
Luxembourg **16** E 4

Luxi (Yunnan, China)
 68 F 6
Luxi (Yunnan, China)
 69 G 6
Luxor **52** F 2
Luza **25** G 2
Luzern **19** D 1
Luzhou **69** H 5
Luziânia **45** G 5
Luzon **73** G 2
Luzon Strait **69** L 6
L'viv **22** B 3
Lycksele **26** J 3
Lydenburg **56** E 5
Lyell Land **33** Ff 4
Lyepyel' **22** C 2
Lynchburg **37** L 4
Lyngdal **27** G 4
Lynx Lake **34** F 2
Lyon **19** C 1
Lys'va **25** J 3
Lyubertsy **22** E 1
Lyudinovo **22** D 2

M

Ma'än **53** G 1
Ma'anshan **69** K 4
Maäraï **53** L 3
Maarianhamina **27** J 3
Maas **16** D 3
Maastricht **16** E 3
Mac. Robertson Land
 80 Q 5
Macadam Plains **76** B 5
Macaiba **45** J 3
Macalpine Lake **34** G 1
Macapá **45** F 1
Macarena, Serranía de
 la **42** E 4
Macau **69** J 6
Macauley Island **79** H 7
Macdonald, Lake **76** D 4
Macdonnell Ranges
 76 E 4
Macedonia **21** D 4
Maceió **45** J 3
Macerata **19** E 2
Macha Kos **55** G 4
Machala **42** C 5
Machar Marshes **52** F 5
Macheng **69** K 4
Machilipatnam **66** E 4
Machiques **42** E 2
Ma-chuan Ho **68** D 5
Machupicchu **44** B 4
Macina **51** F 6
Mackay **77** H 4
Mackay, Lake **76** D 4
Mackenzie King Island
 32 O 3

Mackenzie Mountains
 31 O 3
Mackenzie River **32** K 5
Macmillan Pass **32** L 6
Macon **37** K 5
Mâcon **19** C 1
Macujer **42** E 4
Madagascar **57** G 3
Madang **78** D 4
Madau Island **75** E 4
Madawaska Highlands
 35 M 5
Madeira **50** C 2
Madeira, Rio **44** D 3
Madeleine, Îles de la
 35 P 5
Madera **36** B 4
Madhya Pradesh **66** D 3
Madīnat ash Sha'b
 53 H 5
Madison (Indiana,
 U.S.A.) **37** J 4
Madison (Wisconsin,
 U.S.A.) **37** J 3
Madisonville **37** J 4
Madium **72** E 7
Madrakha, Ra's al
 53 L 4
Madras **66** E 5
Madre, Sierra **73** G 2
Madre de Dios, Rio
 44 C 4
Madre Oriental, Sierra
 38 B 2
Madrid **18** B 2
Madura **72** E 7
Madurai **66** D 6
Mae Sot **67** H 4
Maebashi **70** G 5
Maevatanana **57** H 3
Maéwo **78** F 5
Mafia Island **55** G 5
Mafikeng **56** D 5
Magadan **63** O 5
Magalena **44** D 4
Magburaka **50** D 7
Magdagachi **62** J 6
Magdalena **36** D 5
Magdalena, Isla **47** C 7
Magdalena, Rio **42** E 3
Magdeburg **17** F 3
Magdelena, Isla **36** D 7
Magelang **72** E 7
Magellan, Strait of
 47 C 9
Magerøya **26** L 1
Maghâgha **52** F 2
Maghnia **51** F 2
Magnitogorsk **65** J 2
Magnolia **37** H 5
Magwe **67** H 3
Maha Sarakham **67** J 4
Mahābād **64** G 5
Mahabalipuram **66** E 5
Mahābhārat Lek **66** E 2
Mahaddayweyne **55** J 3
Mahādeo Hills **66** D 3
Mahajanga **57** H 3

Mahalapye 56 D 4
Maḥallāt 64 H 6
Mahanoro 57 H 3
Maharashtra 66 C 3
Mahasamund 66 E 3
Mahbunagar 66 D 4
Mahesana 66 C 3
Mahetia 79 L 5
Mahilyow 22 D 2
Mahón 18 C 3
Mahuva 66 C 3
Mai-Ndombe, Lac
  54 C 4
Maiana 79 G 3
Maicao 42 E 2
Maiduguri 51 J 6
Maigudo 53 G 6
Maikala Range 66 E 3
Maimana 65 K 5
Main Barrier Range
  77 G 6
Maine 37 N 2
Maine, Gulf of 35 O 6
Mainland (Orkney, U.K.)
  16 C 2
Mainland (Shetland,
  U.K.) 16 C 1
Maintirano 57 G 3
Mainz 17 E 3
Maio 50 B 5
Maipú 47 F 6
Maitland 77 J 6
Maizuru 70 G 5
Majene 73 F 6
Majērtēn 55 J 2
Majuro 79 G 3
Makale 53 G 5
Makalu 66 F 2
Makarikari 56 C 4
Makarov 70 H 3
Makar'yev 25 F 3
Makassar 73 F 7
Makassar, Selat 73 F 7
Makat 64 H 3
Makay, Massif du
  57 H 4
Makedonia 21 D 4
Makemo 79 L 5
Makeni 50 D 7
Makgadikgadi Pan
  56 C 4
Makhachkala 23 G 4
Makian 73 H 5
Makin 79 G 3
Makïnsk 65 M 2
Makiyivka 22 E 3
Makkah 53 G 3
Makkovik 35 Q 3
Makó 20 D 3
Makoua 54 C 4
Makrana 66 C 2
Makteir 50 D 4
Makurazuki 71 F 6
Makurdi 51 H 7
Mala 44 A 4
Mala, Punta 39 G 6
Malabar Coast 66 C 5
Malabo 54 A 3

Malacca, Strait of 72 B 5
Maladzyechna 20 E 2
Málaga 18 B 3
Malaita 78 F 4
Malakäl 52 F 6
Malakula 78 F 5
Malang 72 E 7
Malanje 54 C 5
Mälaren 27 J 4
Malargüe 47 D 6
Malaripo 45 F 1
Malaspina 47 D 7
Malaspina Glacier
  31 M 3
Malatya 64 E 5
Mala Vyska 22 D 3
Malawi 56 E 2
Malawi, Lake 56 E 2
Malay Peninsula 72 B 4
Malaya 72 C 5
Malaya Kuril'skaya
  Gr'ada 70 J 4
Malaya Vishera 24 D 3
Malaybalay 73 H 4
Malaysia 72 E 5
Malbork 17 G 3
Malden 79 K 4
Maldives 66 C 6
Maldonado 46 F 5
Malegaon 66 C 3
Mali 50 F 5
Malindi 55 H 4
Malinovoye Ozero
  65 N 2
Mallaig 16 B 2
Mallawï 52 F 2
Mallery Lake 34 H 2
Mallorca 18 C 3
Malmö 27 H 4
Maloca 44 E 1
Maloelap 79 G 3
Malolos 73 G 3
Maloshuyka 24 E 2
Måløy 26 G 3
Malozemel'skaya
  Tundra 25 G 1
Malpelo, Isla del 42 C 4
Malta 19 E 3
Malta, Canale di 19 E 3
Maluku 73 H 6
Maluku, Laut 73 G 6
Malung 27 H 3
Malvan 66 C 4
Malvinas, Islas 47 E 9
Malyn 22 C 2
Malyy Lyakhovskiy,
  Ostrov 62 M 2
Malyy Taymyr, Ostrov
  61 X 2
Malyy Yenisey 61 V 7
Mama 62 F 5
Mamburao 73 G 3
Mamonta, Poluostrov
  61 R 3
Mamou 50 D 6
Mamuju 73 F 6
Man 50 E 7
Man, Isle of 16 C 3

Manacapuru 44 D 2
Manado 73 G 5
Managua 38 E 5
Manakara 57 H 4
Mananjary 57 H 4
Manas 68 D 2
Manãs 67 G 2
Manas Hu 68 D 1
Manãslu 66 E 2
Manaus 44 D 2
Manawoka 73 J 6
Mancha Blanca 47 D 7
Manchester 16 C 3
Mandal 27 G 4
Mandalay 67 H 3
Mandara, Monts 54 B 2
Mandioli 73 H 6
Mandioré, Laguna
  44 E 5
Mandla 66 E 3
Mandsaur 66 D 3
Mandvi 66 B 3
Mandya 66 D 5
Manfalut 52 F 2
Manfredonia 19 F 2
Mangabeiras, Chapada
  das 45 G 3
Mangaia 79 K 6
Mangalia 21 E 4
Mangalore 66 C 5
Mangareya 79 M 6
Mange 68 C 4
Manggar 72 D 6
Mangghystaü Tübegi
  23 H 4
Mangkalihat, Tanjung
  73 F 5
Manglares, Cabo 42 D 4
Mangnai 68 E 3
Mango 51 G 6
Mangoche 56 F 2
Mangole 73 H 6
Mangshi 68 F 6
Manhattan 37 G 4
Manicaland 56 D 3
Manicouagan 35 O 4
Manicouagan, Réservoir
  35 O 4
Manihi 79 L 5
Manihiki 79 J 5
Maniitsoq 33 Aa 5
Manila 73 G 3
Manipur 67 G 3
Manisa 64 C 5
Manitoba 34 H 4
Manitoba, Lake 34 H 4
Manitoulin Island 35 L 5
Manitowoc 37 J 3
Manizales 42 D 3
Manja 57 G 4
Manjimup 76 B 6
Mankato 37 H 3
Manley Hot Springs
  30 K 2
Manmad 66 C 3
Manna 72 C 6
Mannheim 17 E 4
Manning, Cape 32 M 3

Manokwari 73 J 6
Manono 54 E 5
Manp'ojin 70 E 4
Manra 79 H 4
Manresa 18 C 2
Mansa 56 D 2
Mansel Island 35 L 2
Manta 42 C 5
Mantova 19 E 1
Manu 44 B 4
Manua Islands 79 J 5
Manuae 79 K 5
Manuangi 79 L 5
Manui 73 G 6
Manukau 77 N 7
Manus Island 78 D 4
Manyara, Lake 55 G 4
Manyoni 55 F 5
Manzanares 18 C 3
Manzanillo (Cuba)
  39 G 3
Manzanillo (Mexico)
  38 B 4
Manzhouli 70 C 3
Manzini 56 E 5
Mao 39 H 4
Maoke, Pegunungan
  73 K 6
Maoming 69 J 6
Mapaga 73 F 5
Maple Creek 34 F 5
Maputo 56 E 5
Maputo, Baia de
  56 E 5
Maqat 23 H 3
Maqên Gangri 68 F 4
Maquinchao 47 D 7
Mar, Serra do 46 H 4
Mar Chiquita, Laguna
  46 E 5
Mar del Plata 47 F 6
Maraá 44 C 2
Marabá 45 G 3
Maracá, Ilha de 45 F 1
Maracaibo 42 E 2
Maracaibo, Lago de
  42 E 3
Maracaju 45 E 6
Maracaju, Serra de
  45 E 6
Maracay 43 F 2
Maradi 51 H 6
Marägheh 64 G 5
Maragogipe 45 J 4
Marajó, Ilha de 45 F 2
Maramasike Ulawa
  78 F 4
Marãnd 64 G 5
Maranhão 45 G 3
Maranhão, Cachoeira
  44 E 2
Marari 44 C 3
Marathon 36 F 5
Marawi 73 G 4
Marawih 53 K 3
Marbella 18 C 3
Marburg 17 E 3
Marcos Juárez 46 E 5

Marcus Baker, Mount **30** L 3
Mardān **65** M 6
Mardin **64** F 5
Maré **78** F 6
Marechal Deodoro **45** J 3
Mareeba **77** H 3
Margai Caka **68** D 4
Margarita, Isla de **43** G 2
Marghilon **65** M 4
Margie **31** S 4
Maria (French Polynesia) **79** K 6
Maria (French Polynesia) **79** M 6
Maria Island **76** F 2
Maria Theresa Reef **79** K 7
Maria van Diemen, Cape **75** G 7
Mariana Islands **78** D 2
Marianao **38** F 3
Mariar **73** J 6
Mariato, Punta **39** F 6
Maribor **20** C 3
Marico **56** D 4
Marie Byrd Land **80** W 4
Marie-Galante **39** K 4
Mariehamn **27** J 3
Mariental **56** B 4
Marietta **37** K 5
Mariinsk **61** T 6
Marijampolė **27** K 5
Marília **46** G 3
Mar"ina Horka **20** E 2
Marinduque **73** G 3
Marinette **37** J 2
Maringá **46** G 3
Marion Reef **77** J 3
Mariupol' **22** E 3
Marka **55** H 3
Markam **68** F 5
Märkäpur **66** D 4
Markha **62** G 4
Markovo **61** T 5
Marmara **21** E 4
Marmolada **19** E 1
Marmorilik **33** Aa 4
Maroantsetra **57** H 3
Marokau **79** L 5
Maros **73** F 6
Marotiri **79** L 6
Maroua **54** B 1
Marovoay **57** H 3
Marrah, Jabal **52** D 5
Marquises, Archipel des **79** M 4
Marrakech **50** E 2
Marree **77** F 5
Marrupa **57** F 2
Marsabit **55** G 3
Marsala **19** E 3
Marseille **19** D 2
Marshall **37** H 5
Marshall Islands **78** F 2
Marshalltown **37** H 3

Martapura (Indonesia) **72** C 6
Martapura (Indonesia) **72** E 6
Martigues **19** D 2
Martin **17** G 4
Martinez de la Torre **38** C 3
Martinique **39** K 5
Martinsville **37** L 4
Marton **77** O 8
Martre, Lac la **32** N 6
Marutea **79** L 5
Marv Dasht **64** H 7
Mary **65** K 5
Mary River **33** V 4
Maryborough **77** J 5
Maryland **37** L 4
Marysville (California, U.S.A.) **36** B 4
Marysville (Kansas, U.S.A.) **37** G 4
Maryville **37** H 3
Masai Steppe **55** G 4
Masaka **55** F 4
Masalembu Besar **72** E 7
Masan **70** E 5
Masasi **55** G 6
Masaya **38** E 5
Masbate **73** G 3
Masbate (Island) **73** G 3
Mascarene Islands **57** K 3
Mascasin **46** D 5
Masela **73** H 7
Maseru **56** D 5
Mashhad **65** J 5
Masīlah, Wādī al **53** K 4
Masīrah **53** L 3
Masīrah, Khalīj **53** L 4
Masjed Soleymān **64** G 6
Maslyanskiy **60** Q 6
Masoala, Tanjona **57** J 3
Mason City **37** H 3
Masqat **53** L 3
Massa **19** E 2
Massachusetts **37** M 3
Massafra **19** F 2
Massawa **53** G 4
Massena **37** M 3
Massif Central **18** C 1
Massinga **56** F 4
Masterton **77** O 8
Mastung **66** B 2
Masvingo **56** E 4
Mata **73** G 7
Matabeleland **56** D 3
Matachewan **35** L 5
Matadi **54** B 5
Matagalpa **38** E 5
Matagami **35** M 5
Matagorda Island **37** G 6
Mataiva **79** L 5
Matala **56** B 2
Matale **66** E 6

Matam **50** D 5
Matamoros **37** G 6
Matancita **36** D 6
Matane **35** O 5
Matanzas **38** F 3
Matão, Serra do **45** F 3
Matara **66** E 6
Mataram **72** F 7
Matarca **42** E 5
Mataró **18** C 2
Mätätila Dam **66** D 2
Matehuala **36** F 7
Matera **19** F 2
Mathew Town **39** H 3
Mathura **66** D 2
Mati **73** H 4
Mätla **66** F 3
Matochkin Shar **60** N 3
Mato Grosso **44** E 4
Mato Grosso, Planalto do **44** E 4
Mato Grosso do Sul **45** E 6
Matosinhos **18** A 2
Matrüh **52** E 1
Matsu **71** C 7
Matsudo **70** H 5
Matsumoto **70** G 5
Matsuyama **71** F 6
Matsuzaki **70** G 6
Matterhorn **19** D 1
Matua, Ostrov **70** K 3
Maturín **43** G 3
Matyl'ka **61** T 5
Maubeuge **16** D 3
Maués **44** E 2
Maug Islands **78** D 2
Mauganj **66** E 3
Maui **79** K 1
Mauke **79** K 6
Maumere **73** G 7
Maun **56** C 3
Mauna Kea **79** K 2
Mauna Loa **79** K 2
Maunoir, Lac **32** M 5
Maupihaa **79** K 5
Maupiti **79** K 5
Maurice, Lake **76** E 5
Mauritania **50** C 5
Mauritius **57** K 4
Mavuradonha Mountains **56** E 3
Mawlaik **67** G 3
May Pen **39** G 4
Maya **72** D 6
Mayaguana Island **39** H 3
Mayagüez **39** J 4
Mayämey **65** J 5
Mayapán **38** E 3
Maydh **53** J 2
Maykop **23** F 4
Maymyo **67** H 3
Mayn **63** X 4
Mayo **31** N 3
Mayobamba **42** D 6
Mayotte **57** G 2
Mayqayyng **65** N 2

Mayraira Point **73** G 2
Mayumpa **54** B 4
Mayya **62** K 4
Maza **47** E 6
Mazabuka **56** D 3
Mazār-e Sharīf **65** L 5
Mazatenango **38** D 5
Mazatlán **38** A 3
Mazyr **22** C 2
Mbabane **56** E 5
Mbaiki **54** C 3
Mbaké **50** C 6
Mbala **56** E 1
Mbale **55** F 3
Mbalmayo **54** B 3
Mbandaka **54** C 3
Mbanga **54** A 3
Mbanza-Ngungu **54** B 5
Mbarara **55** F 4
Mbeya **55** F 5
Mbinga **55** G 6
Mbini **54** B 3
Mbokou **54** E 2
Mbomou **54** D 3
Mbour **50** C 6
Mbuji-Mayi **54** D 5
McAlester **37** G 5
McAllen **36** G 6
McCarthy **30** M 3
M'Clintock Channel **32** Q 4
McDame **31** P 4
McGrath **30** J 3
McKean Island **79** H 4
McKinley, Mount **30** K 3
McKinley Peak **30** L 3
McLarty Hills **76** C 3
McLeod Lake **31** Q 5
McPherson **37** G 4
McPherson Range **77** J 5
Mdennah **50** E 4
Mead, Lake **36** D 4
Meadow Lake **34** F 4
Meander River **31** R 4
Meaux **18** C 1
Mecca **53** G 3
Medak **66** D 4
Medan **72** B 5
Medellín **42** D 3
Medelpad **26** J 3
Medford **36** B 3
Medgidia **21** E 4
Medicine Hat **31** S 5
Medicine Lodge **36** G 4
Medina **53** G 3
Medina del Campo **18** C 2
Mediterranean Sea **18** B 3
Mednogorsk **65** J 2
Mednyy, Ostrov **63** R 6
Medvezhiy Yar **62** B 2
Medvezh'yegorsk **24** D 2
Meekatharra **76** B 5
Meerut **66** D 2
Mega **73** J 6

Miyake-jima (Japan) **70** G 6
Miyako-jima (Japan) **71** E 8
Miyakonojō **71** F 6
Miyāni **66** B 3
Miyazaki **71** F 6
Mizen Head **16** B 3
Mizil **21** E 3
Mizoram **67** G 3
Mizusawa **70** H 5
Mjölby **27** J 4
Mjösa **27** H 3
Mkomazi **55** G 4
Mladá Boleslav **17** F 3
Mljet **21** C 4
Mo i Rana **26** H 2
Moamba **56** E 5
Moanda **54** B 5
Moba **55** E 5
Moberly **37** H 4
Mobile **37** J 5
Mocambique **57** G 2
Mochudi **56** D 4
Mococa **46** H 3
Moctezuma **36** E 6
Modena **19** E 2
Modesto **36** B 4
Modowi **73** J 6
Moe **77** H 7
Moen-jo-dar **66** B 2
Moero, Lac **56** D 1
Moffat **16** C 2
Mogadishu **55** J 3
Mogdy **62** K 6
Mogocha **62** G 6
Mogoytuy **62** F 6
Moguqi **70** D 3
Mohammedia **50** E 2
Moheli **57** G 2
Mohyliv Podil'skyy
   22 C 3
Mojave Desert **36** C 5
Mokokcghüng **67** G 2
Mokolo **54** B 1
Mokp'o **71** E 6
Molaly **65** N 3
Molde **26** G 3
Moldova **22** C 3
Molfetta **19** F 2
Molina **46** C 6
Mollendo **44** B 5
Molokai **79** K 1
Moloundou **54** C 3
Molucca Sea **73** G 6
Moluccas **73** H 6
Mombasa **55** G 4
Mombetsu **70** H 4
Mompós **42** E 3
Momskiy Khrebet
   62 M 3
Mona, Canal de la
   39 J 4
Monaco **19** D 2
Monarch Mountain
   31 P 5
Monastir **51** J 1
Monchegorsk **24** D 1

Mönchen-Gladbach
   16 E 3
Monclova **36** F 6
Moncton **35** P 5
Mondego, Cabo **18** A 2
Mondy **61** W 7
Money Island **72** E 2
Monfalcone **19** E 1
Monforte de Lemos
   18 B 2
Mong Cai **67** K 3
Mongers Lake **76** B 5
Monghyr **66** F 2
Mongolia **61** W 8
Mõngua **56** B 3
Monjes, Islas los **42** E 2
Mono Lake **36** C 4
Monreal del Campo
   18 C 2
Monroe **37** H 5
Monrovia **50** D 7
Mons **16** D 3
Monsefú **42** D 6
Mont-de-Marsan **18** B 2
Montague, Isla **36** D 5
Montague Island **30** L 4
Montana (Bulgaria)
   21 D 4
Montana (U.S.A.) **36** D 2
Montauban **18** C 2
Montceau-les-Mines
   19 C 1
Monte Albán **38** C 4
Monte Alegre **45** F 2
Monte Azul **45** H 5
Monte Caseros **46** F 5
Monte Cómán **46** D 5
Monte Cristi **39** H 4
Monte Quemado **46** E 4
Montego Bay **39** G 4
Montélimar **19** C 2
Montemayor, Meseta de
   47 D 8
Montemorelos **36** G 6
Montenegro **21** C 4
Monterey **36** B 4
Montería **42** D 3
Montero **44** D 5
Monterotondo **19** E 2
Monterrey **36** F 6
Montes Claros **45** H 5
Montevideo **46** F 5
Montgomery **37** J 5
Monticello **36** E 4
Montluçon **18** C 1
Montmagny **35** N 5
Monto **77** J 4
Montpelier **37** M 3
Montpellier **18** C 2
Montréal **35** N 5
Montserrat **39** K 4
Monumento Natural
   Bosques Petrificados
   47 D 8
Monywa **67** H 3
Monza **19** D 1
Moora **76** B 6
Moore, Lake **76** B 5

Moorea **79** K 5
Moorhead **37** G 2
Moose Jaw **34** F 4
Moosonee **35** L 4
Mopti **50** F 6
Moquegua **44** B 5
Mora **27** H 3
Morado Primero, Cerro
   46 D 3
Moradabad **66** D 2
Moramanga **57** H 3
Morane **79** M 6
Moratuwa **66** D 6
Morava **17** G 4
Morbi **66** C 3
Møre og Romsdal
   26 B 3
Moree **77** H 5
Morelia **38** B 4
Moresby **31** O 5
Moreton Island **77** J 5
Morgantown **37** K 4
Moriki **51** H 6
Morioka **70** H 5
Morjärv **26** K 2
Morkoka **61** X 4
Morlaix **18** C 1
Morne Diablotin **39** K 4
Mornington, Isla **47** B 8
Mornington Island
   77 F 3
Moro Gulf **73** G 4
Morocco **50** E 2
Morogoro **55** G 5
Moroleón **38** B 3
Moron **43** F 2
Morón **39** G 3
Morón de la Frontera
   18 A 3
Morondava **57** G 4
Moroni **57** G 2
Morotai **73** H 5
Moroto, Mount **55** F 3
Morozovsk **23** F 3
Morrinhos **45** G 5
Morris Jesup, Kap
   33 Dd 2
Mors **27** G 4
Morshansk **23** F 2
Mortlock Islands **78** E 3
Morwell **77** H 7
Moscow (Russia) **22** E 1
Moscow (U.S.A.) **36** C 2
Moses Lake **36** C 2
Moshi **55** G 4
Mosjøen **26** H 2
Moskenesøy **26** H 2
Moskva **22** E 1
Mosquitos, Golfo de los
   39 F 6
Mossel Bay **56** C 6
Mossendjo **54** B 4
Mossoró **45** J 3
Most **17** F 3
Mostaganem **51** G 1
Mostar **21** C 4
Mosul **64** F 5
Motala **27** J 4

Mothe **79** H 5
Motherwell **16** C 2
Motril **18** B 3
Motu Ko **79** J 5
Motu One **79** K 5
Motul **38** E 3
Motutunga **79** L 5
Mouila **54** B 4
Mould Bay **32** N 3
Moulins **18** C 1
Moulmein **67** H 4
Moultrie **37** K 5
Moundou **52** C 6
Mount Gambier **77** G 7
Mount Hagen **78** D 4
Mount Isa **77** F 4
Mount Magnet **76** B 5
Mount Roskill **77** N 7
Mount Vernon **36** B 2
Mount Willoughby
   76 E 5
Mountain Home **36** C 3
Moura **44** D 2
Mourdi, Dépression du
   52 D 4
Moutong **73** G 5
Mouydir **51** G 4
Moyale **55** G 3
Moyo **73** F 7
Moyynty **65** M 3
Mozambique **56** E 3
Mozambique Channel
   57 F 4
Mozdok **23** F 4
Mozhga **25** H 3
Mpanda **55** F 5
Mpika **56** E 2
Msäk Mastäfat **52** B 2
Mstislaw **22** D 2
Mtsensk **22** E 2
Mtwara **55** H 6
Mu Us Shamo **69** H 3
Muang Khammouan
   67 J 4
Muang Khongxedon
   67 K 4
Muang Loei **67** J 4
Muang Nan **67** J 4
Muang Pakxan **67** J 4
Muang Phayao **67** H 4
Muang Phrae **67** J 4
Muang Sing **67** J 3
Muang Xaignabouri
   67 J 4
Muar **72** C 5
Muara **72** C 6
Muarabungo **72** C 6
Muaraenim **72** C 6
Muarajuloi **72** E 6
Muaratewe **72** E 6
Muchinga Escarpment
   56 E 2
Mucojo **57** G 2
Mudanjiang **70** E 4
Mudgee **77** H 6
Mudug **55** J 2
Mufu Shan **69** J 5
Mufulira **56** D 2

Muğla **21** E 5
Muhammad, Ra's **52** F 2
Muhu **27** K 4
Mui Bai Bung **67** J 6
Mukacheve **22** B 3
Mukden **70** D 4
Mukomuko **72** C 6
Mulaly **65** N 3
Mulan **70** E 3
Mulanje Mountains **56** F 3
Mulchén **47** C 6
Mulhacén **18** B 3
Mulhouse **19** D 1
Mull **16** B 2
Mullaittivu **66** E 6
Muller, Pegunungan **72** E 6
Mullewa **76** B 5
Multan **66** C 1
Mumbai **66** C 4
Mumra **23** G 3
Muna (Indonesia) **73** G 6
Muna (Russia) **62** H 3
München **17** F 4
Munchique, Cerro **42** D 4
Muncho Lake **31** P 4
Muncie **37** J 3
Mungbere **54** E 3
Munhango **56** B 2
Munku-Sardyk, Gora **61** W 7
Münster **17** E 3
Muntok **72** D 6
Muobezi **56** D 3
Muonio **26** K 2
Muqdisho **55** J 3
Murakami **70** G 5
Murashi **25** G 3
Murchison Falls **55** F 3
Murcia **18** B 3
Murfreesboro **37** J 4
Muriaé **45** H 6
Murmansk **24** D 1
Murom **23** F 1
Muroran **70** H 4
Muros **18** B 2
Murray **37** J 4
Murray (River) **77** G 6
Murray Islands **78** D 4
Mururoa **79** M 6
Murwara **66** E 3
Muş **64** F 5
Musala (Bulgaria) **21** D 4
Musala (Indonesia) **72** B 5
Musan **70** E 4
Muscat **53** L 3
Musgrave **77** G 2
Musgrave Ranges **76** E 5
Muskogee **37** G 4
Musoma **55** F 4
Musrakaman **73** F 6
Musters, Lago **47** D 8

Muswellbrook **77** J 6
Mutare **56** E 3
Mutoray **61** W 5
Mutsu **70** H 4
Mũynoq **65** J 4
Muzaffarnagar **66** D 2
Muzaffarpur **66** F 2
Muzhi **25** K 1
Muztag Feng **68** D 3
Muztaū Biigi **65** P 3
Muzuzu **56** E 2
Mwali **57** G 2
Mwanza **55** F 4
Mweka **54** D 4
Mwene Ditu **54** D 5
My Tho **67** K 5
Myadzyel **22** C 2
Myanaung **67** H 4
Myanmar **67** G 3
Myaungmya **67** G 4
Myingyan **67** H 3
Myitkyinā **67** H 2
Mykines **21** D 5
Mykolayiv **22** D 3
Mykonos **21** E 5
Mylius Erichsen Land **33** Ff 2
Mymensingh **67** G 3
Mynbulak **65** K 4
Myndagayy **62** K 4
Mýrdalsjökull **26** B 3
Myrhorod **22** D 3
Myrtle Beach **37** L 5
Mys Shmidta **63** U 3
Mys Zhelaniya **60** P 2
Mysore **66** D 5
Myszków **17** G 3
Mytilini **21** E 5

N

Naas **16** B 3
Nabberu, Lake **76** C 5
Naberezhnyye Chelny **25** H 3
Nabī Shu'ayb, Jabal an **53** H 4
Nabire **73** K 6
Nābul **51** J 1
Nabulus **53** G 1
Nachuge **67** G 5
Nada **67** K 4
Nadiad **66** C 3
Nador **51** F 1
Nadu **66** D 5
Nadvirna **22** B 3
Nadym **60** Q 4
Næstved **27** H 4
Nafada **51** J 6
Naga **73** G 3
Naga Hills **67** G 2

Nagai Island **30** J 5
Nāgāland **67** G 2
Nagano **70** G 5
Nagaoka **70** G 5
Nagasaki **71** E 6
Nagaur **66** C 2
Nagda **66** D 3
Nagercoil **66** D 6
Nago **71** E 4
Nagoya **70** G 5
Nagpur **66** D 3
Nagqu **68** E 4
Nagykanizsa **20** C 3
Naha **71** E 7
Nahanni Butte **32** M 6
Nahanni National Park **32** L 6
Nahāvand **64** G 6
Nahuel Huapi, Lago **47** C 7
Nahuel Huapi, Parçue Nacional **47** C 7
Nahuel Niyeu **47** D 7
Naiman Qi **70** D 4
Nairobi **55** G 4
Naissaar **27** K 4
Naivasha **55** G 4
Najafābād **64** H 6
Najd **53** G 2
Najin **70** F 4
Najrān **53** H 4
Nakhodka **70** F 4
Nakhon Nayok **67** J 5
Nakhon Phanom **67** J 4
Nakhon Ratchasima **67** J 5
Nakhon Sawan **67** J 4
Nakhon Si Thammarat **67** H 6
Nakuru **55** G 4
Nalayh **61** X 8
Nal'chik **23** F 4
Nallamalla Range **66** D 4
Nālūt **52** B 1
Nam Co **68** D 4
Nam Dinh **67** K 3
Namacurra **57** F 3
Namaland **56** B 5
Namangan **65** M 4
Namaqualand **56** B 5
Nameh **73** F 5
Namhkam **67** H 3
Namib Desert **56** A 3
Namibe **56** A 3
Namibia **56** A 4
Namjagbarwa Feng **68** F 5
Namlea **73** H 6
Nampa **36** C 3
Namp'o **70** E 5
Nampula **57** F 3
Namsos **26** H 3
Namtsy **62** J 4
Namu **78** F 3
Namur **16** D 3
Nan Hai **69** J 6
Nan Hulsan Hu **68** F 3

Nanaimo **31** Q 6
Nanam **70** E 4
Nanao **70** G 5
Nancha **70** E 3
Nanchang **69** K 5
Nancheng **69** K 5
Nanchong **69** H 4
Nanchuan **69** H 5
Nancowry **67** G 6
Nancy **19** D 1
Nanda Devi **66** D 1
Nānded **66** D 4
Nandurbār **66** C 3
Nandyāl **66** D 4
Nanfeng **69** K 5
Nānga Parbat **65** M 5
Nangatayap **72** E 6
Nangong **69** K 3
Nangpinch **72** E 6
Nanhua **68** G 5
Nanjing **69** K 4
Nanning **69** H 6
Nanpan Jiang **69** G 6
Nanping **69** K 5
Nanran Nil **52** F 2
Nansei-shotō **71** E 7
Nansen Land **33** Cc 2
Nantes **18** B 1
Nantong **69** L 4
Nantucket Island **37** N 3
Nanumea **79** G 4
Nanuque **45** H 5
Nanusa, Kepulauan **73** H 5
Nanxiong **69** J 5
Nanyang **69** J 4
Nanyuki **55** G 3
Nanzhang **69** J 4
Nanzhao **69** J 4
Nao, Cabo de la **18** C 3
Napas **61** S 6
Napier **77** O 7
Naples **19** E 2
Napoli **19** E 2
Napuka **79** L 5
Narasapur **66** E 4
Narathiwat **67** J 6
Narayanganj **67** G 3
Narbonne **18** C 2
Nares Land **33** Bb 2
Narimanov **23** G 3
Närke **27** H 4
Naro-Fominsk **22** E 1
Narrabri **77** H 6
Narrandera **77** H 6
Narrogin **76** B 6
Narsaq **33** Bb 6
Narsimhapur **66** D 3
Narva **27** L 4
Narvik **26** J 2
Nar'yan Mar **25** H 1
Naryn **65** N 4
Naryn Qum **64** G 3
Nāsāud **20** D 3
Nashta Rūd **64** H 5
Nashville **37** J 4
Näsijärvi **26** K 3
Nasik **66** C 3

Orkney Islands **16** C 2
Orlando **37** K 6
Orléans **18** C 1
Ormara **66** A 2
Ormoc **73** G 3
Örnsköldsvik **26** J 3
Oro, Rio de **50** C 4
Oroluk **78** E 3
Oron **51** H 8
Orona **79** H 4
Oroqen Zizhiqi **70** D 2
Orsa **27** H 3
Orsha **22** D 2
Orsk **65** J 2
Ortegal, Cabo **18** A 2
Ortigueira **18** B 2
Orulgan, Khrebet **62** J 3
Orümïyeh **64** G 5
Oruro **44** C 5
Ōsaka **70** G 5
Osbourne **36** G 4
Osen **26** H 3
Osh **65** M 4
Oshakati **56** B 3
Oshawa **35** M 6
Oshkosh **37** J 3
Oshogbo **51** G 7
Oshtorān Kūh **53** J 1
Osijek **21** C 3
Osinniki **61** T 7
Osinovka **65** O 3
Oskarshamn **27** J 4
Öskemen **65** O 2
Oslo **27** H 4
Oslofjorden **27** H 4
Osmānābād **66** D 4
Osmaniye **64** E 5
Osnabrück **17** E 3
Osorno **47** C 7
Ossora **63** Q 5
Ostashkov **24** D 3
Östergötland **27** H 4
Östersjön **27** J 4
Östersund **26** H 3
Ostrava **17** G 4
Ostróda **22** A 2
Ostrogozhsk **23** E 2
Ostrołęka **22** B 2
Ostrov **24** C 3
Ostrów Mazowiecka
   17 H 3
Ostrów Wielkopolski
   17 G 3
Osuna **18** A 3
Otaru **70** H 4
Otavi **56** B 3
Otjiwarongo **56** B 4
Otranto **19** F 2
Ōtsu **70** G 5
Otta **26** G 3
Ottawa (Canada) **35** M 5
Ottawa (U.S.A.) **37** G 4
Ottawa Islands **35** L 3
Ottenby **27** J 4
Ottumwa **37** H 3
Otway, Cape **77** G 7
Otwock **17** H 3
Ouadda **54** D 2

Ouaddaï **52** D 5
Ouagadougou **51** F 6
Ouahigouya **51** F 6
Oualata **50** E 5
Ouanary **43** J 4
Ouaqui **43** J 4
Ouarane **50** D 4
Ouargla **51** H 2
Ouarzazate **50** E 2
Oubangui **54** C 3
Oudtshoorn **56** C 6
Oued Zem **50** E 2
Ouessant, Île d' **18** A 1
Ouezzane **50** E 2
Ouidah **51** G 7
Oujda **51** F 2
Oulu **26** L 3
Oulujärvi **26** L 3
Oum Chalouba **52** D 4
Oumé **50** E 7
Ounianga **52** D 4
Ourense **18** A 2
Ouricuri **45** H 3
Ourinhos **46** H 3
Outjo **56** B 4
Ouvéa **78** F 6
Ouyen **77** G 7
Ovalle **46** C 5
Ovamboland **56** A 3
Oviedo **18** A 2
Ovruch **22** C 2
Owen Sound **35** L 6
Owen Stanley Range
   78 D 4
Owensboro **37** J 4
Owerri **51** H 7
Owo **51** H 7
Oxford **16** C 3
Oyem **54** B 3
Oymayakonskoye
   Nagor'ye **62** M 4
Oyotung **62** N 2
Oyun Khomoto **62** L 3
Oyyl **64** H 3
Ozamiz **73** G 4
Ozark **37** J 5
Özd **20** D 3
Ozernoy, Zaliv **63** Q 5
Ozinki **23** G 2
Ozurget'i **64** F 4

P

Paarl **56** B 6
Paamiut **33** Bb 6
Pabna **67** F 3
Pacajus **45** J 2
Pacasmayo **42** D 6
Pachacamac **44** A 4
Pachuca **38** C 3
Pacific Ocean **78** G 3

Padang **72** C 6
Padang (Island) **72** C 5
Padangpanjang **72** C 6
Padangsidempuan
   72 B 5
Paderborn **17** E 3
Padova **19** E 1
Padrauna **66** E 2
Padre Island **37** G 6
Paducah **37** J 4
Paektu-San **70** E 4
Pag **21** B 4
Pagadian **73** G 4
Pagai Selatan **72** C 6
Pagai Utara **72** B 6
Pagalu **54** A 4
Pagan **78** D 2
Pagani **55** G 5
Pagoda Point **67** G 4
Päijänne **26** L 3
Painan **72** C 6
Painted Desert **36** D 4
Pajala **26** K 2
Pak Phanang **67** J 6
Pakistan **66** A 2
Pakokku **67** H 3
Paks **20** C 3
Pakse **67** K 4
Pala **52** B 6
Palana **63** P 5
Palanan Point **73** G 2
Palangkaraya **72** E 6
Palani **66** D 5
Palanpur **66** C 3
Palapye **56** D 4
Palatka **63** O 4
Palau **78** C 3
Palau Islands **78** C 3
Palawan **73** F 4
Palawan Passage
   73 F 4
Palayankottai **66** D 6
Paleleh **73** G 5
Palembang **72** C 6
Palena **47** C 7
Palencia **18** B 2
Palenque **38** E 4
Palermo **19** E 3
Palestine **37** G 5
Paletwa **67** G 3
Pälghät **66** D 5
Pali **66** C 2
Palime **51** G 7
Pälitäna **66** C 3
Pallasovka **23** G 2
Palliser, Îles **79** L 5
Palm Bay **37** K 6
Palm Springs **36** C 5
Palma de Mallorca
   18 C 3
Palma Soriano **39** G 3
Palmares **45** J 3
Palmas **45** G 3
Palmeira da Missões
   46 G 4
Palmeira dos Indios
   45 J 3
Palmer **30** L 3

Palmerston **79** J 5
Palmerston North
   77 O 8
Palmira **42** D 4
Palopo **73** G 6
Palos, Cabo de **18** B 3
Palpalá **46** D 3
Palpetu, Tanjung **73** H 6
Palu **73** F 6
Pama **51** G 6
Pamekasan **72** E 7
Pamirs **65** M 5
Pampa **36** F 4
Pampa Grande **44** D 5
Pamplona **42** E 3
Pamplona-Iruña **18** B 2
Panaji **66** C 4
Panamá **39** G 6
Panamá, Golfo de
   39 F 6
Panamá Canal **39** F 5
Panama City **37** J 5
Panay **73** G 3
Pančevo **21** D 4
Pandharpur **66** D 4
Pando **46** F 5
Panevežys **27** K 4
Pangani **55** G 4
Pangkadjene **73** F 6
Pangkalpinang **72** D 6
Pangnirtung **35** O 1
Pangutaran Group
   73 F 4
Panié, Mont **78** F 6
Panipat **66** D 2
Panna **66** E 3
Panshi **70** E 4
Pantar **73** G 7
Pantelleria, Isola di
   19 E 3
Panxian **69** G 5
Pápa **20** C 3
Papantla **38** C 3
Papar **72** F 4
Papeete **79** L 5
Papua New Guinea
   78 D 4
Pará **45** F 3
Parabel' **61** S 6
Paracatu **45** G 5
Paracel Islands **72** E 2
Paracuru **45** J 2
Pāradwïp **66** F 3
Paragould **37** H 4
Paraguai **44** E 4
Paraguari **46** F 4
Paraguay **46** E 3
Paraiba **45** K 3
Parakou **51** G 7
Paramaribo **43** H 3
Paramirim **45** H 4
Páramo Frontino
   42 D 3
Paramushir, Ostrov
   63 P 6
Paraná (Argentina)
   46 E 5
Paranã (Brazil) **45** G 4

Porto Alegre (Rio
 Grande do Sul, Brazil)
 46 G 5
Porto Amboim **56** A 2
Pôrto de Meinacos
 45 F 4
Pôrto de Moz **45** F 2
Pôrto Esperidiã **44** E 5
Pôrto Grande **45** F 1
Pôrto Jofre **44** E 5
Pôrto Nacional **45** G 4
Porto Novo **51** G 7
Pôrto Santo **50** C 2
Pôrto União **46** G 4
Pôrto Valter **44** B 3
Pôrto Velho **44** D 3
Portoviejo **42** C 5
Portsmouth (New
 Hampshire, U.S.A.)
 37 M 3
Portsmouth (Ohio,
 U.S.A.) **37** K 4
Portsmouth (U.K.)
 16 C 3
Portsmouth (Virginia,
 U.S.A.) **37** L 4
Portugal **18** A 2
Porvenir **47** C 9
Posadas **46** F 4
Poso **73** G 6
Posse **45** G 4
Poste-de-la-Baleine
 35 M 3
Potchefstroom **56** D 5
Potenza **19** F 2
P'ot'i **64** F 4
Potiskum **51** J 6
Potosí **44** C 5
Potro, Cerro el **46** D 4
Potsdam **17** F 3
Poughkeepsie **37** M 3
Povazská Bystrica
 17 G 4
Powell, Lake **36** D 4
Poza Rica de Hidalgo
 38 C 3
Požarevac **21** D 4
Poznań **17** G 3
Pozo del Tigre **44** D 5
Pozoblanco **18** C 3
Prachuap Khiri Khan
 67 H 5
Pradera **42** D 4
Pradesh **66** D 1
Prague **17** F 3
Praha **17** F 3
Praia **50** B 6
Praia Grande **46** G 4
Pratapgarh **66** C 3
Prato **19** E 2
Pratt **36** G 4
Praya **73** F 7
Prenzlau **17** F 3
Preparis Island **67** G 5
Preparis South Channel
 67 G 5
Prescott **36** D 5
Prescott Island **32** R 4

Presidencia Roque
 Sáenz Peña **46** E 4
Presidente Epitácio
 46 G 3
Presidente Prudente
 46 G 3
Prešov **17** H 4
Presque Isle **37** N 2
Prestea **51** F 7
Prestonburg **37** K 4
Pretoria **56** D 5
Preveza **21** D 5
Priangarskoye Plato
 61 V 6
Pribilof Islands **63** U 5
Priboj **21** C 4
Příbram **17** F 4
Prichard **37** J 5
Prieska **56** C 5
Prievidza **17** G 4
Prilep **21** D 4
Priluki **22** D 2
Primorsko-Akhtarsk
 22 E 3
Prince Albert **34** F 4
Prince Albert National
 Park **34** F 4
Prince Alfred, Cape
 32 M 4
Prince Charles Island
 33 V 5
Prince Edward Island
 (Island) **35** P 5
Prince Edward Island
 (Province) **35** P 5
Prince George **31** Q 5
Prince of Wales, Cape
 30 G 2
Prince of Wales Island
 (Australia) **77** G 2
Prince of Wales Island
 (Canada) **32** R 4
Prince of Wales Island
 (U.S.A.) **31** O 4
Prince Patrick Island
 32 N 3
Prince Regent Inlet
 32 S 4
Prince Rupert **31** O 5
Princess Charlotte Bay
 77 G 2
Princess Royal Island
 31 P 5
Príncipe **54** A 3
Príncipe da Beira **44** D 4
Prinsesse Astrid Kyst
 80 P 5
Prinsesse Ragnhild Kyst
 80 P 5
Prinzapolca **38** F 5
Priozersk **24** D 2
Pripolyarnyy Ural **25** J 2
Priština **21** D 4
Privas **19** D 2
Privolzhskaya
 Vozvyshennost' **23** G 2
Priyutovo **23** H 2
Prizren **21** D 4

Proddatür **66** D 5
Progreso **38** E 3
Prokhladnyy **23** F 4
Prokop'yevsk **61** T 7
Prokuplje **21** D 4
Proletarsk **23** F 3
Prome **67** H 4
Propria **45** J 4
Proven **33** Z 4
Provence **19** D 2
Providence **37** M 3
Providencia, Isla de
 39 F 5
Provideniya **63** V 4
Provo **36** D 3
Prudentópolis **46** G 4
Prudhoe Bay **30** L 1
Pruszków **17** H 3
Pruzhany **22** B 2
Prypyats' **22** C 2
Przemyśl **17** H 4
Pskov **24** C 3
Pucallpa **42** E 6
Pucheng **69** K 5
Pudasjärvi **26** L 2
Pudino **61** R 6
Pudops Dam **35** Q 5
Pudozh **24** E 2
Puebla **38** C 4
Pueblo **36** F 4
Puente Alto **46** C 5
Puente-Genil **18** C 3
Puerto Armuelles **38** F 6
Puerto Ayacucho **43** F 3
Puerto Barrios **38** E 4
Puerto Cabello **43** F 2
Puerto Cabezas **38** G 5
Puerto Chicama **42** D 6
Puerto Cisnes **47** C 7
Puerto Coig **47** D 9
Puerto Colombia **42** D 2
Puerto Cortés **38** E 4
Puerto Cumarebo
 43 F 2
Puerto Deseado **47** D 8
Puerto Escondito **38** D 4
Puerto Heath **44** C 4
Puerto la Cruz **43** G 2
Puerto Lempira **38** F 4
Puerto Limón **38** F 6
Puerto Madryn **47** D 7
Puerto Maldonado
 44 C 4
Puerto Montt **47** C 7
Puerto Natales **47** C 9
Puerto Pirámides **47** E 7
Puerto Plata **39** H 4
Puerto Princesa **73** F 4
Puerto Rico **39** J 4
Puerto Sastre **46** F 3
Puerto Suárez **44** E 5
Puerto Vallarta **38** A 3
Puerto Varas **47** C 7
Puerto Villazón **44** D 4
Puerto Williams
 47 D 10
Puertollano **18** B 3
Pugachev **23** G 2

Pukapuka (Cook
 Islands) **79** J 5
Pukapuka (French
 Polynesia) **79** M 5
Pukaruha **79** M 5
Pukch'ŏng **70** E 4
Pula **21** B 4
Pulap **78** D 3
Púlar, Cerro **46** D 3
Puławy **22** B 2
Pullman **36** C 2
Pulupandan **73** G 3
Puluwat **78** D 3
Puna, Isla **42** C 5
Puna de Atacama
 46 D 4
Puncak Jaya **73** K 6
Puncak Trikora **78** C 4
Pune **66** C 4
Punjab (India) **66** D 1
Punjab (Pakistan)
 66 C 1
Puno **44** B 5
Punta, Cerro de **39** J 4
Punta Alta **47** E 6
Punta Arenas **47** C 9
Punta de Mata **43** G 3
Punta Delgada **47** E 7
Punta Gorda (Belize)
 38 E 4
Punta Gorda
 (Nicaragua) **38** F 5
Punta Lempira **38** F 4
Puntarenas **38** F 5
Punto Fijo **43** E 2
Puper **73** J 6
Puqi **69** J 5
Puquio **44** B 4
Puquios **46** D 4
Pur **61** R 4
Purekkari neem **27** L 4
Puri **66** F 4
Purnea **66** F 2
Purtuniq **35** N 2
Purwakarta **72** D 7
Purwokerto **72** D 7
Pusan **70** E 5
Pushkin **24** D 3
Putian **69** K 5
Puting, Tanjung **72** E 6
Putla de Guerrero
 38 C 4
Putorana, Plato **61** U 4
Puttalan **66** D 6
Puttgarden **17** F 3
Puvirnituq **35** M 2
Puyang **69** J 3
Pwllheli **16** C 3
Pyandzh **65** L 5
Pyapon **67** H 4
Pyasina **61** T 3
Pyasino, Ozero **61** T 4
Pyatigorsk **23** F 4
Pyatistennoy **63** Q 3
P''yatykhatky **22** D 3
Pye **67** H 4
Pyhäjärvi **26** L 3
Pyinmana **67** H 4

Pylos **21** D 5
P'yŏngyang **70** E 5
Pyramid Lake **36** C 3
Pyramids Memphis
   52 F 2
Pyrénées **18** B 2
Pyrgos **21** D 5
Pyryatyn **22** D 2
Pyu **67** H 4

Q

Qaanaaq **33** X 3
Qabanbay **65** O 3
Qābis **51** H 2
Qaidam Pendi **68** E 3
Qala Nau **65** K 6
Qamar, Ghubbat al
   53 K 4
Qamashi **65** L 5
Qamdo **68** F 4
Qandahār **65** L 6
Qapshaghay **65** N 4
Qapshaghay Bögeni
   65 N 4
Qaqortoq **33** Bb 6
Qarabutaq **65** K 3
Qaraghandy **65** M 3
Qaraghayly **65** N 3
Qaraqum **64** H 3
Qaratöbe **64** H 3
Qarataū **65** M 4
Qarataū Zhotasy **65** L 4
Qarazhal **65** M 3
Qarsaqbay **65** L 3
Qarshi **65** L 5
Qasigiannguit **33** Aa 5
Qaskeleng **65** N 4
Qatar **53** K 3
Qaynar **65** N 3
Qawz Abū Ūlū **52** F 4
Qazaqtyng
   Usaqshoqylyghy
   65 J 3
Qazvin **64** G 5
Qeqertarsuaq **33** Aa 5
Qeqertarsuaq (Island)
   33 Aa 5
Qeshm **53** L 2
Qeshqantengiz **65** M 3
Qian Gorlos **70** D 3
Qianwei **69** G 5
Qianxi **69** H 5
Qiemo **68** D 3
Qijiang **69** H 5
Qijiaojing **68** E 2
Qikiqtarjuaq **33** Y 5
Qilian Shan **68** F 3
Qinā **52** F 2
Qin'an **69** H 4
Qingdao **69** L 3

Qinggang **70** E 3
Qinghai **68** E 3
Qinghai Hu **68** F 3
Qinghe **68** E 1
Qingjiang **69** K 4
Qingyuan **69** J 6
Qinhuangdao **69** K 3
Qinling Shan **69** H 4
Qinzhou **69** H 6
Qionghai **67** L 4
Qionglai **69** G 4
Qiongshan **67** L 4
Qiqihar **70** D 3
Qitai **68** D 2
Qitaihe **70** F 3
Qiyang **69** J 5
Qom **64** H 6
Qomsheh **64** H 6
Qorakül **65** K 5
Qosköl **65** L 3
Qosshaghyl **23** H 3
Qostanay **65** K 2
Qotanqaraghay **65** P 3
Quan Dao Nam Du
   67 J 6
Quang Ngai **67** K 4
Quanjyang **69** J 5
Quanzhou (Fujian,
   China) **69** K 6
Quanzhou (Guangxi,
   China) **69** J 5
Quaqtaq **35** O 2
Quarai **46** F 5
Quartu Sant'elena
   19 D 3
Quartzsite **36** D 5
Qüchän **65** J 5
Quebec **35** N 5
Quebec (State) **35** M 4
Queen Charlotte Islands
   31 O 5
Queen Elizabeth Islands
   32 S 3
Queen Mary Land
   80 S 5
Queen Maud Gulf
   32 Q 5
Queensland **77** F 4
Queenstown (Australia)
   76 H 8
Queenstown (South
   Africa) **56** D 6
Quela **54** C 5
Quelimane **57** F 3
Quellon **47** C 7
Quelmadas **45** J 4
Quemado, Monte **46** E 4
Querétaro **38** B 3
Quesada **38** G 5
Quesnel **31** Q 5
Quetta **66** B 1
Quevedo **42** D 5
Quezaltenango **38** D 5
Quezon City **73** G 3
Qui Nhon **67** K 5
Quibdó **42** D 3
Quiberon **11** C 1
Quillabamba **44** B 4

Quillota **46** C 5
Quilon **66** D 6
Quilpie **77** G 5
Quimen **69** K 5
Quimii **46** E 4
Quimper **18** B 1
Quincy **37** H 4
Quiriguá **38** E 4
Quirinopólis **45** F 5
Quitasueño, Banco
   39 F 5
Quito **42** D 5
Quixadá **45** J 2
Quixeramobim **45** J 3
Qujing **69** G 5
Qulsary **23** H 3
Qumarlêb Jiuzhi **68** F 4
Qūnghirot **65** J 4
Qūqon **65** M 4
Qürghonteppa **65** L 5
Quryq **23** H 4
Qūs **52** F 2
Qusmurun Köli **65** K 2
Quxian **69** K 5
Qyzylorda **65** L 4

R

Raba **73** F 7
Rabak **52** F 5
Rabat **50** E 2
Rabaul **78** E 4
Râbniţa **22** C 3
Rach Gia **67** K 5
Rădăuţi **20** E 3
Radom **17** H 3
Radomsko **17** G 3
Radøy **27** F 3
Radviškis **27** K 4
Rae **32** N 6
Raevavae **79** L 6
Rafael, Cachoeira do
   44 D 4
Rafaela **46** E 5
Rafsanjän **53** L 1
Ragged Island Range
   39 G 3
Ragusa **19** E 3
Rahallamane **50** D 4
Rahat, Harrat **53** G 3
Rahīmyär Khän **66** C 2
Raiatea **79** L 5
Raichur **66** D 4
Raigarh **66** E 3
Rainy Lake **34** J 5
Raipur **66** E 3
Rāj Gangpur **66** E 3
Raj Nandgaon **66** E 3
Rajabasa **72** C 7
Rājahmundry **66** E 4
Rajanpur **66** C 2

Rājapālaiyam **66** D 6
Rajasthan **66** C 2
Rajkot **66** C 3
Rājmahal Hills **66** E 3
Rajshahi **67** F 3
Rakahanga **79** J 4
Raleigh **37** L 4
Rama **38** G 5
Ramādah **51** J 2
Ramirez, Isla **47** B 9
Ramlat al Wigh
   52 C 3
Ramlat Rabyānah
   52 C 3
Ramlat Yām **53** J 4
Ramm, Jabal **53** G 2
Râmnicu Sārat **21** E 3
Râmnicu Vâlcea **21** D 3
Rampur **66** D 2
Ramree Island **67** G 4
Ramsgate **16** D 3
Rāna Pratāp Sāgar
   66 D 3
Rancagua **46** C 5
Ranchi **66** F 3
Rancho de Caça dos
   Tapiúnas **44** E 4
Ranco, Lago **47** C 7
Randers **27** H 4
Rangiroa **79** L 5
Rangkasbitung **72** D 7
Rangoon **67** H 4
Rangpur **67** F 2
Rangsang **72** C 5
Ranibennur **66** D 5
Rankin Inlet **34** J 2
Ranong **67** H 6
Ransiki **73** J 6
Rantau **72** C 5
Rantauprapat **72** B 5
Raoul Island **79** H 6
Rapa **79** L 6
Raper, Cape **33** X 5
Rapid City **36** F 3
Raraka **79** L 5
Raroia **79** L 5
Rarotonga **79** K 6
Ra's al Khaymah **53** L 2
Rās Koh **66** B 2
Rasa, Punta **47** E 7
Rashīd **52** F 1
Rasht **64** G 5
Rasskazovo **23** F 2
Rat Island **30** D 5
Ratak Chain **79** G 2
Ratangarh **66** C 2
Rath **66** D 2
Rathenow **17** F 3
Rathlin Island **16** B 2
Ratlam **66** D 3
Ratnagiri **66** C 4
Rättvik **27** J 3
Raub **72** C 5
Rauch **47** F 6
Raumo **27** K 3
Raurkela **66** E 3
Ravahere **79** L 5
Ravenna **19** E 2

Ravensthorpe **76** C 6
Rawaki **79** H 4
Rāwalpindi **65** M 6
Rawlinna **76** D 6
Rawlins **36** E 3
Rawson **47** D 7
Rāyadrug **66** D 5
Rāyagarha **66** E 4
Raychikhinsk **62** J 7
Rayong **67** J 5
Raz, Pointe du **18** B 1
Razgrad **21** E 4
Ré, Île de **18** B 1
Reading **16** C 3
Real, Cordillera **44** C 5
Reao **79** M 5
Rebecca, Lake **76** C 6
Rebi **73** J 7
Rebojo, Cachoeira do **44** E 3
Reboly **24** D 2
Rebun-To **70** H 3
Recherche, Archipelago of the **76** C 6
Rechna Doab **66** C 1
Rechytsa **22** D 2
Recife **45** K 3
Reconquista **46** F 4
Red Basin **69** H 4
Red Bluff **36** B 3
Red Cloud **36** G 3
Red Deer **31** S 5
Red Deer River **31** S 5
Red Devil **30** J 3
Red Lake **34** J 4
Red River **37** H 5
Red Sea **53** G 2
Redcliffe **77** J 5
Redding **36** B 3
Redfield **36** G 3
Redon **18** C 1
Redoubt Volcano **30** K 3
Reef Islands **78** F 4
Regensburg **17** F 4
Reggane **51** G 3
Reggio di Calabria **19** F 3
Reggio nell'Emilia **19** E 2
Reghin **20** D 3
Regina **34** G 4
Registro **46** H 3
Regresso, Cachoeira do **45** E 2
Reims **18** C 1
Reina Adelaida, Archipielago **47** C 9
Reindeer Lake **34** G 3
Reine **26** H 2
Reinosa **18** C 2
Reitoru **79** L 5
Rekinniki **63** Q 4
Reliance **34** F 2
Remanso **45** H 3
Rembang **72** E 7
Remontnoye **23** F 3
Rendsburg **17** E 3
Rengat **72** C 6

Rengo **46** C 5
Renland **33** Ff 4
Renmark **77** G 6
Rennell Island **78** F 5
Rennes **18** B 1
Reno **36** C 4
Reo **73** G 7
Replot **26** K 3
Repulse Bay **32** T 5
Reshteh-ye Kūhhā-ye Alborz **64** H 5
Resistencia **46** F 4
Reşiţa **21** D 3
Resolution Island (Canada) **35** P 2
Resolution Island (New Zealand) **77** M 9
Rethymno **21** D 5
Retkucha **63** S 3
Réunion **57** K 4
Reus **18** C 2
Revda **25** J 3
Revelstoke **31** R 5
Revillagigedo Island **31** O 4
Rewa **66** E 3
Rexburg **36** D 3
Rey **64** H 5
Rey, Isla del **39** G 6
Reykjavík **26** A 3
Reynosa **36** G 6
Rezh **25** K 3
Rēzekne **27** L 4
Rhein **17** E 4
Rhir, Cap **50** E 2
Rhode Island **37** M 3
Rhondda **16** C 3
Rhône **19** C 2
Riau, Kepulauan **72** C 5
Ribadeo **18** B 2
Ribaue **57** F 2
Ribe **27** G 4
Ribeirão Prêto **46** H 3
Riberalta **44** C 4
Richard-Toll **50** C 5
Richards, Cape **33** V 2
Richland **36** C 2
Richmond **37** L 4
Riding Mountain National Park **34** G 4
Riesa **17** F 3
Riesco, Isla **47** C 9
Rieti **19** E 2
Rīga **27** K 4
Riga, Gulf of **27** K 4
Rigolet **35** Q 4
Rijeka **21** B 3
Riksgränsen **26** J 2
Riley **36** C 3
Rimatara **79** K 6
Rimini **19** E 2
Rimouski **35** O 5
Rinbung **68** D 5
Rinca **73** F 7
Ringkøbing **27** G 4
Ringvassøy **26** J 2
Rio Branco **44** C 3

Rio Bravo **36** G 6
Rio Bueno **47** C 7
Rio Claro **46** H 3
Rio Colorado **47** E 6
Rio Cuarto **46** E 5
Rio de Janeiro (Brazil) **45** H 6
Rio de Janeiro (State, Brazil) **45** H 6
Rio do Sul **46** H 4
Rio Gallegos **47** D 9
Rio Grande **47** D 9
Rio Grande do Norte **45** J 3
Rio Grande do Sul **46** G 5
Rio Lagartos **38** F 3
Rio Largo **45** J 3
Rio Mayo, Paso **47** C 8
Rio Negro **46** H 4
Rio Negro, Embalse del **46** F 3
Rio Negro, Pantanal do **44** E 5
Rio Secundo **46** E 5
Rio Tercero **46** E 5
Riobamba **42** D 5
Riohacha **42** E 2
Rioverde **38** B 3
Ripon **16** C 3
Rishiri-Tô **70** H 3
Rivas **38** F 5
Riverside **36** C 5
Rivière-du-Loup **35** O 5
Rivne **22** C 2
Rivoli **19** D 1
Riyadh **53** J 3
Rize **64** F 4
Rizhao **69** K 3
Roan Plateau **36** E 4
Roanne **18** C 1
Roanoke **37** L 4
Roanoke Rapids **37** L 4
Robeson Channel **33** Y 2
Robinson Crusoe, Isla **46** B 5
Robinson Ranges **76** B 5
Robstown **37** G 6
Rocha **46** G 5
Rochefort **18** B 1
Rochester **37** L 3
Rock Hill **37** K 5
Rock Springs **36** E 3
Rockford **37** J 3
Rockhampton **77** J 4
Rocklands Reservoir **77** G 7
Rocky Mountain National Park **36** E 4
Rocky Mountains (Canada) **31** Q 4
Rocky Mountains (U.S.A.) **36** D 2
Rodez **18** D 2
Rodney, Cape **30** G 3
Rodos **21** E 5

Rodos (Island) **21** E 5
Rogaland **27** G 4
Roggeveldberg **56** B 6
Rohri **66** B 2
Rohtak **66** D 2
Roi Et **67** J 4
Roi Georges, Îles du **79** L 5
Roldal **27** G 4
Rolla **37** H 4
Rolvsøya **26** K 1
Roma (Australia) **77** H 5
Roma (Italy) **19** E 2
Roman **20** E 3
Romang **73** H 7
Romania **20** D 3
Romanovka **62** F 6
Rome (Italy) **19** F 2
Rome (U.S.A.) **37** J 5
Romny **22** D 2
Rømø **27** G 4
Rona **16** B 2
Roncador, Cayos de **39** F 5
Roncador, Serra do **45** F 4
Roncador Reef **78** E 4
Rondônia (Brazil) **44** D 4
Rondônia (State, Brazil) **44** D 4
Rondonópolis **45** F 5
Rongan **69** H 5
Rongelap **78** F 2
Rongerik **78** F 2
Rongjiang **69** H 5
Rongxian (Guangxi, China) **69** J 6
Rongxian (Sichuan, China) **69** G 5
Rønne **27** H 4
Ronneby **27** H 4
Roosevelt, Rio **44** D 3
Roquefort **18** C 2
Roraima **44** D 1
Roraima, Mount **43** G 3
Røros **26** H 3
Rosa, Monte **19** D 1
Rosario (Argentina) **46** E 5
Rosario (Mexico) **38** B 3
Rosario (Paraguay) **46** F 3
Rosario de la Frontera **46** D 4
Rosário do Sul **46** G 5
Rose Island **79** J 5
Roseau **39** K 4
Roseburg **36** B 3
Rosenberg **37** G 6
Rosenheim **17** F 4
Rosetown **34** F 4
Roşiorii-de-Vede **21** E 4
Roskilde **27** H 4
Roslavl' **22** D 2
Ross River **31** O 3
Rossel Island **77** J 2
Rossosh' **23** E 2

S

Salihli **64** C 5
Salihorsk **22** C 2
Salima **56** E 2
Salina **37** G 4
Salina del Gualicho
  47 D 7
Salina Grande **47** D 6
Salinas (Brazil) **45** H 5
Salinas (U.S.A.) **36** B 4
Salinas, Pampa de las
  46 D 5
Salinas, Ponta das
  56 A 2
Salinas Grandes **46** E 4
Salines, Cap de ses
  18 C 3
Salisbury (Australia)
  77 F 6
Salisbury (U.K.) **16** C 3
Salisbury Island **35** M 2
Salluyo, Nevado
  44 C 4
Salmon **36** D 2
Salon-de-Provence
  19 E 2
Sal'sk **23** F 3
Salt Lake City **36** D 3
Salta **46** D 3
Saltillo **36** F 6
Salto **46** F 5
Salton Sea **36** C 5
Sälür **66** E 4
Salvador **45** J 4
Salvatierra **38** B 3
Salween **67** H 3
Salzburg **19** E 1
Salzgitter **17** F 3
Salzwedel **17** F 3
Samales Group **73** G 4
Samälüt **52** F 2
Samar **73** H 3
Samar Sea **73** G 3
Samara **23** H 2
Samarinda **73** F 6
Samarqand **65** L 5
Sambalpur **66** E 3
Sambas **72** D 5
Sambir **22** B 3
Samboja **73** F 6
Samburg **61** R 4
Samch'ŏk **70** E 5
Samch'ŏnp'o **71** E 6
Samoa **79** H 5
Samoa Islands **79** H 5
Samokov **21** D 4
Samos **21** E 5
Samothraki **21** E 4
Sampit **72** E 6
Samsang **68** C 4
Samsun **64** E 4
Samut Songkhram
  67 H 5
San **50** F 6
San Agustin, Cape
  73 H 4
San Andrés **38** F 5
San Andrés Tuxtla
  38 C 4

San Andrés y
  Providencia **39** G 5
San Angelo **36** F 5
San Antonio (Peru)
  46 C 5
San Antonio (U.S.A.)
  36 G 6
San Antonio
  (Venezuela) **43** F 4
San Antonio, Cabo
  38 F 3
San Augustin, Cape
  73 H 4
San Benedetto del
  Tronto **19** E 2
San Bernardino
  36 C 5
San Bernardo **46** C 5
San Boria **44** C 4
San Carlos (Falkland
  Islands) **47** F 9
San Carlos (Nicaragua)
  38 G 5
San Carlos (Uruguay)
  46 G 5
San Carlos de Bariloche
  47 C 7
San Carlos de Rio
  Negro **44** C 1
San Carlos del Zulia
  42 E 3
San Clemente **36** C 5
San Cristobal **78** F 5
San Cristóbal
  (Argentina) **46** E 5
San Cristóbal
  (Dominican Republic)
  39 H 4
San Cristóbal
  (Galápagos Islands)
  42 B 5
San Cristóbal
  (Venezuela) **42** E 3
San Cristóbal de las
  Casas **38** D 4
San Diego **36** C 5
San Felipe (Mexico)
  36 D 5
San Felipe (Peru)
  46 C 5
San Felipe (Venezuela)
  43 F 2
San Fernando (Peru)
  46 C 5
San Fernando
  (Philippines) **73** G 2
San Fernando (Spain)
  18 B 3
San Fernando de Apure
  43 F 3
San Francisco
  (Argentina) **46** E 5
San Francisco (U.S.A.)
  36 B 4
San Francisco de
  Macoris **39** H 4
San Francisco del Oro
  36 E 6

San Gottardo, Passo del
  19 D 1
San Ignacio **46** F 4
San Ignacio de Velasco
  44 D 5
San Isidro **38** F 6
San Jacinto **42** D 3
San Joaquin Valley
  36 B 4
San Jorge **46** E 5
San Jorge, Golfo **47** D 8
San Jorge Island **78** E 4
San Jose **73** G 2
San José (Costa Rica)
  38 F 6
San José (U.S.A.)
  36 B 4
San José, Isla **36** D 6
San Jose de Buenavista
  73 G 3
San Jose de Chiquitos
  44 D 5
San Jose de Guanipa
  43 G 3
San José de Jáchal
  46 D 5
San José del Guaviare
  42 E 4
San Juan (Argentina)
  46 D 5
San Juan (Puerto Rico)
  39 K 4
San Juan del Norte
  38 F 5
San Juan del Norte,
  Bahía de **38** F 5
San Juan del Rio
  38 C 3
San Julián **47** D 8
San Justo **46** F 5
San Lorenzo **46** E 5
San Lorenzo, Cerro
  47 C 8
San Lucas, Cabo
  36 E 7
San Luis **46** D 5
San Luis, Sierra de
  46 D 5
San Luis de la Paz
  38 B 3
San Luis Obispo **36** B 4
San Luis Potosi **38** B 3
San Marcos (Colombia)
  42 D 3
San Marcos (Mexico)
  38 D 4
San Marcos (U.S.A.)
  37 G 6
San Marino **19** E 2
San Martin **46** D 5
San Martín **42** E 4
San Martin, Lago
  47 C 8
San Mateo **36** B 4
San Matías **44** E 5
San Matias, Golfo
  47 E 7
San Miguel **38** E 5

San Miguel de Allende
  38 B 3
San Miguel de Tucumán
  46 D 4
San Miguel Islands
  73 F 4
San Nicolas **36** F 6
San Nicolás **46** E 5
San Onofre **42** D 3
San Pablo (Bolivia)
  44 C 6
San Pablo (Philippines)
  73 G 3
San Pedro (Argentina)
  46 F 5
San Pedro (Mexico)
  36 F 6
San Pedro (Paraguay)
  46 F 3
San Pédro **50** E 8
San Pedro Pochutia
  43 C 4
San Pedro Sula **38** E 4
San Pietro, Isola di
  19 D 3
San Rafael **46** D 5
San Ramón de la Nueva
  Orán **46** E 3
San Remo **19** D 2
San Roque **46** F 4
San Salvador **38** E 5
San Salvador de Jujuy
  46 D 3
San Sebastian **47** D 9
San Severo **19** F 2
San Valentin, Monte
  47 C 8
San Vincente **73** G 2
San Vito, Capo **19** E 3
San'a' **53** H 4
Sanaga **54** B 3
Sanak Island **30** H 5
Sanana **73** H 6
Sanandaj **64** G 5
Sancti Spiritus **39** G 3
Sand **27** G 4
Sand Cay **66** C 5
Sandakan **73** F 4
Sandane **26** G 3
Sandanski **21** D 4
Sandbukt **26** K 2
Sandefjord **27** H 4
Sanderson **36** F 5
Sandnes **27** G 4
Sandoway **67** G 4
Sandoy **16** B 1
Sandstone (Australia)
  76 B 5
Sandstone (U.S.A.)
  37 H 2
Sandusky **37** K 3
Sandviken **27** J 3
Sandy Cape **77** J 4
Sandy Lake **34** J 4
Sanford, Mount **30** M 3
Sangamner **66** C 4
Sanger **36** C 4
Sanggau **72** E 5

Sangha 54 B 3
Sangha (River) 54 C 3
Sangir 73 H 5
Sangir, Kepulauan 73 H 5
Sangiyn Dalay Nuur 61 V 8
Sangju 70 E 5
Sangli 66 C 4
Sangmélima 54 B 3
Sanikiluaq 35 M 4
Sanjo 70 G 5
Sankt Gallen 19 D 1
Sankt Michel 26 L 3
Sankt-Peterburg 24 D 3
Sankt Pölten 19 F 1
Sankuru 54 D 4
Sanlúcar de Barrameda 18 B 3
Sanmenxia 69 J 4
Sanming 69 K 5
Sannär 52 F 5
Sannikova 62 L 2
Sanok 17 H 4
Santa, Pico de 54 A 3
Santa Ana (Bolivia) 44 C 4
Santa Ana (El Salvador) 38 E 5
Santa Ana (Solomon Islands) 78 F 5
Santa Ana (U.S.A.) 36 C 5
Santa Barbara (Mexico) 36 E 6
Santa Barbara (U.S.A.) 36 C 5
Santa Catarina, Ilha de 46 H 4
Santa Clara 39 G 3
Santa Clara Los Gatos 36 B 4
Santa Cruz (Argentina) 47 D 9
Santa Cruz (Bolivia) 44 D 5
Santa Cruz (U.S.A.) 36 B 4
Santa Cruz de la Palma 50 C 3
Santa Cruz de Tenerife 50 C 3
Santa Cruz del Sur 39 G 3
Santa Cruz do Sul 46 G 4
Santa Cruz Islands 78 F 5
Santa Elena (Argentina) 46 F 5
Santa Elena (Venezuela) 43 G 4
Santa Elena, Cabo 38 E 5
Santa Fe 36 E 4
Santa Fé 46 E 5
Santa Fe do Sul 46 G 3

Santa Helena 45 G 2
Santa Helena de Goiás 45 F 5
Santa Inés, Isla 47 C 9
Santa Isabel 47 D 6
Santa Isbel Island 78 E 4
Santa Júlia 44 E 3
Santa Margarita, Isla de 36 D 7
Santa Maria (Amazonas, Brazil) 44 E 2
Santa Maria (Azores) 50 B 1
Santa Maria (Rio Grande do Sul, Brazil) 46 G 4
Santa Maria (U.S.A.) 36 B 5
Santa Maria, Cabo de 56 E 5
Santa Maria di Leuca, Capo 19 F 3
Santa María, Isla 42 A 5
Santa Marta 42 E 2
Santa Marta, Cabo de 56 A 2
Santa Rosa (Argentina) 47 E 6
Santa Rosa (Bolivia) 44 D 5
Santa Rosa (Brazil) 46 G 4
Santa Rosa (U.S.A.) 36 B 4
Santa Rosa Island 36 B 5
Santa Rosalla 36 D 6
Santa Vitória do Palmar 46 G 5
Santai 69 H 4
Santana 45 H 4
Santana, Cachoeira 45 G 4
Santana do Livramento 46 F 5
Santander (Colombia) 42 D 4
Santander (Spain) 18 B 2
Santanghon 68 E 2
Santarém 45 F 2
Santiago (Brazil) 46 G 4
Santiago (Dominican Republic) 39 H 4
Santiago (Panamá) 39 F 6
Santiago (Peru) 46 C 5
Santiago de Compostela 18 A 2
Santiago de Cuba 39 G 3
Santiago del Estero 46 E 4
Santiago do Cacém 18 B 3
Santo André 46 H 3

Santo Ângelo 46 G 4
Santo Antao 50 A 5
Santo Antonio, Cachoeira 44 D 3
Santo Antonio de Jesus 45 J 4
Santo Antonio do Içá 44 C 2
Santo Domingo (Dominican Republic) 39 J 4
Santo Domingo (Mexico) 36 D 6
Santo Tomé 46 F 4
Santos 46 H 3
Sany-Tash 65 M 5
São Bento 45 H 2
São Borja 46 F 4
São Carlos 46 H 3
São Cristóvão Estancia 45 J 4
São Felix do Xingu 45 F 3
São Francisco 45 H 5
São Francisco, Rio 45 G 5
São Francisco do Sul 46 H 4
São Gabriel 46 G 5
São João del Rei 45 H 6
São João dos Patos 45 H 3
São Jorge 50 A 1
São José do Río Prêto 46 H 3
São José dos Campos 45 G 6
São Leopoldo 46 G 4
São Lourénço, Pantanal de 44 E 5
São Lourenço do Sul 46 G 5
São Luís 45 H 2
São Luís Gonzaga 46 F 4
São Mateus 45 J 5
São Miguel 50 A 1
São Miguel d'Oeste 46 G 4
São Miguel do Araguaia 45 F 4
São Nicolau 50 B 5
São Paulo 46 H 3
São Paulo (State) 46 H 3
São Paulo de Olivença 44 C 2
São Tiago 50 B 6
São Tomé and Príncipe 54 A 3
São Vicente (Brazil) 46 H 3
São Vicente (Cape Verde) 50 A 5
Sapele 51 H 7
Sapporo 70 H 4
Sapulpa 37 G 4
Saqqaq 33 Aa 4

Saraburi 67 J 5
Sarajevo 21 C 4
Sarakhs 65 K 5
Sarangani 73 H 4
Sarangarh 66 E 3
Saransk 23 G 2
Sarapul 25 H 3
Sarasota 37 K 6
Saratov 23 G 2
Saravan 67 K 4
Sarawak 72 E 5
Sardarshahr 66 C 2
Sardegna 19 D 3
Sardinia 19 D 3
Sargodha 66 C 1
Sarh 52 C 6
Sārī 64 H 5
Sarigan 78 D 2
Sarikei 72 E 5
Sarīr Kalanshiyū 52 D 2
Sarīr Tibesti 52 C 3
Sariwon 70 E 5
Sarmiento 47 D 8
Sarny 22 C 2
Sarowbī 65 L 6
Sarqan 65 N 3
Sarych, Mys 22 D 4
Saryesik-Atyraū Qumy 65 N 3
Saryözek 65 N 4
Saryshaghan 65 M 3
Sāsarām 66 E 3
Sasebo 71 E 6
Saskatchewan 34 F 4
Saskatchewan River 34 G 4
Saskatoon 34 F 4
Saskylakh 61 Y 3
Sasovo 23 F 2
Sassari 19 D 2
Sassnitz 17 F 3
Sasyqköl 65 O 3
Sātāra 66 C 4
Sätbaev 65 L 3
Satna 66 E 3
Satpura Range 66 C 3
Satu Mare 20 D 3
Satun 67 J 6
Saudárkrókur 26 B 2
Saudi Arabia 53 H 3
Sault Sainte Marie 35 L 5
Saumarez Reef 78 E 6
Saumur 18 B 1
Saunders Island 47 E 9
Saurimo 54 D 5
Sava 20 C 3
Savaii 79 H 5
Savalou 51 G 7
Savanna la Mar 39 G 4
Savannah 37 K 5
Savannakhet 67 J 4
Savda 26 G 3
Sāveh 64 H 5
Savona 19 D 2
Savonlinna 26 L 3
Savu 73 G 8
Sawāi Mādhopur 66 D 2

Sherekhov **61** W 7
Sheridan **36** E 3
Sherlovaya Gora **62** G 6
Sherman **37** G 5
Shetland Islands **16** D 1
Shibarghan **65** L 5
Shibīn al Kawn **52** F 1
Shidao **69** L 3
Shīeli **65** L 4
Shiguaigou **70** B 4
Shijiazhuang **69** J 3
Shikapur **66** D 5
Shikarpur **66** B 2
Shikoku **71** F 6
Shikotan, Ostrov **70** J 4
Shilka **62** G 6
Shilla **66** D 1
Shillong **67** G 2
Shilovo **23** F 2
Shimbiris **53** J 5
Shimizu **70** G 5
Shimoga **66** D 5
Shimonoseki **71** F 6
Shingai **70** G 6
Shingbwiyang **67** H 2
Shinjo **70** H 5
Shinyanga **55** F 4
Shiping **69** G 6
Shippagan **35** P 5
Shipunovo **65** O 2
Shīr Kūh **53** K 1
Shira **61** T 7
Shiranuka **70** H 4
Shīrāz **53** K 2
Shirokostan Poluostrov
    62 L 2
Shīrvān **65** J 5
Shivpuri **66** D 2
Shiwan Dashan **69** H 6
Shizunai **70** H 4
Shizuoka **70** G 6
Shkodër **21** C 4
Shmidta, Ostrov **61** U 1
Shmidta, Poluostrov
    62 M 6
Shoa **53** G 6
Shokal'skogo, Ostrov
    60 Q 3
Sholapur **66** D 4
Sholaqqkorghan **65** L 4
Shoshone **36** D 3
Shoshoni **36** E 3
Shostka **22** D 2
Shou Xian **69** K 4
Shouchang **69** K 5
Shouguang **69** K 3
Shoyna **24** F 1
Shreveport **37** H 5
Shrewsbury **16** C 3
Shū **65** M 4
Shuangcheng **70** E 3
Shuangliao **70** D 4
Shuangyashan **70** F 3
Shuguri Falls **55** G 5
Shuicheng **69** G 5
Shulan **70** E 4
Shule **68** B 3
Shumagin Islands **30** J 4

Shumen **21** E 4
Shumerlya **23** G 1
Shumshu, Ostrov **63** P 6
Shuoxian **69** J 3
Shurab **65** M 4
Shūshtar **64** G 6
Shuwak **53** G 5
Shuya **24** F 3
Shuyak Island **30** K 4
Shuyang **69** K 4
Shymkent **65** L 4
Si Racha **67** J 5
Siähän Range **66** A 2
Siälkot **66** C 1
Siargao **73** H 4
Siau **73** H 5
Siauliai **27** K 4
Sibay **65** J 2
Šibenik **21** C 4
Siberut **72** B 6
Sibi **66** B 2
Sibirskiye Uvaly **60** P 5
Sibirskoye **61** V 4
Sibiryakova, Ostrov
    61 R 3
Sibiu **20** D 3
Sibolga **72** B 5
Sibsagar **67** G 2
Sibu **72** E 5
Sibutu **73** F 5
Sibuyan **73** G 3
Sibuyan Sea **73** G 3
Sichuan Pendi **69** H 4
Sicilia **19** E 3
Sicilia, Canale di **19** E 3
Sicuani **44** B 4
Sidamo **53** G 7
Siddhapur **66** C 3
Siddipet **66** D 4
Siderno **19** G 3
Sidi-Bel-Abbès **51** F 1
Sidi Kacem **50** E 2
Sidney **31** Q 6
Sidra, Gulf of **52** C 1
Siedlce **17** H 3
Siegen **17** E 3
Siena **19** E 2
Sieradz **17** G 3
Sierra Colorada **47** D 7
Sifnos **21** D 5
Sigep **72** B 6
Sighetu Marmaţiei
    20 D 3
Sigli **72** B 4
Siglufjörður **26** B 2
Siguiri **50** E 6
Sigulda **27** K 4
Siirt **64** F 5
Sikar **66** D 2
Sikaram **65** L 6
Sikasso **50** E 6
Sikeston **37** J 4
Sikhote-Alin **70** G 3
Sikkim **66** F 2
Siktyach **62** H 3
Silchar **67** G 3
Siletitengiz Köli **65** M 2
Silicon Valley **36** B 4

Siliguri **66** F 2
Siling Co **68** D 4
Silistra **21** E 4
Siljan **27** H 3
Silkeborg **27** G 4
Sillem Island **33** W 4
Sillon de Talbert **18** B 1
Sillustani **44** B 5
Silvassa **66** C 3
Silver City **36** E 5
Simao **68** G 6
Simeulue **72** B 5
Simferopol' **22** D 4
Simla **66** D 1
Simplon Pass **19** D 1
Simpson Desert **76** F 4
Simpson Desert
    National Park **77** F 5
Simrishamn **27** H 4
Sinā **52** F 2
Sinabang **72** B 5
Since **42** D 3
Sincelejo **42** D 3
Sinch'ang **70** E 4
Sindjai **73** G 7
Sines, Cabo de **18** A 3
Sinfra **50** E 7
Singapore **72** C 5
Singaradja **72** F 7
Singkang **73** G 6
Singkawang **72** D 5
Singkep **72** C 6
Singö **27** J 3
Sinnūris **52** F 2
Sinop **64** E 4
Sinp'o **70** E 4
Sintang **72** E 5
Sinüiju **70** D 4
Sioux City **37** G 3
Sioux Falls **37** G 3
Sipalay **73** G 4
Siping **70** D 4
Sipura **72** B 6
Siquijor **73** G 4
Sir Banī Yās **53** K 3
Sir Edward Pellew
    Group **76** F 3
Sira **66** D 5
Siracusa **19** F 3
Sirevåg **27** G 4
Sirhan, Wādī as **53** G 1
Sirohi **66** C 3
Sironj **66** D 3
Sirr, Nafūd as **53** H 2
Sirsa **66** D 2
Sirt **52** C 1
Sirt, Gulf of **52** C 1
Sisak **21** C 3
Sisaket **67** J 4
Sissimiut **33** Aa 5
Sitapur **66** E 2
Siteia **21** E 5
Sitka **31** N 4
Sitkalidak Island **30** K 4
Sittwe **67** G 3
Sivas **64** E 5
Siverek **64** E 5
Sīwah, Wāhāt **52** E 2

Siwalik Range **66** D 1
Siwan **66** E 2
Sjælland **27** H 4
Skadovsk **22** D 3
Skagen **27** H 4
Skagerrak **27** G 4
Skagway **31** N 4
Skåne **27** H 4
Skardu **65** N 5
Skarodnaye **22** C 2
Skarżysko Kamienna
    22 B 2
Skegness **1** D 3
Skeiðarárjökull **26** B 3
Skellefteå **26** K 3
Skellefteälven **26** L 2
Ski **27** H 4
Skibotn **26** K 2
Skien **27** G 4
Skikda **51** H 1
Skomvær **26** H 2
Skopelos **21** D 5
Skopje **21** D 4
Skövde **27** H 4
Skovhøj **26** B 4
Skovorodino **62** H 6
Skowhegan **37** N 3
Skvyra **22** C 3
Skye **16** B 2
Skyros **21** D 5
Slamet, Gunung **72** D 7
Slantsy **24** C 3
Slatina **21** D 4
Slave Coast **51** G 8
Slave River **32** O 6
Slavgorod **65** N 2
Slavonski Brod **21** C 3
Slavuta **22** C 2
Slavyansk-na Kubani
    22 E 3
Sleeper Islands **35** L 3
Slettuheiði **26** B 2
Sligo **16** B 3
Sliven **21** E 4
Slonim **22** C 2
Slovakia **17** G 4
Slovenia **20** B 3
Slov"yans'k **22** E 3
Slozhnyy, Ostrov **61** T 2
Słupsk **17** G 3
Slutsk **22** C 2
Slyudyanka **61** W 7
Småland **27** J 4
Smallwood Reservoir
    35 P 4
Smederevo **21** D 4
Smila **22** D 3
Smirnykh **70** H 3
Smith **31** S 4
Smithton **76** H 8
Smokey Falls **35** L 4
Smøla **26** G 3
Smolensk **22** D 2
Smolyan **21** D 4
Smythe, Mount
    31 Q 4
Snag **30** M 3
Snake River **36** C 3

Snake River Plain **36** D 3
Snihurivka **22** D 3
Snowville **36** D 3
Snyder **36** F 5
Sobral **45** H 2
Soc Trang **67** K 6
Sochi **23** E 4
Société, Archipel de la **79** K 5
Society Islands **79** K 5
Socorro **42** E 3
Socotra **53** K 5
Sodankylä **26** L 2
Soddu **53** G 6
Söderhamn **27** J 3
Södermanland **27** J 4
Södertälje **27** J 4
Soe **73** G 7
Sofala, Baía de **56** F 4
Sofia **21** D 4
Sofie Christensen Reef **79** L 8
Sofiya **21** D 4
Sofiysk **62** K 6
Sofporog **24** D 1
Sofronovo **24** E 3
Sogamoso **42** E 3
Sogn og Fjordane **26** G 3
Sogndal **27** G 3
Sognefjorden **27** G 3
Soissons **18** C 1
Sôjosôn-man **70** D 5
Sokch'o **70** E 5
Söke **64** C 5
Sokodé **51** G 7
Sokółka **17** H 3
Sokoto **51** H 6
Sokhumi **23** F 4
Solano **73** G 2
Soldotna **30** K 3
Soledad **43** G 3
Solenoye **23** F 3
Solikamsk **25** J 3
Sol'-Iletsk **23** H 2
Solingen **17** E 3
Sollefteå **26** J 3
Solomon Islands **78** E 5
Solomon Sea **78** E 4
Solon **70** D 3
Solonchak Arys **65** L 3
Somalia **55** J 2
Sombor **20** C 3
Sombrerete **36** F 7
Somerset **37** K 4
Somerset Island **32** S 4
Son La **67** J 3
Son Tay **67** K 3
Sônch'ôn **70** D 5
Sønderborg **27** G 5
Søndre Strømfjord **33** Aa 5
Sonepur **66** E 3
Song Cau **67** K 5
Song Ma **67** J 3
Songea **55** G 6
Songhua Hu **70** E 4

Songjiang **69** L 4
Songkhla **67** J 6
Songnim **70** E 5
Sonmiani Bay **66** B 2
Sonneberg **17** F 3
Sonoita **36** D 5
Sonora **36** F 5
Sonoran Desert **36** D 5
Sonqor **64** G 6
Sonsonate **38** E 5
Sonsorol Islands **73** J 4
Sopka Shiveluch **63** Q 5
Sopot **17** G 3
Sopron **20** C 3
Sorang **65** M 3
Sor Kajdak **64** H 4
Sør-Trøndelag **26** H 3
Sorada **66** E 4
Sorel **35** N 5
Soria **18** B 2
Soroca **22** C 3
Sorocaba **46** H 3
Sorochinsk **23** H 2
Soroti **55** F 3
Sørøya **26** K 1
Sorsele **26** J 2
Sorsogon **73** G 3
Sorta **27** F 3
Sortavala **24** D 2
Sortland **26** J 2
Sos'va **25** K 3
Sosnogorsk **25** H 2
Sosnovo-Ozerskoye **62** F 6
Sosnowiec **17** G 3
Sotsial **65** N 3
Soudan **76** F 4
Soufrière **39** K 4
Souk Ahras **51** H 1
Sôul **70** E 5
Soulac-sur-Mer **18** C 1
Soure **45** G 2
Sousa **45** J 3
South Africa **56** B 6
South Andaman **67** G 5
South Aulatsivik Island **35** P 3
South Australia **76** E 6
South Bend **37** J 3
South Carolina **37** K 5
South China Sea **72** D 4
South Dakota **36** F 3
South East Cape **76** H 8
South East Point **77** H 7
South Georgia **47** K 9
South Island **77** M 8
South Korea **70** F 5
South Ronaldsay **16** C 2
South Shields **16** C 2
South Stradbroke Island **77** J 5
South Uist **16** B 2
Southampton **16** C 3
Southampton Island **34** K 2
Southend **34** G 3
Southend-on-Sea **16** D 3

Southern Alps **77** M 8
Southern Cook Islands **79** K 5
Southern Cross **76** B 6
Southern Indian Lake **34** H 3
Southport **77** J 5
South West Cape **77** M 9
Soutpansberg **56** D 4
Sovetskaya Gavan' **70** H 3
Sovetskiy **25** G 3
Spain **18** A 2
Spanish Town **39** G 4
Sparks **36** C 4
Spartanburg **37** K 5
Sparti **21** D 5
Spartivento, Capo **19** D 3
Spassk-Dal'niy **70** F 4
Spearfish **36** F 3
Speke Gulf **55** F 4
Spence Bay **32** S 5
Spencer **37** G 3
Spencer, Cape **76** F 7
Split **21** C 4
Spokane **36** C 2
Springbok **56** B 5
Springdale **37** H 4
Springfield (Colorado, U.S.A.) **35** F 4
Springfield (Illinois, U.S.A.) **37** J 4
Springfield (Massachusetts, U.S.A.) **37** M 3
Springfield (Mississippi, U.S.A.) **37** H 4
Springfield (Oregon, U.S.A.) **36** B 3
Springfontein **56** D 6
Springs **56** D 5
Springsure **77** H 4
Spurn Head **16** D 3
Squillace, Golfo di **19** F 3
Srebrenica **21** C 4
Sredinnyy Khrebet **63** P 6
Sredne Sibirskoye Ploskogor'ye **61** W 4
Srednekolymsk **63** O 3
Sremska Mitrovica **21** C 4
Sretensk **62** G 6
Sri Jayawardenepura **66** E 6
Sri Kālahasti **66** D 5
Sri Lanka **66** E 6
Srīkākulam **66** E 4
Srinagar **65** M 6
Staaten River National Park **77** G 3
Stade **17** E 3
Stafford **16** C 3
Stakhanov **23** E 3

Stallworthy, Cape **32** S 2
Stalowa Wola **17** H 3
Stamford **37** M 3
Stanke Dimitrov **21** D 4
Stanley **36** F 2
Stanley Falls **54** E 3
Stanovoy Khrebet **62** H 5
Stanovoye Nagor'ye **62** F 5
Stanthorpe **77** J 5
Stara Planina **21** D 4
Stara Zagora **21** E 4
Staraya Russa **24** D 3
Starbuck Island **79** K 4
Stargard Szczeciński **17** G 3
Starobil's'k **23** E 3
Starodub **22** D 2
Starogard Gdański **17** G 3
Staryy Oskol **22** E 2
State College **37** L 3
Staten Island **47** E 10
Statesboro **37** K 5
Staunton **37** L 4
Stavanger **27** G 4
Stavropol' **23** F 3
Stavropolka **65** L 2
Steelpoort **56** E 4
Steenstrup Gletscher **33** Z 3
Stefanie, Lake **53** G 6
Stefansson Island **32** P 4
Steilrand Mountains **56** A 3
Steinkjer **26** H 3
Stellenbosch **56** B 6
Stendal **17** F 3
Stepnyak **65** M 2
Sterling **36** F 3
Sterlitamak **23** J 2
Stevens Point **37** J 3
Stewart Crossing **31** N 3
Stewart Island **77** M 9
Stewart Islands **78** F 4
Stewart River **30** N 3
Steyr **19** E 1
Stillwater **37** G 4
Štip **21** D 4
Stirling (Australia) **76** B 6
Stirling (U.K.) **16** C 2
Stirling Range **76** B 6
Stirling Range National Park **76** B 6
Stockholm **27** J 4
Stockton Plateau **36** F 5
Stoke-on-Trent **16** C 3
Stolbovoy, Ostrov **62** L 2
Stora Lulevatten **26** J 2
Stora Sjöfallet **26** J 2
Storavan **26** J 2
Stord **27** F 4
Store Bælt **27** H 4
Store Koldewey **33** Hh 3

T

Ta'izz 53 H 5
Taj Mahal 66 D 2
Tajikistan 65 L 5
Tajo, Río 18 B 3
Tajrīsh 64 H 5
Tajumulco, Volcán 38 D 4
Tak 67 H 4
Takalar 73 F 7
Takamatsu 70 F 6
Takaoka 70 G 5
Takapuna 77 N 7
Takara-jima 71 E 7
Takasaki 70 G 5
Takengon 72 B 5
Takhli 67 J 4
Takijuk Lake 32 O 5
Takikawa 70 H 4
Takla Landing 31 P 4
Takla Makan 68 C 3
Taklimakan Shamo 68 C 3
Takume 79 L 5
Takutea 79 K 5
Tala 38 B 3
Talagbetutu 72 C 6
Talaimannar 66 D 6
Talak 51 G 5
Talamanca, Cordillera de 38 E 5
Talara 42 C 5
Talas 65 M 4
Talata Mafara 51 H 6
Talaud, Kepulauan 73 H 5
Talavera de la Reina 18 B 3
Talca 47 C 6
Talcahuano 47 C 6
Tälcher 66 F 3
Taldyqorghan 65 N 3
Talence 18 B 2
Talghar 65 N 4
Taliabu 73 G 6
Taliquin 65 L 5
Taliwang 73 F 7
Talkeetna 30 K 3
Tallahassee 37 K 5
Tallinn 27 K 4
Tal'menka 65 O 2
Talnakh 61 T 4
Tal'ne 22 D 3
Talok 73 F 5
Talovka 23 G 4
Talsi 27 K 4
Taltal 46 C 4
Talu 72 B 5
Taluk 72 C 6
Taluma 62 H 5
Tam Ky 67 K 4
Tama Abu Range 72 F 5
Tamale 51 F 7
Tamanrasset 51 H 4
Tamarugal, Pampa del 46 C 2
Tamazunchale 38 C 3
Tambacounda 50 D 6

Tambalan 72 F 5
Tambalan, Kepulauan 72 D 5
Tamberías 46 D 5
Tambo Grande 42 C 5
Tambov 23 F 2
Tambura 52 E 6
Tamgue, Massif du 50 D 6
Tamil 66 D 5
Tammerfors 26 K 3
Tampa 37 K 6
Tampere 26 K 3
Tampico 38 C 3
Tamsagbulag 70 C 3
Tamworth 77 J 6
Tana (Kenya) 55 G 3
Tana (Norway) 26 L 2
Tana, Lake 53 G 5
Tanaga Island 30 E 5
Tanahbala 72 B 6
Tanahgrogot 73 F 6
Tanahjampea 73 G 7
Tanahmasa 72 B 6
Tanama 61 R 3
Tanami Desert Wildlife Sanctuary 76 D 3
Tanana 30 K 2
Tanch'ön 70 E 4
Tandag 73 H 4
Tandil 47 F 6
Tando Adam 66 B 2
Tando Muhammad Khan 66 B 2
Tandsjöborg 26 H 3
Tane-ga-shima 71 F 6
Tanezrouft 51 F 4
Tanga (Russia) 62 F 6
Tanga (Tanzania) 55 G 5
Tanganyika, Lake 55 E 4
Tanger 50 E 1
Tanggerang 72 D 7
Tanggu 69 K 3
Tanggula Shan 68 E 4
Tanggula Shankou 68 E 4
Tanghe 69 J 4
Tangmai 68 F 4
Tangra Yumco 68 D 4
Tangshan 69 K 3
Tangwanghe 70 E 3
Tangyin 69 J 3
Tangyuan 70 E 3
Tanimbar, Kepulauan 73 J 7
Tanjungbalai 72 B 5
Tanjungpandan 72 D 6
Tanjungpinang 72 C 5
Tanjungredep 73 F 5
Tanjungselor 73 F 5
Tänk 66 C 1
Tankovo 61 T 5
Tanna 78 F 5
Tännäs 26 H 3
Tannu Ola, Khrebet 61 U 7

Tanout 51 H 6
Tantä 52 F 1
Tantoyuca 38 C 3
Tanzania 55 F 5
Tao'an 70 D 3
Taourirt 51 F 2
T'ao-yüan 69 L 5
Tapa 27 L 4
Tapachula 38 D 5
Tapajós, Rio 45 E 2
Tapaktuan 72 B 5
Tapauá 44 D 3
Tapul Group 73 G 4
Tapurucuara 44 C 2
Taqtabrod 65 L 2
Tara 60 Q 6
Tara Vai 79 M 6
Tarabuco 44 D 5
Tarābulus 52 B 1
Tarābulus 64 E 6
Tarakan 73 F 5
Taranto 19 F 2
Taranto, Golfo di 19 F 2
Tarapoto 42 D 6
Tarauacá 44 B 3
Tarawa 79 G 3
Taraz 65 M 4
Tarbes 18 C 2
Tarcoola 76 E 6
Taree 77 J 6
Tarfaya 50 D 3
Târgovişte 21 E 4
Târgu Jiu 21 D 3
Târgu Mureş 20 D 3
Tarija 44 D 6
Tarīm 53 J 4
Tarkhankut, Mys 22 D 3
Tarko-Sale 61 R 5
Tarkwa 51 F 7
Tarlac 73 G 2
Tarlton, Isla 47 C 9
Tarma 44 A 4
Tärnaby 26 J 2
Tarnobrzeg 17 H 3
Tarnów 17 H 4
Taroom 77 H 5
Taroudant 50 E 2
Tarpon Springs 37 K 6
Tarragona 18 C 2
Tarrassa 18 C 2
Tarsus 64 D 5
Tart 68 E 3
Tartagal 46 E 3
Tartu 27 L 4
Tartus 64 E 6
Tarutung 72 B 5
Tas-Kystaby, Khrebet 62 M 4
Tas-Tumus 62 J 4
Taseyevo 61 U 6
Tash-Kömür 65 M 4
Tashkurgan 65 L 5
Tashtagol 61 T 7
Tashtyp 61 T 7
Tasiilap Karra 33 Ee 5
Tasiilaq 33 Dd 5
Tasikmalaja 72 D 7

Tasman Peninsula 76 H 8
Tasman Sea 77 J 7
Tasmania (Island) 76 G 8
Tasmania (State) 76 G 8
Tassili-Oua-n-Ahaggar 51 G 5
Tata 20 C 3
Tatabánya 20 C 3
Tatarsk 61 R 6
Tatarskiy Proliv 62 M 7
Tatau 72 E 5
Tataurovo 61 X 7
Tathlina Lake 32 N 6
Tathlith 53 H 4
Tatnam, Cape 34 J 3
Tatry 17 G 4
Tatta 66 B 3
Tau 79 J 5
Tauá 45 H 3
Taubaté 45 G 6
Tauere 79 L 5
Taunggyi 67 H 3
Taupo 77 O 7
Taurag 27 K 4
Tauranga 77 O 7
Taūshyq 23 H 4
Tavastehus 27 K 3
Tavda 60 P 6
Taveta 55 G 4
Taveuni 79 H 5
Tavoy 67 H 5
Tavşanli 21 E 5
Tawau 73 F 5
Tawitawi Group 73 F 4
Taxco de Alarcón 38 C 4
Tay Ninh 67 K 5
Tayabamba 42 D 6
Tayga 61 T 6
Taygonos, Mys 63 P 4
Taygonos, Poluostrov 63 Q 4
Taylor 30 H 2
Taymä 53 G 2
Taymyr, Ozero 61 W 3
Taymyr, Poluostrov 61 U 3
Taypaq 23 H 3
Tayshet 61 V 6
Taz 61 S 5
Taza 51 F 2
Tazovskiy 61 R 4
Tazumal 38 E 5
T'bilisi 64 F 4
Tczew 17 G 3
Te Araroa 77 O 7
Teapa 38 E 4
Tebingtinggi 72 B 5
Tecate 36 C 5
Tecka 47 C 7
Tecomán 38 B 4
Tecuala 38 A 3
Tecuci 20 E 3
Tefé 44 D 2
Tegal 72 D 7
Tegucigalpa 38 E 5

Uryupinsk 23 F 2
Urzhum 25 G 3
Urziceni 21 E 4
Uşak 64 C 5
Usakos 56 B 4
Ushakova, Ostrov
 61 R 1
Üsharal 65 O 3
Ushki, Zaliv 63 N 5
Ushtöbe 65 N 3
Ushuaia 47 D 9
Ush-Urekchen, Khrebet
 63 Q 3
Usman' 23 E 2
Usol'ye-Sibirskoye
 61 W 7
Ussuriysk 70 F 4
Ust'-Ilimsk 61 W 6
Ust'-Ilimskoye
 Vodokhranilishche
 61 W 6
Üstirt 64 H 4
Ust'-Ishim 60 Q 6
Ust'-Kamchatsk 63 Q 5
Ust'-Kara 60 P 4
Ust'-Katav 25 J 4
Ust'-Khayryuzovo 63 P 5
Ust'-Kulom 25 H 2
Ust'-Kut 61 X 6
Ust'-Labinsk 23 E 3
Ust'-Maya 62 K 4
Ust'-Mil' 62 K 5
Ust'-Muya 62 G 5
Ust'-Nera 62 M 4
Ust'-Omchug 63 N 4
Ust'-Paden'ga 24 F 2
Ust'-Penzhino 63 R 4
Ust'-Port 61 S 4
Ust'-Sopochnoye 63 P 5
Ust'-Tatta 62 K 4
Ust'-Tsil'ma 25 H 1
Ust'-Urgal 62 K 6
Ust'-Usa 25 J 1
Ust'-Vaga 24 F 2
Ust'-Voyampolka 63 P 5
Usu 68 C 2
Usulután 38 E 5
Utah 36 D 4
Utica 37 L 3
Utirik 78 G 2
Utrecht 16 E 3
Utsunmiya 70 G 5
Uttar Pradesh 66 D 2
Uttaradit 67 J 4
Utupua 78 F 5
Uuldza 70 B 3
Uummannaq 33 Aa 4
Uummannaq 33 Cc 6
Üüreg Nuur 61 U 8
Uusikaupunki 27 K 3
Uusimaa 27 K 3
Uva 25 H 3
Uvalde 36 G 6
Uvarovo 23 F 2
Uvdal 27 G 3
Uvs Nuur 61 U 7
Uwayl 52 E 6
Uxmal 38 E 3

Uyedineniya, Ostrov
 61 S 2
Uyuni 44 C 6
Uyuni, Salar de 44 C 6
Uzbekistan 65 K 4
Uzhhorod 22 B 3
Uzhur 61 T 6
Užice 21 C 4
Uzlovaya 22 E 2

V

Vaal 55 C 5
Vaal Dam 56 D 5
Vaasa 26 K 3
Vác 20 C 3
Vacaria 46 G 4
Vache, Île-à 39 H 4
Vadodara 66 C 3
Vaduz 19 D 1
Vágar 16 B 1
Vaghena Island 78 E 4
Vakh 61 R 5
Valday 24 D 3
Valdayskaya
 Vozvyshennost' 24 D 3
Valdermarsvik 27 J 4
Valdez 30 L 3
Valdivia 47 C 6
Val-d'Or 35 M 5
Valdosta 37 K 5
Valença 45 J 4
Valence 19 C 2
Valencia (Spain) 18 B 3
Valencia (Venezuela)
 43 F 2
Valera 42 E 3
Valga 27 L 4
Valjevo 21 C 4
Valladolid (Mexico)
 38 F 3
Valladolid (Spain)
 18 B 2
Valle 27 G 4
Valle de la Pascua
 43 F 3
Valledupar 42 E 2
Vallenar 46 C 4
Valletta 19 E 3
Valley City 36 G 2
Valmiera 27 L 4
Valparaíso 46 C 5
Vals, Tanjung 73 K 7
Valuyki 22 E 2
Van 64 F 5
Van Dieman, Cape
 76 E 2
Van Diemen Gulf 76 E 2
Van Gölü 64 F 5
Vanadzor 64 F 4

Vanavara 61 W 5
Vancouver 31 Q 6
Vancouver Island 31 P 5
Vanderbijlpark 56 D 5
Vanderhoof 31 Q 5
Vanderlin Island 76 F 3
Vanduzi 56 E 3
Vänern 27 H 4
Vänersborg 27 H 4
Vangunu Island 78 E 4
Vanikoro Islands 75 F 5
Vankarem 63 U 3
Vanna 26 J 1
Vännäsby 26 J 3
Vannes 18 B 1
van Rees, Pegunungan
 73 K 6
Vansittart Island 35 L 1
Vanua Lava 78 F 5
Vanuatu 78 F 5
Vārānasi 66 E 2
Varangerhalvøya 26 L 1
Varaždin 20 C 3
Varberg 27 H 4
Varde 27 G 4
Vardø 26 M 1
Vârful Moldoveanu
 21 D 3
Varginha 45 G 6
Värmland 27 H 4
Varna 21 E 4
Várnamo 27 H 4
Varsinais Suomi 27 K 3
Várzea Grande 44 E 5
Varzuga 24 E 1
Vasa 26 K 3
Vaşac 21 D 3
Vasai 66 C 4
Vaslui 20 E 3
Vasta 23 G 3
Västerås 27 J 4
Västerbotten 26 J 3
Västerdalälven 27 H 3
Västergötland 27 H 4
Västervik 27 J 4
Västmanland 27 J 4
Vasyl'kiv 22 D 2
Vasyugan 61 R 6
Vatican State 19 E 2
Vatnajökull 26 B 3
Vatoa 79 H 5
Vatomandry 57 H 3
Vatra Dornei 20 E 3
Vättern 27 H 4
Vava'u Group 79 H 5
Vavuniya 66 E 6
Vawkavysk 22 B 2
Växjö 27 H 4
Vaygach 60 N 3
Vega 26 H 2
Veinticinco de Mayo
 47 E 6
Vejle 27 G 4
Veles 21 D 4
Velikiy Ustyug 25 G 2
Velikiye-Luki 24 D 3
Veliko Tŭrnovo 21 E 4
Velikonda Range 66 D 4

Vellore 66 D 5
Vel'sk 24 F 2
Venado Tuerto 46 E 5
Vendinga 25 G 2
Vendôme 18 D 1
Venetie 30 L 2
Venezia 19 E 1
Venezuela 43 F 3
Venezuela, Golfo de
 42 E 2
Venice, Gulf of 19 E 1
Ventspils 27 K 4
Ventura 36 C 5
Venustiano Carranza
 38 D 4
Vera 46 E 4
Veracruz 38 C 4
Veraval 66 C 3
Vereeniging 56 D 5
Vereshchagino 25 H 3
Verkhneangarskiy
 Khrebet 62 E 5
Verkhneimbatskoye
 61 T 5
Verkhnevilyuysk 62 H 4
Verkhniy Ufaley 25 K 3
Verkhn'odniprovs'k
 22 D 3
Verkhnyaya Amga
 62 J 5
Verkhnyaya Salda
 60 O 6
Verkhnyaya Toyma
 25 F 2
Verkhotur'ye 25 K 3
Verkhoyansk 62 K 3
Verkhoyanskiy Khrebet
 62 J 3
Vermillion Bay 34 J 5
Vermont 37 M 3
Vernal 36 E 3
Vernon (Canada) 31 R 5
Vernon (U.S.A.) 36 G 5
Vero Beach 37 K 6
Veroia 21 D 4
Verona 19 E 1
Versailles 18 C 1
Vert, Cap 50 C 6
Veshenskaya 23 F 3
Vest-Agder 27 G 4
Vesterålen 26 H 2
Vestfjorden 26 H 2
Vestmannaeyjar 26 A 3
Vestvågøy 26 H 2
Ves'yegonsk 24 E 3
Vétaoundé 78 F 5
Vetlanda 27 J 4
Vevelstad 26 H 2
Vezh'ydor 25 H 2
Viana do Castelo
 18 B 2
Viangchan 67 J 4
Vibo Valentia 19 F 3
Viborg 27 G 4
Vic 18 C 2
Vicenza 19 E 1
Vichuga 24 F 3
Vichy 18 C 1

Victoria (Australia) **77** G 7
Victoria (Canada) **36** B 2
Victoria (Chile) **47** C 6
Victoria (Hong Kong) **69** J 6
Victoria (Malaysia) **72** F 4
Victoria (U.S.A.) **37** G 6
Victoria, Lake **55** F 4
Victoria de las Tunas **39** G 3
Victoria Island **32** O 4
Victoria Nile **55** F 3
Victoria River Downs **76** E 3
Victoria Strait **32** Q 5
Victoria West **56** C 6
Victorias **73** G 3
Victorville **36** C 5
Vicuña Mackenna **46** E 5
Vidin **21** D 4
Vidisha **66** D 3
Vidra **21** E 4
Viedma **47** E 7
Viedma, Lago **47** C 8
Vienna **19** F 1
Vienne **19** C 1
Vientiane **67** J 4
Vieques, Isla de **39** K 4
Vierzon **18** C 1
Viet Triu **67** K 3
Vietnam **67** K 4
Vigan **73** G 2
Vigo **18** A 2
Vihari **66** C 1
Vihorlát **17** H 4
Vijayawāda **66** E 4
Vík **26** B 3
Viña del Mar **46** C 5
Vikna **26** H 3
Vila-real **18** B 2
Vila Velha **45** H 6
Vilalba **18** A 2
Vilanandro, Tanjona **57** G 3
Vilanova i la Geltrú **18** C 2
Vilhelmina **26** J 3
Vilhena **44** D 4
Viliga-Kushka **63** P 4
Viljandi **27** L 4
Vil'kitskogo, Ostrov **61** R 3
Vil'kitskogo, Proliv **61** W 2
Villa Alemana **46** C 5
Villa Ángela **46** E 4
Villa Constitución **46** E 5
Villa del Rosario **42** E 2
Villa Dolores **46** D 5
Villa Frontera **36** F 6
Villa Maria **46** E 5
Villa Minetti **46** E 4
Villa Montes **44** D 6

Villa Nueva **46** D 5
Villa Ocampo **46** F 4
Villa Ojo de Agua **46** E 4
Villa Regina **47** D 6
Villa Tunari **44** C 5
Villach **19** E 1
Villaguay **46** F 5
Villahermosa **38** D 4
Villarrica (Paraguay) **46** F 4
Villarrica (Peru) **47** C 6
Villavicencio **42** E 4
Villeurbanne **19** C 1
Villmanstrand **27** L 3
Villupuram **66** D 5
Vilnius **27** L 5
Vilyeyka **22** C 2
Vilyuy **62** G 4
Vilyuyskoye Plato **61** X 4
Vilyuyskoye Vodokhranilishche **61** X 5
Vimmerby **27** J 4
Vina **54** B 2
Vinaròs **18** C 2
Vincennes **37** J 4
Vindhya Range **66** C 3
Vinh **67** K 4
Vinh Loi **67** K 6
Vinkovci **21** C 3
Vinnytsya **22** C 3
Virac **73** G 3
Viramgam **66** C 3
Virgin Islands **39** J 4
Virginia (South Africa) **56** D 5
Virginia (State, U.S.A.) **37** L 4
Virginia (U.S.A.) **37** H 2
Virginia Beach **37** L 4
Virginia Falls **32** L 6
Virudunager **66** D 6
Visalia **36** C 4
Visayan Sea **73** G 3
Visby **27** J 4
Viscount Melville Sound **32** O 4
Viseu **18** B 2
Viseul-de-Sus **20** D 3
Vishakhapatnam **66** E 4
Visnagar **66** C 3
Viso, Monte **19** D 2
Vistula **17** G 3
Vitarte **44** A 4
Viterbo **19** E 2
Viti Levu **79** G 5
Vitim **62** G 5
Vitimskoye Ploskogor'ye **62** F 6
Vitória (Amazonas, Brazil) **45** F 2
Vitória (Espírito Santo, Brazil) **45** H 6
Vitória da Conquista **45** H 4

Vitoria-Gasteiz **18** B 2
Vitsyebsk **22** D 1
Vittoria **19** E 3
Vittorio Veneto **19** E 1
Vivi **61** V 5
Vizcaíno, Desierto de **36** D 6
Vize, Ostrov **61** R 2
Vizianagaram **66** E 4
Vladikavkaz **23** F 4
Vladimir **23** F 1
Vladivostok **70** F 4
Vlissingen **16** D 3
Vlorë **21** C 4
Vogan **51** G 7
Voi **55** G 4
Vojvodina **21** C 3
Volga **23** G 3
Volgo-Balt Kanal **24** E 2
Volgodonsk **23** F 3
Volgograd **23** F 3
Volkhov **24** D 3
Volksrust **56** D 5
Volnovakha **22** E 3
Volochanka **61** U 3
Volodymyr-Volyns'kyy **22** B 2
Vologda **24** E 3
Volos **21** D 5
Volosovo **24** C 3
Vol'sk **23** G 2
Volta **51** G 7
Volta, Lake **51** F 7
Volta Blanche **51** F 6
Volta Redonda **45** H 6
Volzhsk **23** G 1
Volzhskiy **23** F 3
Vongping **68** F 5
Voranava **22** C 2
Voreioi Sporades **21** D 5
Vorkuta **25** K 1
Vormsi **27** K 4
Voronezh **23** E 2
Voronina, Ostrov **61** U 2
Võru **27** L 4
Voss **27** G 3
Vostochno-Sibirskoye More **63** P 2
Vostochnyy Sayan **61** U 7
Vostok Island **79** K 5
Votkinsk **25** H 3
Votuporanga **46** G 3
Voyvozh **25** J 2
Vozhgora **25** G 2
Voznesens'k **22** D 3
Vozrozhdeniya **65** J 3
Vrangelya, Ostrov **63** T 2
Vranje **21** D 4
Vratsa **21** D 4
Vrsac **21** D 3
Vryburg **56** C 5
Vryheid **56** E 5
Vsetín **17** G 4
Vsevolozhsk **24** D 3
Vukovar **21** C 3

Vung Tau **67** K 5
Vyatka **25** G 3
Vyatskiye Polyany **25** H 3
Vyaz'ma **22** D 1
Vyborg **24** C 2
Vyksa **23** F 1
Vyshniy Volochek **24** D 3
Vysokiy, Mys **62** N 1
Vytegra **24** E 2

W

W.J. van Blommestein Meer **43** H 4
Wa **51** F 6
Waboden **34** H 4
Wabowden **34** H 4
Waco **37** G 5
Wad Madanī **52** F 5
Waddenzee **16** D 3
Waddington, Mount **31** P 5
Wādī Halfā **52** F 3
Wagga Wagga **77** H 7
Wagin **76** B 6
Wāh Cantonment **65** M 6
Wahai **73** H 6
Wahiawa **79** K 1
Wahībah **53** L 3
Waibeem **73** J 4
Waigeo **73** J 5
Waija **73** H 6
Wainwright **30** H 1
Waitemata **77** N 7
Waiwo **73** J 6
Wajir **55** H 3
Wakasa-wan **70** G 5
Wakayama **70** G 6
Wakema **67** H 4
Wakkanai **70** H 3
Walaga **53** G 6
Wałbrzych **17** G 3
Wałcz **17** G 3
Wales (U.K.) **16** C 3
Wales (U.S.A.) **30** G 2
Wales Island **32** T 5
Walker Lake **36** C 4
Walla Walla **36** C 2
Wallachia **21** D 4
Wallaroo **77** F 6
Wallel **52** F 6
Wallis, Îles **79** H 5
Wallis and Futuna **79** H 5
Walrus Islands **30** H 4

Waltershausen Gletscher **33** Ff 4
Walvis Bay **56** A 4
Wamba **54** C 5
Wandel Sea **33** Gg 2
Wanganui **77** O 7
Wangaratta **77** H 7
Wangiwangi **73** G 7
Wangkui **70** E 3
Wangqing **70** E 4
Wanneroo **76** B 6
Wanning **67** L 4
Wanxian **69** H 4
Wanyuan **69** H 4
Warangal **66** D 4
Warburton Range **76** D 5
Ware **31** P 4
Waren **73** K 6
Warin Chamrap **67** J 4
Warming Land **33** Aa 2
Warner Robins **37** K 5
Warrenton **56** C 5
Warri **51** H 7
Warrnambool **77** G 7
Warrumbungle Range **77** H 6
Warsaw **17** H 3
Warszawa **17** H 3
Warwick **77** J 5
Wasgomuwa National Park **66** E 6
Washburn Lake **32** P 4
Washim **66** D 3
Washington **36** B 2
Washington D.C. **37** L 4
Washington Land **33** X 2
Wasior **73** J 6
Waspán **38** G 5
Watampone **73** G 6
Waterford **16** B 3
Waterloo (Belgium) **16** D 3
Waterloo (U.S.A.) **37** H 3
Waterton Lakes National Park **31** R 6
Watertown **37** G 3
Waterville **37** N 3
Watsa **55** E 3
Watson Lake **31** P 3
Watubela, Kepulauan **73** J 6
Waukara, Gunung **73** F 6
Waukarlycarly, Lake **76** C 4
Waukegan **37** J 3
Wausau **37** J 3
Wave Hill **76** E 3
Wäw **52** E 6
Wawa **34** L 5
Way, Lake **76** B 5
Waycross **37** K 5
Wayne **37** K 4
Webbe Shibeli **53** H 6
Webi Shabeelle **55** H 3
Weda **73** H 5

Weddell Island **47** E 9
Weh **72** B 4
Wei He **69** J 4
Weichang **70** C 4
Weiden **17** F 4
Weifang **69** K 3
Weihai **69** L 3
Weinan **69** H 4
Weishan Hu **69** K 4
Weißwasser **17** F 3
Wejherowo **17** G 3
Welkom **56** D 5
Wellesley Islands **77** F 3
Wellington **77** N 8
Wellington, Isla **47** C 8
Wels **19** E 1
Wenchang **67** L 4
Wenchi **51** F 7
Wendeng **69** L 3
Wenling **69** L 5
Wenshan **69** G 6
Wentworth **77** G 6
Wenzhou **69** L 5
Weri **73** J 6
Wessel, Cape **76** F 2
Wessel Islands **76** F 2
West Bengal **66** F 3
West Cape Howe **76** B 7
West Falkland **47** E 9
West Indies **39** J 3
West Memphis **37** H 4
West Nicholson **56** D 4
West Palm Beach **37** K 6
West Virginia **37** K 4
West Wyalong **77** H 6
West Yellowstone **36** D 3
Western Australia **76** B 4
Western Ghâts **66** C 4
Western Port **77** G 7
Western Sahara **50** D 4
Westminister **36** B 2
Weston-super-Mare **16** C 3
Westport **77** N 8
Westray **16** C 2
Wetar **73** H 7
Wetzlar **17** E 3
Wewak **78** D 4
Wexford **16** B 3
Weyburn **34** G 5
Whakatane **77** O 7
Whale Cove **34** J 2
Whalsay **16** C 1
Whangarei **77** N 7
Wharton Lake **34** G 2
Wheeler **36** B 2
White Island **34** K 1
White Nile **52** E 6
White River **34** K 5
White Volta **51** F 7
Whitecourt **31** R 5
Whitehaven **16** C 3
Whitehorse **31** N 3
Whitney, Mount **36** C 4

Whitsunday Island **77** H 4
Whittier **30** L 3
Wholdaia Lake **34** F 2
Whyalla **76** F 6
Wichita **37** G 4
Wichita Falls **36** G 5
Wick **16** C 2
Wickham, Cape **77** G 7
Wien **19** F 1
Wiener Neustadt **19** F 1
Wiesbaden **17** E 3
Wight, Isle of **16** C 3
Wilcannia **77** G 6
Wilhelm, Mount **78** D 4
Wilhelm II Land **80** R 5
Wilhelmshaven **17** E 3
Willemstad **39** J 3
Williams Lake **31** Q 5
Williamsport **37** L 3
Willis Group **77** J 3
Williston (South Africa) **56** C 6
Williston (U.S.A.) **36** F 2
Williston Lake **31** Q 4
Willow Springs **37** H 4
Wilmington **37** L 4
Wilson, Cape **33** U 5
Wilson's Promontory National Park **77** H 7
Wiluna **76** C 5
Winchester (U.K.) **16** C 3
Winchester (U.S.A.) **37** K 4
Windhoek **56** B 4
Windorah **77** G 5
Windsor **35** L 6
Windward Islands (Caribbean) **39** K 5
Windward Islands (French Polynesia) **79** K 5
Winfield **37** G 4
Winisk **34** K 3
Winnebago **51** F 7
Winnipeg **34** H 5
Winnipeg, Lake **34** H 4
Winnipegosis, Lake **34** G 4
Winona **37** H 3
Winslow Reef **79** H 4
Winston-Salem **37** K 4
Winter Park **37** K 6
Winton **77** G 4
Wisconsin **37** H 2
Wiseman **30** K 2
Wisła **17** G 3
Wismar **17** F 3
Witbank **56** D 5
Wittenberg **17** F 3
Wittenberge **17** F 3
Witwatersrand **56** D 5
Włocławek **17** G 3
Wokam **73** J 7
Wolf Point **36** E 2
Wolfsberg **19** E 1

Wollaston Forland **33** Gg 4
Wollaston Lake **34** G 3
Wollongong **77** J 6
Wolverhampton **16** C 3
Wonju **70** E 5
Wŏnsan **70** E 5
Wood Buffalo National Park **31** S 4
Woodland **36** B 4
Woodlark Island **75** E 4
Woods, Lake **76** E 3
Woods, Lake of the **34** H 5
Woodward **36** G 4
Woomera **76** F 6
Worcester (South Africa) **56** B 6
Worcester (U.K.) **16** C 3
Wordie Gletscher **33** Gg 4
Workington **16** C 3
Worland **36** E 3
Worthington **37** G 3
Wosi **73** H 6
Wosu **73** G 6
Wotho **78** F 2
Wotje **78** G 3
Wotu **73** G 6
Wowoni **73** G 6
Woy Woy **77** J 6
Wozrojdeniye Orol **65** J 3
Wrangell **31** O 4
Wrangell, Cape **30** C 5
Wrangell Mountains **30** M 3
Wrangell Saint Elias National Park **30** M 3
Wrath, Cape **16** B 2
Wrigley **32** M 6
Wrocław **17** G 3
Wu Shan **69** J 4
Wuchang (Heilongjiang, China) **70** E 4
Wuchang (Hubei, China) **69** J 4
Wuchuan **69** J 6
Wuda **69** H 3
Wudu **69** G 4
Wugang **69** J 5
Wuhai **69** H 3
Wuhan **69** J 4
Wuhu **69** K 4
Wuji Shan **69** K 5
Wulff Land **33** Aa 2
Wuling Shan **69** H 5
Wumeng **69** G 5
Wunnummin Lake **34** K 4
Wuppertal **17** E 3
Wuqing **69** K 3
Wurno **51** H 6
Würzburg **17** E 4
Wutai Shan **69** J 3
Wutunghliao **69** G 5
Wuwei (Anhui, China) **69** K 4

York **16** C 3
York, Cape **77** G 2
York Factory **34** J 3
Yorke Peninsula **76** F 6
Yorkton **34** G 4
Yosemite National Park
  36 B 4
Yoshkar-Ola **25** G 3
Yŏsu **71** E 6
Youghal **16** B 3
Youllemmedeue **51** G 5
Youngstown **37** K 3
Youyi Feng **61** T 8
Yozgat **64** D 5
Yrghyz **65** K 3
Ystad **27** H 4
Ysyk-Köl **65** N 4
Ytterhogdal **26** H 3
Ytyk-Kyuyel' **62** K 4
Yü Shan **69** L 6
Yuanping **69** J 3
Yuanqu **69** J 3
Yübari **70** H 4
Yucatán, Canal de
  38 E 3
Yucatán Peninsula
  38 E 3
Yuci **69** J 3
Yueqing **69** L 5
Yuexi **69** G 5
Yueyang **69** J 5
Yugo-Tal **63** O 3
Yugorskiy Poluostrov
  60 O 4
Yugoslavia **21** C 4
Yukhnov **22** E 2
Yukogirskoye
  Ploskogor'ye **63** O 3
Yukon **30** N 2
Yukon Flats **30** L 2
Yukon Flats National
  Monument **30** L 2
Yukon Plateau **31** N 3
Yukon River (Canada)
  31 N 3
Yukon River (U.S.A.)
  30 H 3
Yukon Territory **31** N 2
Yuli **68** D 2
Yulin (Guangxi, China)
  69 J 6
Yulin (Shaanxi, China)
  69 H 3
Yuma **36** D 5
Yumen **68** F 3
Yumenzhen **68** F 2
Yun Xian **69** J 4
Yunaska Island **30** F 5
Yuncheng **69** J 3
Yün-lin **69** L 6
Yunnan **69** G 6
Yunxiao **69** K 6
Yurga **61** S 6
Yurimaguas **42** D 6
Yushan **69** K 5
Yushkozero **24** D 2
Yushu **70** E 4

Yutian **68** C 3
Yuxi **69** G 6
Yuxian **69** J 3
Yuyao **69** L 4
Yuzhno-Aleksandrovka
  61 V 6
Yuzhno Muyskiy
  Khrebet **62** F 5
Yuzhno-Sakhalinsk
  70 H 3
Yuzhnoural'sk **25** K 4
Yuzhnyy Anyuyskiy
  Khrebet **63** Q 3

Z

Zabol **65** K 6
Zabrze **17** G 3
Zabürün'e **23** H 3
Zacapa **38** E 5
Zacápu **38** B 4
Zacatecas **38** B 3
Zachodnyaya Dzvina
  27 L 4
Zadar **21** C 4
Zafra **18** B 3
Zagreb **20** C 3
Zagros, Kühhā-ye **53** J 1
Zahlah **64** E 6
Zakamensk **61** W 7
Zakopane **17** G 4
Zakynthos **21** C 5
Zalaegerszeg **20** C 3
Zalari **61** W 7
Zalew Szczeciński
  17 F 3
Zalingei **52** D 5
Zambeze **56** E 3
Zambezi **56** C 3
Zambia **56** C 2
Zamboanga **73** G 4
Zambonga Peninsula
  73 G 4
Zambrów **20** D 2
Zamora **18** A 2
Zamora de Hidalgo
  38 B 4
Zanesville **37** K 4
Zanjän **64** G 5
Zanul'ye **25** G 2
Zanzibar **55** G 5
Zanzibar Channel
  55 G 5
Zanzibar Island **55** G 5
Zaoyang **69** J 4
Zaozhuang **69** K 4
Zapadno-Sibirskaya
  Ravnina **60** O 5
Zapadnyy Sayan **61** T 7
Zapala **47** C 6
Zaporizhzhya **22** E 3

Zaragoza **18** B 2
Zarasai **27** L 4
Zárate **46** F 5
Zaraza **43** F 3
Zarghün Shahr **65** L 6
Zaria **51** H 6
Zarumilla **42** C 5
Żary **17** G 3
Zäskär Mountains
  65 N 6
Zatoka Pomorska **17** F 3
Zavitinsk **62** J 6
Zavodoukovsk **60** P 6
Zav'yalova, Ostrov
  63 N 5
Zaysan **65** O 3
Zduńska Wola **17** G 3
Zeerust **56** D 5
Zeitz **17** F 3
Zelenodol'sk **23** G 1
Zelenokumsk **23** F 4
Żepa **21** C 4
Zenica **21** C 4
Zeya **62** J 6
Zeya (River) **62** J 6
Zeyskoye
  Vodokhranilishche
  62 J 6
Zgorzelec **17** G 3
Zhalaghash **65** L 3
Zhalpaqtal **64** G 3
Zhangaözen **64** H 4
Zhangaqala **23** G 3
Zhangatas **65** L 4
Zhangbei **70** B 4
Zhangguangcai Ling
  70 E 4
Zhangjiakou **70** B 4
Zhangpu **69** K 6
Zhangwu **70** D 4
Zhangye **68** G 3
Zhangzhou **69** K 6
Zhänibek **23** G 3
Zhanjiang **69** J 6
Zhaoan **69** K 6
Zhaodong Hulan **70** E 3
Zhaojue **69** G 5
Zhaoqing **69** J 6
Zhaotong **69** G 5
Zhaoyuan **70** E 3
Zharkent **65** N 4
Zhashkiv **22** D 3
Zhaysang Köli **65** O 3
Zhayylma **65** K 2
Zhayyq **64** H 3
Zhejiang **69** K 5
Zhelezinka **65** N 2
Zheleznogorsk **22** E 2
Zheleznogorsk-Ilimskiy
  61 W 6
Zhenghe **69** K 5
Zhengzhou **69** J 4
Zhenjiang **69** K 4
Zhenlai **70** D 3
Zhenning **69** H 5
Zhenxiong **69** G 5
Zhenyuan **69** H 5
Zherdevka **23** F 2

Zhetiqara **65** K 2
Zhezkazgan **65** L 3
Zhigalovo **61** W 7
Zhigansk **62** H 3
Zhigulevsk **23** G 2
Zhijiang **69** H 5
Zhmerynka **22** C 3
Zhob **66** B 1
Zhodzina **22** C 2
Zholymbet **65** M 2
Zhong Xian **69** H 4
Zhongshan **69** J 6
Zhongwei **69** H 3
Zhongxiang **69** J 4
Zhosaly **65** K 3
Zhou Shan Dao **69** L 4
Zhou Shan Quandao
  69 L 4
Zhoukouzhen **69** J 4
Zhovtnevoye **22** D 3
Zhujiang Kou **69** J 6
Zhukovka **22** D 2
Zhumadian **69** J 4
Zhuolu **70** C 4
Zhuòxian **69** K 3
Zhushan **69** J 4
Zhuzhou **69** J 5
Zhytomyr **22** C 2
Zibo **69** K 3
Zielona Góra **17** G 3
Zighan, Wāhāt **52** D 2
Zigong **69** G 5
Ziguinchor **50** C 6
Žile **64** E 4
Žilina **17** G 4
Zima **61** W 7
Zimba **56** D 3
Zimbabwe **56** D 3
Zinder **51** H 6
Zitácuaro **38** B 4
Ziwa Magharibi **55** F 4
Ziyang **69** G 4
Zlatoust **25** J 3
Zmeinogorsk **65** O 2
Znamenka (Kazakhstan)
  65 N 2
Znamenka (Ukraine)
  22 D 3
Znojmo **17** G 4
Zomba **56** F 3
Zonguldak **64** D 4
Zouar **52** C 3
Zrenjanin **21** D 3
Zuera **18** C 2
Zufär **53** K 4
Zugdidi **64** F 4
Zugspitze **19** E 1
Zujevka **25** H 3
Zunyi **69** H 5
Zürich **19** D 1
Zvishavane **56** D 3
Zvolen **17** G 4
Zwickau **17** F 3
Zwolle **16** E 3
Zyryanka **63** O 3
Zyryanovsk **65** O 3
Żywiec **17** H 4

STATISTICAL SECTION

This statistical section consists of 192 entries - one for each independent country. Each entry consists of basic information designed to give a general overview, with an illustration of the current national flag.
Using Afghanistan as an example:

 Statistical Panel

AFGHANISTAN: English short form.
Jamhuria Afghanistan: local long form.
The Islamic State of Afghanistan: long form in English.
Area: given in both square miles (mi^2) and square kilometers (km^2).
Highest point: Highest mountain or hill.
Population: year in brackets (1998) refers to the latest United Nations official estimate of population.
Capital, population: country capital with its population from the latest census or official estimate.
Other important cities: by population.
Population growth per annum: average annual rate of population change 1995-2000.
Life expectancy at birth: the average length of time a baby born today can expect to live.
Official languages: the national language or that language used in education.
Literacy rate: percentage of the population with the ability to read and write.
Religion(s): predominant.
Currency: name of money in actual use.
Main exports: most important exported products.

The sources used to compile these panels for each country are numerous and varied to ensure that only the most current information is provided (where available). The main references include The Statesman's Yearbook, 1998/1999 and The UN Statistical Yearbook, 42nd edition.

AFGHANISTAN
Jamburia Afghanistan
The Islamic State of Afghanistan

Area: 251,773 mi² / 652,090 km²

Highest point: Nowshak

Population: 23,346,000 (1998)

Capital, population: Kabul, 2,000,000

Other important cities, population: Qandahār / Kandahar, 225,500, Herat, 177,300, Mazār-e Sharīf, 130,600

Population growth per annum: 5.27%

Life expectancy at birth: 45 male, 46 female

Official Language: Pushtu, Dari

Literacy: 44% male, 14% female

Religion: 99% Muslim

Currency: one Afghani = 100 puls

Main exports: Fruit, nuts, carpets, wool, cotton & natural gas

ALBANIA
Republic e Shqipërisë
Republic of Albania

Area: 11,101 mi² / 28,748 km²

Highest point: Korab

Population: 3,445,000 (1998)

Capital, population: Tiranë(Tirana), 257,000 (1996)

Other important cities, population: Durrës, 869,000, Shkodër, 837,000, Elbasan, 832,000

Population growth per annum: 0.6%

Life expectancy at birth: 70 male, 76 female

Official Language: Albanian (Gheg, Tosk)

Literacy: 85% male, 85% female

Religion: 70% Muslim, 20% Orthodox, 10% R.C.

Currency: one Lek = 100 qindars

Main exports: Chromium & chrome products, foodstuffs, plant & animal products, bitumen, electricity, tobacco & fuels

ALGERIA
Jumhuriya al-Jazairiya
ad-Dimuqratiya ash-Shabiya
The Democratic & Popular Republic of Algeria

Area: 919,595 mi² / 2,381,741 km²

Highest point: Mt Tahat

Population: 30,175,000 (1998)

Capital, population: Al Jazā'ir (Algiers), 2,168,000

Other important cities, population: Oran, 609,823, Constantine, 440,842, Annaba, 222,518

Population growth per annum: 2.3%

Life expectancy at birth: 67 male, 70 female

Official Language: Arabic

Literacy: 64% male, 45% female

Religion: 98% Muslim

Currency: one Algerian Dinar = 100 centimes

Main exports: Crude oil, gas, condensates & refined products

ANDORRA
Principat d"Andorra
Principality of Andorra

Area: 175 mi² / 453 km²

Highest point: Pla del' Estany

Population: 72,766 (1996)

Capital, population: Andorra la Vella 22,386

Other important cities, population: Escaldes-Engordany, 13,177

Population growth per annum: 2.8%

Life expectancy at birth: 86 male, 95 female

Official Language: Catalan

Literacy: 99% male, 99% female

Religion: Roman Catholic

Currency: French Franc, Spanish Peseta

Main exports: Cigarettes, cigars, electricity & furniture

ANGOLA

República de Angola
Republic of Angola

Area: 481,559 mi² / 1,246,700 km²

Highest point: Moco

Population: 11,967,000 (1998)

Capital, population: Luanda, 2,250,000 (1995)

Other important cities, population: Huambo, 400,000, Lobito, 59,258, Benguela, 40,996

Population growth per annum: 3.3%

Life expectancy at birth: 47 male, 51 female

Official Language: Portuguese

Literacy: 56% male, 28% female

Religion: 64% Christian, 34% Animist

Currency: one Kwanza = 100 lwei

Main exports: Crude oil, diamonds, refined oil & gas

ANTIGUA AND BARBUDA

State of Antigua and Barbuda

Area: 171 mi² / 442 km²

Highest point: Boggy Peak

Population: 69,000 (1996)

Capital, population: St John's, 30,000

Other important cities, population: Codrington (Barbuda), 1,200

Population growth per annum: 0.6%

Life expectancy at birth: 70 male, 74 female

Official Language: English

Literacy: 92% male, 88% female

Religion: Christian

Currency: one East Caribbean Dollar = 100 cents

Main exports: Tourism

ARGENTINA

República Argentina
The Argentine Republic

Area: 1,073,859 mi² / 2,780,092 km²

Highest point: Cerro Aconcagua

Population: 36,123,000 (1998)

Capital, population: Buenos Aires, 11,662,050

Other important cities, population: Córdoba, 1,179,420, Rosario, 1,157,372, Mendoza, 801,920

Population growth per annum: 1.3%

Life expectancy at birth: 70 male, 77 female

Official Language: Spanish

Literacy: 95% male, 95% female

Religion: 93% Roman Catholic, 2% Protestant

Currency: one Peso = 100 centavos = 10,000 australs

Main exports: Cereals, waste from the food industry, oils, fruit & fish

ARMENIA

Hayastani Hanrapetoutioun
The Republic of Armenia

Area: 11,490 mi² / 29,800 km²

Highest point: Aragats Lerr

Population: 36,450,000 (1998)

Capital, population: Yerevan, 1,254,400 (1994)

Other important cities, population: Vanadzor, 170,200, Gyumri, 120,000

Population growth per annum: 0.2%

Life expectancy at birth: 76 male, 70 female

Official Language: Armenian

Literacy: 99% male, 99% female

Religion: Armenian Orthodox

Currency: one Dram = 100 lumma

Main exports: Machinery, metal working products, chemicals & petroleum products

AUSTRALIA

The Commonwealth
of Australia

Area: 2,966,368 mi² / 7,682,300 km²

Highest point: Mt Kosciusko

Population: 18,490,000 (1998)

Capital, population: Canberra, 332,100 (1995)

Other important cities, population: Sydney, 3,770,100, Melbourne, 3,217,400, Brisbane, 1,488,900

Population growth per annum: 1%

Life expectancy at birth: 75 male, 81 female

Official Language: English

Literacy: 99% male, 99% female

Religion: 74% Christian, Muslim, Jewish, Buddhist

Currency: one Australian Dollar = 100 cents

Main exports: Metal ores and scrap, coal and coal products, gold, non-ferrous metals & textile fibres

AUSTRIA

Republik Österreich
The Republic of Austria

Area: 32,377 mi² / 83,859 km²

Highest point: Großglockner

Population: 8,210,000 (1998)

Capital, population: Wien (Vienna), 1,539,848 (1991)

Other important cities, population: Graz, 237,810, Linz, 203,044, Salzburg, 143,978

Population growth per annum: 0.6%

Life expectancy at birth: 74 male, 80 female

Official Language: German

Literacy: 99% male, 99% female

Religion: 78% Roman Catholic, 5% Protestant

Currency: one Schilling = 100 groschen

Main exports: Processed goods, machinery and transport equipment, other finished goods, raw materials, chemical products & foodstuffs

AZERBAIJAN

Azarbaijchan Respublikasy
The Azerbaijani Republic

Area: 33,430 mi² / 86,600 km²

Highest point: Bazardüzü dağ

Population: 7,714,000 (1998)

Capital, population: Bakı (Baku), 1,720,000 (1997)

Other important cities, population: Gäncä, 295,000, Sumqayıt, 271,000

Population growth per annum: 1.2%

Life expectancy at birth: 68 male, 75 female

Official Language: Azerbaijani

Literacy: 96% male, 96% female

Religion: 88% Muslim, Christian

Currency: one Manat = 100 gyapics

Main exports: Petroleum products, machinery, foodstuffs &

THE BAHAMAS

Commonwealth of
The Bahamas

Area: 5,353 mi² / 13,864 km²

Highest point: Mt Alvernia

Population: 293,000 (1998)

Capital, population: Nassau, 178,000 (1996)

Other important cities, population: Freeport, 45,000

Population growth per annum: 1.6%

Life expectancy at birth: 70 male, 79 female

Official Language: English

Literacy: 98% male, 95% female

Religion: 95% Christian

Currency: one Bahamian dollar = 100 cents

Main exports: Oil products, chemicals, fish, rum & salt

BAHRAIN
Dawlat Al Bahrayn
State of Bahrain

Area: 265 mi² / 688 km²

Highest point: Jabal al-Dukhan

Population: 594,000 (1998)

Capital, population: Al Manāmah, 140,401 (1995)

Other important cities, population: Al Muharraq, 78,000, Jidhafs, 48,000, Rifa'a, 28,150

Population growth per annum: 2.1%

Life expectancy at birth: 71 male, 75 female

Official Language: Arabic

Literacy: 89% male, 79% female

Religion: 85% Muslim, 7% Christian

Currency: one Bahraini dinar = 100 fils

Main exports: Oil and petroleum products

BANGLADESH
Gana Prajatantri Bangladesh
People's Republic of
Bangladesh

Area: 57,295 mi² / 148,393 km²

Highest point: Keokradong

Population: 124,043,000 (1998)

Capital, population: Dhaka (Dacca), 3,397,187 (1991)

Other important cities, population: Chittagong, 1,363,998, Khulna, 545,849, Rajshahi, 299, 671

Population growth per annum: 1.6%

Life expectancy at birth: 58 male, 58 female

Official Language: Bengali

Literacy: 57% male, 22% female

Religion: 87% Muslim, 12% Hindu,

Currency: one Taka = 100 paisas

Main exports: Jute and jute goods, tea, hides and skins, newsprint, fish and garments

BARBADOS
Barbados

Area: 166 mi² / 430 km²

Highest point: Mt Hillaby

Population: 263,000 (1998)

Capital, population: Bridgetown, 6,720 (1990)

Other important cities, population: N/A

Population growth per annum: 0.3%

Life expectancy at birth: 74 male, 79 female

Official Language: English

Literacy: 98% male, 97% female

Religion: 71% Protestant, 5% Roman Catholic

Currency: one Barbados dollar = 100 cents

Main exports: Electrical components, chemicals, foodstuffs, cars and other durables

BELARUS
Republika Belarus
Republic of Belarus

Area: 801,134 mi² / 207,600 km²

Highest point: Hora Dzyarzhynskaya

Population: 10,323,000 (1998)

Capital, population: Minsk, 1,700,000 (1994)

Other important cities, population: Homyel', 503,300, Vitsyebsk, 369,200, Mahilyow, 363,000

Population growth per annum: -0.1%

Life expectancy at birth: 68 male, 75 female

Official Language: Belorussian

Literacy: 98% male, 98% female

Religion: Belorussian Orthodox, Roman Catholic

Currency: one Ruble = 100 kopeks

Main exports: Machinery, chemicals, petrochemicals, iron & steel

BELGIUM

Royaume de Belgique-Koninkrijk
België
Kingdom of Belgium

Area: 11,778 mi² / 30,518 km²

Highest point: Botrange

Population: 10,213,000 (1998)

Capital, population: Bruxelles, 950,597 (1997)

Other important cities, population: Antwerpen, 453,030, Gent, 225,469, Charleroi, 204,899

Population growth per annum: 0.2%

Life expectancy at birth: 74 male, 81 female

Official Language: French, Flemish (Dutch)

Literacy: 99% male, 99% female

Religion: 72% Roman Catholic, Protestant

Currency: one Belgian franc = 100 centimes

Main exports: Foodstuffs, livestock, diamonds, iron & steel

BELIZE

Belize

Area: 8,866 mi² / 22,963 km²

Highest point: Victoria Peak

Population: 230,000 (1998)

Capital, population: Belmopan, 3,852 (1993)

Other important cities, population: Belize City, 47,724

Population growth per annum: 2.5%

Life expectancy at birth: 73 male, 76 female

Official Language: English

Literacy: 93% male, 93% female

Religion: 58% Roman Catholic, 34% Protestant

Currency: one Belize dollar = 100 cents

Main exports: Sugar, clothes, citrus products, fish & bananas

BENIN

République du Bénin
The Republic of Benin

Area: 43,502 mi² / 112,622 km²

Highest point: Atacora Massif

Population: 8,771,000 (1998)

Capital, population: Porto Novo, 177,660 (1992)

Other important cities, population: Cotonou, 533,212, Parakou, 106,708, Abomey, 65,725

Population growth per annum: 2.8%

Life expectancy at birth: 47 male, 51 female

Official Language: French

Literacy: 32% male, 16% female

Religion: 70% Traditional, 15% Christian, 15% Muslim

Currency: one CFA franc = 100 centimes

Main exports: Cotton & crude oil

BHUTAN
Druk-yul
The Kingdom of Bhutan

Area: 18,000 mi² / 46,500 km²

Highest point: Kula Kangri

Population: 1,917,000 (1998)

Capital, population: Thimphu (Thimbu), 30,340 (1993)

Other important cities, population: N/A

Population growth per annum: 2.7%

Life expectancy at birth: 52 male, 55 female

Official Language: Dzongkha, English, Nepali

Literacy: 51% male, 25% female

Religion: 70% Buddhist, 25% Hindu

Currency: one Ngultrum = 100 chetrum

Main exports: Fruit & timber

BOLIVIA

República de Bolivia
Republic of Bolivia

Area: 424,346 mi² / 1,098,581 km²

Highest point: Nevado Sajama

Population: 7,958,000 (1998)

Capital, population: Sucre, 130,952 (1992)

Other important cities, population: Santa Cruz, 694,616, Cochabamba, 404,102, Seat of Government La Paz, 711,036

Population growth per annum: 2.3%

Life expectancy at birth: 60 male, 63 female

Official Language: Spanish

Literacy: 85% male, 71% female

Religion: 94% Roman Catholic

Currency: one Boliviano = 100 centavos

Main exports: Timber, zinc, gold, tin, natural gas & jewellery

BOSNIA-HERZEGOVINA

Republika Bosnia I Hercegovina
The Republic of Bosnia & Herzegovina

Area: 19,741 mi² / 51,129 km²

Highest point: Maglic

Population: 3,994,000 (1998)

Capital, population: Sarajevo, 526,000

Other important cities, population: Banja Luka, 190,000, Zenica, 147,000, Tuzla, 132,000, Mostar, 126,000

Population growth per annum: 3.9%

Life expectancy at birth: 70 male, 76 female

Official Language: Serbo-Croat

Literacy: 90% male, 90% female

Religion: 40% Muslim, 31% Orthodox

Currency: Dinar

Main exports: Coal & domestic appliances

BOTSWANA

Republic of Botswana

Area: 224,808 mi² / 582,000 km²

Highest point: Tsodilo Hill

Population: 1,551,000 (1998)

Capital, population: Gaborone, 138,471 (1991)

Other important cities, population: Mahalapye, 104,450, Serowe, 95,041, Tutume, 86,405

Population growth per annum: 2.2%

Life expectancy at birth: 65 male, 69 female

Official Language: English, Setswana

Literacy: 84% male, 65% female

Religion: 50% Traditional, 50% Christian

Currency: one Pula = 100 thebe

Main exports: Diamonds, copper, nickel & beef

BRAZIL

República Federativa do Brasil
The Federative Republic of Brazil

Area: 3,287,893 mi² / 8,511,996 km²

Highest point: Pico de Neblina

Population: 165,158,000 (1998)

Capital, population: Brasília, (Federal District), 1,821,946 (1996)

Other important cities, population: São Paulo, 9,839,436, Rio de Janeiro, 5,551,538, Belo Horizonte, 2,091,448

Population growth per annum: 1.2%

Life expectancy at birth: 65 male, 70 female

Official Language: Portuguese

Literacy: 82% male, 80% female

Religion: 89% Roman Catholic, 7% Protestant

Currency: one Real = 100 centavos

Main exports: Soya, iron, manganese and other ores, coffee, orange juice, tobacco & cocoa beans

BRUNEI

Negara Brunei Darussalam
State of Brunei Darussalam

Area: 2,226 mi² / 5,765 km²

Highest point: Bukit Pagon

Population: 333,000 (1998)

Capital, population: Bandar Seri Begawan, 45,867 (1991)

Other important cities, population: Seria, 21,082, Kuala Belait, 21,163

Population growth per annum: 2.1%

Life expectancy at birth: 73 male, 77 female

Official Language: Malay

Literacy: 93% male, 83% female

Religion: 67% Muslim, 13% Buddhist, 10% Christian

Currency: one Brunei Dollar or Ringgit = 100 cents

Main exports: Crude oil & natural gas

BULGARIA

Republika Bulgaria
The Republic of Bulgaria

Area: 42,855 mi² / 110,994 km²

Highest point: Musala

Population: 8,387,000 (1998)

Capital, population: Sofiya (Sofia), 1,141,712 (1996)

Other important cities, population: Plovdiv, 344,326, Varna, 301,421, Burgas, 199,470

Population growth per annum: -0.5%

Life expectancy at birth: 68 male, 75 female

Official Language: Bulgarian

Literacy: 93% male, 93% female

Religion: 80% Eastern Orthodox, Sunni Muslim

Currency: one Lev = 100 stotinki

Main exports: Pork and poultry, livestock, tomatoes, cheese, wine, tobacco, soda ash, ammonium nitrate & polyethylene

BURKINA FASO

République Démocratique
de Burkina Faso
The Republic of Burkina

Area: 105,884 mi² / 274,122 km²

Highest point: Téna Kourou

Population: 11,402,000 (1998)

Capital, population: Ouagadougou, 442,223 (1985)

Other important cities, population: Bobo-Dioulasso, 231,162, Koudougou, 51,670, Ouahigouya, 38,604

Population growth per annum: 2.8%

Life expectancy at birth: 46 male, 49 female

Official Language: French

Literacy: 28% male, 12% female

Religion: 40% Muslim, 12% Roman Catholic, 40% Traditional

Currency: one CFA franc = 100 centimes

Main exports: Cotton & gold

BURUNDI

Republika y'Uburundi
The Republic of Burundi

Area: 10,751 mi² / 27,834 km²

Highest point: Mt Hela

Population: 6,526,000 (1998)

Capital, population: Bujumbura, 300,000 (1996)

Other important cities, population: N/A

Population growth per annum: 2.8%

Life expectancy at birth: 50 male, 53 female

Official Language: French

Literacy: 61% male, 40% female

Religion: 78% Roman Catholic

Currency: one Burundi franc = 100 centimes

Main exports: Coffee, manufactured goods & tea

CAMBODIA

Preah Reach Ana Pak Kampuchea
Kingdom of Cambodia

Area: 69,898 mi² / 181,035 km²

Highest point: Phnum Aôral

Population: 10,751,000 (1998)

Capital, population: Phnom Penh, 920,000 (1994)

Other important cities, population: Kompong Cham, Batdambang

Population growth per annum: 2.2%

Life expectancy at birth: 53 male, 55 female

Official Language: Khmer

Literacy: 48% male, 65% female

Religion: 88% Buddhist, 2% Muslim

Currency: one Riel = 100 sen

Main exports: Timber, rubber, soya beans & sesame

CAMEROON

République du Cameroun
Republic of Cameroon

Area: 183,648 mi² / 475,442 km²

Highest point: Cameroun Mountain

Population: 14,323,000 (1998)

Capital, population: Yaoundé, 750,000 (1981)

Other important cities, population: Douala, 884,000, Garoua, 177,000, Maroua, 143,000

Population growth per annum: 2.7%

Life expectancy at birth: 57 male, 60 female

Official Language: French, English

Literacy: 66% male, 43% female

Religion: 33% Roman Catholic, 21% Muslim, 17% Protestant

Currency: one CFA franc = 100 centimes

Main exports: Logs, cocoa, coffee, aluminium, timber products, cotton & bananas

CANADA

Canada

Area: 3,851,320 mi² / 9,970,610 km²

Highest point: Mt Logan

Population: 30,194,000 (1998)

Capital, population: Ottawa, 920,857

Other important cities, population: Toronto, 4,344,300, Montréal, 3,337,200, Vancouver, 1,831,000, (1995)

Population growth per annum: 0.9%

Life expectancy at birth: 75 male, 81 female

Official Language: English, French

Literacy: 99% male, 99% female

Religion: 47% Roman Catholic, 41% Protestant

Currency: one Canadian dollar = 100 cents

Main exports: Motor vehicles and parts, machinery and equipment, industrial goods and materials & forestry products

CAPE VERDE

República de Cabo Verde
The Republic of Cape Verde

Area: 1,557 mi² / 4,033 km²

Highest point: Mt Fogo

Population: 217,000 (1998)

Capital, population: Praia, 61,707 (1990)

Other important cities, population: Mindelo, 47,080 (1990)

Population growth per annum: 2.5%

Life expectancy at birth: 65 male, 67 female

Official Language: Portuguese

Literacy: 80% male, 60% female

Religion: 93% Roman Catholic, 7% Protestant

Currency: one Cape Verde Escudo = 100 centavos

Main exports: Fish, salt, volcanic rock & bananas

CENTRAL AFRICAN REPUBLIC

République Centrafricaine
The Central African Republic

Area: 240,324 mi² / 622,984 km²

Highest point: Mt Gaou

Population: 3,489,000 (1998)

Capital, population: Bangui, 451,690 (1988)

Other important cities, population: M'baiki, 189,554, ossangoa, 120,330, Bouar, 105,782

Population growth per annum: 2.1%

Life expectancy at birth: 48 male, 53 female

Official Language: French

Literacy: 52% male, 25% female

Religion: 45% Protestant, 30% Roman Catholic

Currency: one CFA franc = 100 centimes

Main exports: Coffee, diamonds & timber

CHAD

République du Tchad
The Republic of Chad

Area: 496,000 mi² / 1,284,000 km²

Highest point: Emi Koussi

Population: 6,887,000 (1998)

Capital, population: N'Djamena, 530,965 (1993)

Other important cities, population: Moundou, 282,103, Sarh, 193,753, Bongor, 196,713

Population growth per annum: 2.7%

Life expectancy at birth: 48 male, 51 female

Official Language: French, Arabic

Literacy: 42% male, 18% female

Religion: 37% Muslim, 30% Christian

Currency: one CFA franc = 100 centimes

Main exports: Cotton, cattle, textiles & fish

CHILE

República de Chile
Republic of Chile

Area: 292,383 mi² / 756,945 km²

Highest point: Cerro Ojos del Salado

Population: 14,824,000 (1998)

Capital, population: Santiago, 5,180,757 (1992)

Other important cities, population: Concepción, 330,448, Valparaíso, 276,736, Temuco, 240,880

Population growth per annum: 1.3%

Life expectancy at birth: 71 male, 78 female

Official Language: Spanish

Literacy: 93% male, 93% female

Religion: 80% Roman Catholic, 6% Protestant

Currency: one Chilean peso = 100 centavos

Main exports: Agricultural products, minerals & manufactured goods

CHINA

Zhonghua Renmin Gonghe Guo
The People's Republic of China

Area: 3,696,100 mi² / 9,572,900 km²

Highest point: Qomolangma Feng (Mt. Everest)

Population: 1,261,389,000 (1998)

Capital, population: Beijing (Peking), 6,560,000 (1996)

Other important cities, population: Shanghai, 8,760,000, Tianjin (Tientsin), 4,970,000, Shenyang, 3,860,000

Population growth per annum: 0.9%

Life expectancy at birth: 68 male, 72 female

Official Language: Mandarin Chinese

Literacy: 84% male, 72% female

Religion: 20% Confucian, 6% Buddhist, 2% Taoist, 2% Muslim

Currency: one Yuan = 10 jiao, one Jiao = 10 fen

Main exports: Crude oil, silk and satin, coal, cotton & cement

COLOMBIA
República de Colombia
Republic of Colombia

Area: 441,020 mi² / 1,141,748 km²

Highest point: Picó Cristóbal Colón

Population: 37,685,000 (1998)

Capital, population: Bogotá, 6,004,782 (1997)

Other important cities, population: Cali, 1,985,906, Medellín, 1,970,691, Barranquilla, 1,157,826

Population growth per annum: 1.7%

Life expectancy at birth: 67 male, 73 female

Official Language: Spanish

Literacy: 87% male, 86% female

Religion: 95% Roman Catholic

Currency: one Colombian peso = 100 centavos

Main exports: Coffee, petroleum & mineral products

COMOROS
République Fédérale Islamique des Comores
The Federal Islamic Republic of the Comoros

Area: 719 mi² / 1,862 km²

Highest point: Mt Kartala

Population: 672,000 (1998)

Capital, population: Moroni, 22,000 (1988)

Other important cities, population: Fomboni, 7,000, Mutsamudu, 14,000

Population growth per annum: 3.1%

Life expectancy at birth: 58 male, 59 female

Official Language: Arabic, French

Literacy: 64% male, 50% female

Religion: 86% Muslim, 14% Roman Catholic

Currency: one Comorian franc = 100 centimes

Main exports: Vanilla, cloves, ylang-ylang, essences, cocoa, copra & coffee

CONGO
République du Congo
The Republic of Congo

Area: 132,103 mi² / 342,000 km²

Highest point: Mt Lékéti

Population: 2,822,000 (1998)

Capital, population: Brazzaville, 937,579 (1992)

Other important cities, population: Pointe Noire, 576,206, Loubomo, 83,605, Nkayi, 42,465

Population growth per annum: 2.8%

Life expectancy at birth: 48 male, 52 female

Official Language: French

Literacy: 70% male, 44% female

Religion: 55% Roman Catholic, 22% Protestant

Currency: one CFA franc = 100 centimess

Main exports: Crude oil, lumber, plywood, sugar, cocoa, coffee & diamonds

CONGO (DEM. REP.)
République Democratique du Congo
The Democratic Republic of the Congo

Area: 905,365 mi² / 2,344,885 km²

Highest point: Mt Ngaliema

Population: 49,208,000 (1998)

Capital, population: Kinshasa, 4,655,313

Other important cities, population: Kananga, 393,030, Lubumbashi, 851,381, Mbuji-Mayi, 806,475

Population growth per annum: 2.6%

Life expectancy at birth: 50 male, 53 female

Official Language: French

Literacy: 84% male, 61% female

Religion: 48% Roman Catholic, 29% Protestant

Currency: one Zaire = 100 Makuta

Main exports: Diamonds, copper, coffee, cobalt & crude oil

COSTA RICA
República de Costa Rica
The Republic of Costa Rica

Area: 19,730 mi² / 51,100 km²

Highest point: Cerro Chirripó

Population: 3,650,000 (1998)

Capital, population: San José, 296,625 (1984)

Other important cities, population: Limón, 67,784, Alajuela, 44,358, Puntarenas, 37,390

Population growth per annum: 2.9%

Life expectancy at birth: 76 male, 79 female

Official Language: Spanish

Literacy: 93% male, 93% female

Religion: 92% Roman Catholic

Currency: one Costa Rican colón = 100 céntimos

Main exports: Manufactured and other goods, coffee, bananas, sugar & cocoa

CÔTE D'IVOIRE
République de la Côte d'Ivoire
Republic of the Ivory Coast

Area: 124,557 mi² / 322,463 km²

Highest point: Mt Nimba

Population: 14,567,000 (1998)

Capital, population: Yamoussoukro, 120,000 (1986)

Other important cities, population: Abidjan, 2,534,000, Bouaké, 390,000, Daloa, 102,000

Population growth per annum: 2.0%

Life expectancy at birth: 49 male, 51 female

Official Language: French

Literacy: 67% male, 40% female

Religion: 44% Traditional, 32% Christian, 24% Muslim

Currency: one CFA franc = 100 centimes

Main exports: Cocoa, petroleum products, cotton & tinned tuna

CROATIA
Republika Hrvatska
The Republic of Croatia

Area: 20,812 mi² / 56,538 km²

Highest point: Troglav

Population: 4,494,000 (1998)

Capital, population: Zagreb, 726,770 (1991)

Other important cities, population: Split, 189,388, Rijeka, 167,964, Osijek, 104,761

Population growth per annum: -0.1%

Life expectancy at birth: 68 male, 77 female

Official Language: Croatian

Literacy: 97% male, 97% female

Religion: 77% Roman Catholic, 8% Orthodox

Currency: one Kuna = 100 lipa

Main exports: Machinery, transport equipment, chemicals & foodstuffs

CUBA
República de Cuba
The Republic of Cuba

Area: 44,237 mi² / 114,524 km²

Highest point: Pico Turquino

Population: 11,115,000 (1998)

Capital, population: La Habana (Havana), 2,124,000 (1991)

Other important cities, population: Santiago de Cuba, 418,000, Camagüey, 289,000, Holguín, 206,000

Population growth per annum: 0.4%

Life expectancy at birth: 74 male, 78 female

Official Language: Spanish

Literacy: 95% male, 93% female

Religion: 60% Roman Catholic, 4% Protestant

Currency: one Cuban peso = 100 centavos

Main exports: Sugar, minerals, tobacco, citrus fruit & fish

CYPRUS

**Kypriaki Dimokratia-Kibris
Çumhuriyeti
Republic of Cyprus**

Area: 3,572 mi² / 9,251 km²

Highest point: Mt Olympus

Population: 775,000 (1998)

Capital, population: Lefkosia (Nicosia), 177,451 (1992)

Other important cities, population: Lemesos (Limassol), 136,741, Larnaka, 60,557, Pafos, 32,575

Population growth per annum: 1.3%

Life expectancy at birth: 76 male, 80 female

Official Language: Greek, Turkish

Literacy: 94% male, 94% female

Religion: 76% Greek Orthodox, 23% Muslim

Currency: one Cyprus pound = 100 cents

Main exports: Clothing, potatoes, medicinal products, fruit & cement

CZECH REPUBLIC

**Česká Republika
The Czech Republic**

Area: 30,449 mi² / 78,864 km²

Highest point: Snezka

Population: 10,223,000 (1998)

Capital, population: Praha (Prague), 1,217,000 (1993)

Other important cities, population: Brno, 390,000, Ostrava 327,000, Plzeň, 172,000

Population growth per annum: -0.1%

Life expectancy at birth: 68 male, 75 female

Official Language: Czech

Literacy: 99% male, 99% female

Religion: Roman Catholic

Currency: one Koruna = 100 halura

Main exports: Manufactured goods

DENMARK

**Kongeriget Danmark
The Kingdom of Denmark**

Area: 16,631 mi² / 43,075 km²

Highest point: Yding Skovhøj

Population: 5,258,000 (1998)

Capital, population: København (Copenhagen), 1,372,768 (1997)

Other important cities, population: Århus, 215,045, Odense, 145,354, Ålborg, 191,118

Population growth per annum: 0.2%

Life expectancy at birth: 73 male, 79 female

Official Language: Danish

Literacy: 99% male, 99% female

Religion: 99% Lutheran

Currency: one Danish krone = 100 øre

Main exports: Machinery, electrical goods, equipment, live animals, meat and meat products & metals

DJIBOUTI

**Jumhouriyya Djibouti
Republic of Djibouti**

Area: 8,961 mi² / 23,200 km²

Highest point: Musa Ali Terra

Population: 651,000 (1998)

Capital, population: Djibouti, 383,000 (1995)

Other important cities, population: N/A

Population growth per annum: 2.7%

Life expectancy at birth: 49 male, 52 female

Official Language: French, Arabic

Literacy: 60% male, 33% female

Religion: 96% Muslim, Roman Catholic

Currency: one Djibouti franc = 100 centimes

Main exports: Hides, cattle & coffee

DOMINICA

**he Commonwealth of
ominica**

rea: 290 mi² / 751 km²

ighest point: Morne Diablotin

pulation: 75,000 (1998)

apital, population: Roseau, 15,853 (1991)

ther important cities, population: N/A

pulation growth per annum: 0.1%

ife expectancy at birth: 72 male, 76 female

fficial Language: English

iteracy: 94% male 94% female

eligion: 77% Roman Catholic, Protestant

urrency: one East Caribbean dollar = 100 cents

ain exports: Bananas, soap, fruit juices, essential oils,
conuts, vegetables & fruit

DOMINICAN REPUBLIC

**República Dominicana
The Dominican Republic**

Area: 18,700 mi² / 48,442 km²

Highest point: Duarte

Population: 8,232,000 (1998)

Capital, population: Santo Domingo, 2,055,000 (1991)

Other important cities, population: Santiago, 375,000, La
Romana, 136,000, San Pedro de Macoris, 162,000

Population growth per annum: 1.6%

Life expectancy at birth: 69 male, 73 female

Official Language: Spanish

Literacy: 85% male, 82% female

Religion: 93% Roman Catholic

Currency: one Peso Oro = 100 centavos

Main exports: Sugar, molasses, coffee, cocoa, tobacco, ferro-
nickel, gold & silver

CUADOR

**epública del Ecuador
Republic of Ecuador**

rea: 104,551 mi² / 270,670 km²

ighest point: Cerro Chimborazo

opulation: 12,175,000 (1998)

apital, population: Quito, 1,100,847 (1990)

ther important cities, population: Guayaquil, 1,508,444,
uenca, 194,981, Machala, 144,197

opulation growth per annum: 1.8%

ife expectancy at birth: 67 male, 73 female

fficial Language: Spanish

iteracy: 88% male, 84% female

Religion: 90% Roman Catholic, 6% Protestant

Currency: one Sucre = 100 centavos

Main exports: Shrimps, bananas, coffee beans, cocoa beans
nd products & cut flowers

EGYPT

**Jumhuriyat Misr al-Arabiya
The Arab Republic of Egypt**

Area: 386,900 mi² / 1,002,000 km²

Highest point: Mt Catherine (Jabal Katrina)

Population: 65,675,000 (1998)

Capital, population: Al Qāhirah (Cairo), 6,452,000 (1990)

Other important cities, population: Al Iskandarīyah
(Alexandria), 3,170,000, Al Jīzah (Giza), 2,156,000, Shubra Al
Khayma, 811,000

Population growth per annum: 1.9%

Life expectancy at birth: 65 male, 67 female

Official Language: Arabic

Literacy: 63% male, 34% female

Religion: 94% Muslim

Currency: one Egyptian pound = 100 piastres

Main exports: Crude oil, cotton goods, refined petroleum,
aluminium, oranges & potatoes

EL SALVADOR
República de El Salvador
The Republic of El Salvador

Area: 8,124 mi² / 21,041 km²

Highest point: Volcán de Santa Ana

Population: 6,059,000 (1998)

Capital, population: San Salvador, 1,522,126 (1992)

Other important cities, population: Santa Ana, 202,337, San Miguel, 182,817, Nueva San Salvador, 116,575

Population growth per annum: 2.2%

Life expectancy at birth: 66 male, 71 female

Official Language: Spanish

Literacy: 76% male, 70% female

Religion: 90% Roman Catholic

Currency: one Colón = 100 centavos

Main exports: Coffee

EQUATORIAL GUINEA
República de Guinea Ecuatorial
The Republic of Equatorial Guinea

Area: 10,831 mi² / 28,051 km²

Highest point: Pico de Moca

Population: 430,000 (1998)

Capital, population: Malabo, 10,000 (1986)

Other important cities, population: Bata, 17,000 (1986)

Population growth per annum: 2.5%

Life expectancy at birth: 48 male, 52 female

Official Language: Spanish

Literacy: 89% male, 67% female

Religion: 89% Roman Catholic

Currency: one CFA franc = 100 centimes

Main exports: Timber, textile fibres, cocoa & coffee

ERITREA
Hagere Ertra
The State of Eritrea

Area: 36,171 mi² / 93,679 km²

Highest point: Ramlo

Population: 3,548,000 (1998)

Capital, population: Asmara, 367,300 (1991)

Other important cities, population: N/A

Population growth per annum: 3.7%

Life expectancy at birth: 51 male, 55 female

Official Language: Tigrinya, English, Arabic

Literacy: 23% male, 7% female

Religion: 50% Muslim, 50% Christian

Currency: Nakfa

Main exports: Drinks, leather and leather products, textiles & oil products

ESTONIA
Eesti Vabariik
The Republic of Estonia

Area: 17,413 mi² / 45,100 km²

Highest point: Suur Munamägi

Population: 1,442,000 (1998)

Capital, population: Tallinn, 420,470 (1997)

Other important cities, population: Tartu, 101,901, Kohtla-Järve, 53,485, Narva, 75,211

Population growth per annum: -1.0%

Life expectancy at birth: 64 male, 75 female

Official Language: Estonian

Literacy: 99% male, 99% female

Religion: Christian (Lutheran & Orthodox)

Currency: one Kroon = 100 sents

Main exports: Foodstuffs, animal products, timber products, base metals, mineral products & machinery

ETHIOPIA

Ityopia
Federal Democratic
Republic of Ethiopia

Area: 471,800 mi² / 1,221,900 km²

Highest point: Ras Dashen

Population: 62,111,000 (1998)

Capital, population: Addis Ababa, 1,700,000 (1990)

Other important cities, population: Diredawa, 98,104, Nazret, 76,284, Bahr Dar, 54,800

Population growth per annum: 3.2%

Life expectancy at birth: 48 male, 52 female

Official Language: Amharic

Literacy: 45% male, 25% female

Religion: 53% Ethiopian Orthodox, 30% Muslim

Currency: one Ethiopian birr = 100 cents

Main exports: Coffee

FIJI

Republic of Fiji

Area: 7,098 mi² / 18,376 km²

Highest point: Tomaniivi

Population: 822,000 (1998)

Capital, population: Suva, 71,608 (1986)

Other important cities, population: Lautoka, 28,728 (1986)

Population growth per annum: 1.6%

Life expectancy at birth: 71 male, 75 female

Official Language: English

Literacy: 94% male, 89% female

Religion: 52% Christian, 40% Hindu, 8% Muslim

Currency: one Fiji dollar = 100 cents

Main exports: Sugar, fish, timber, ginger & molasses

FINLAND

Suomen Tasavalta:
Republiken Finland
The Republic of Finland

Area: 130,614 mi² / 338,145 km²

Highest point: Haltiatuntura

Population: 5,156,000 (1998)

Capital, population: Helsinki (Helsingfors), 525,031 (1995)

Other important cities, population: Espoo (Esbo), 191,247, Tampere (Tammerfors), 182,742, Turku (Åbo), 164,370

Population growth per annum: 0.3%

Life expectancy at birth: 73 male, 80 female

Official Language: Finnish, Swedish

Literacy: 100% male, 100% female

Religion: 89% Lutheran, 1% Greek Orthodox

Currency: Euro / one Markka = 100 pennis

Main exports: Metal, engineering, electronics & forestry

FRANCE

Republique Française
The French Republic

Area: 210,033 mi² / 543,965 km²

Highest point: Mt Blanc

Population: 58,733,000 (1998)

Capital, population: Paris, 9,318,821 (1990)

Other important cities, population: Lyon, 1,262,223, Marseille, 1,230,936, Lille, 959,234

Population growth per annum: 0.3%

Life expectancy at birth: 74 male, 81 female

Official Language: French

Literacy: 100% male, 100% female

Religion: 76% Roman Catholic

Currency: Euro / one French franc = 100 centimes

Main exports: Metals, chemicals, machinery and equipment, iron and steel & foodstuffs

GABON

République Gabonaise
The Gabonese Republic

Area: 103,391 mi² / 267,667 km²

Highest point: Mt Iboundji

Population: 1,171,000 (1998)

Capital, population: Libreville, 419,596 (1993)

Other important cities, population: Port-Gentil, 123,300, Masuku, 38,030, Lambaréné, 26,257

Population growth per annum: 2.8%

Life expectancy at birth: 54 male, 57 female

Official Language: French

Literacy: 73% male, 84% female

Religion: 65% Roman Catholic

Currency: one CFA franc = 100 centimes

Main exports: Crude oil, natural gas, timber and wood products, manganese & uranium

THE GAMBIA

The Republic of The Gambia

Area: 4,363 mi² / 11,294 km²

Highest point: Unnamed

Population: 1,194,000 (1998)

Capital, population: Banjul, 44,188 (1983)

Other important cities, population: Serekunda, 68,433, Brikama, 19,584, Bakau, 19,309

Population growth per annum: 2.3%

Life expectancy at birth: 45 male, 47 female

Official Language: English

Literacy: 53% male, 25% female

Religion: 90% Muslim, Christian

Currency: one Dalasi = 100 butut

Main exports: Groundnuts, groundnut oil and cake, cotton lint, fish, hides & skins

GEORGIA

Sakartvelos Respublika
The Republic of Georgia

Area: 26,900 mi² / 69,700 km²

Highest point: Gora Kazbek

Population: 5,428,000 (1998)

Capital, population: T'bilisi, 1,300,000 (1994)

Other important cities, population: K'ut'aisi, 235,000, Rust'avi, 159,000, Bat'umi, 136,000

Population growth per annum: -0.1%

Life expectancy at birth: 70 male, 78 female

Official Language: Georgian

Literacy: 99% male, 99% female

Religion: 83% Orthodox, 11% Muslim

Currency: one Lari = 100 tetri

Main exports: Iron and steel products, food and drink, machinery, textiles & chemicals

GERMANY

Bundesrepublik Deutschland
The Federal Republic
of Germany

Area: 137,781 mi² / 356,854 km²

Highest point: Zugspitze

Population: 82,401,000 (1998)

Capital, population: Berlin, 3,470,200 (1995)

Other important cities, population: Hamburg, 1,706,800, München, 1,240,600, Köln, 955,500

Population growth per annum: 0.3%

Life expectancy at birth: 74 male, 80 female

Official Language: German

Literacy: 100% male, 100% female

Religion: 45% Protestant, 37% Roman Catholic, 2% Muslim

Currency: Euro / one Deutsche mark = 100 pfennig

Main exports: Live animals, foodstuffs, drinks, tobacco, raw materials, semi-finished & finished goods

GHANA

The Republic of Ghana

Area: 92,456 mi² / 239,460 km²

Highest point: Afadjato

Population: 18,857,000 (1998)

Capital, population: Accra, 949,113 (1988)

Other important cities, population: Kumasi, 385,192, Tamale, 151,069, Téma, 109,975

Population growth per annum: 2.3%

Life expectancy at birth: 57 male, 60 female

Official Language: English

Literacy: 71% male, 51% female

Religion: 38% Traditional, 30% Muslim, 24% Christian

Currency: one Cedi = 100 pesewas

Main exports: Gold, cocoa and cocoa products, timber, tuna, bauxite and aluminium, manganese ore & diamonds

GREECE
Elliniki Dimokratia
The Hellenic Republic

Area: 50,949 mi² / 131,957 km²

Highest point: Olympos (Olympus)

Population: 10,551,000 (1998)

Capital, population: Athina (Athens), 3,096,775 (1991)

Other important cities, population: Thessaloniki, 377,951, Peiraias, 169,622, Patra, 155,180

Population growth per annum: 0.3%

Life expectancy at birth: 76 male, 81 female

Official Language: Greek

Literacy: 98% male, 89% female

Religion: 98% Greek Orthodox, Muslim

Currency: one Drachma = 100 lepta

Main exports: Manufactured articles, clothing and accessories, food and live animals, vegetables and fruit & refined petroleum products

GRENADA

Grenada

Area: 133 mi² / 344 km²

Highest point: Mt St Catherine

Population: 92,000 (1996)

Capital, population: St George's, 35,742 (1989)

Other important cities, population: N/A

Population growth per annum: -1.3%

Life expectancy at birth: 69 male, 74 female

Official Language: English

Literacy: 85%

Religion: 53% Roman Catholic, 30% Protestant

Currency: one East Caribbean dollar = 100 cents

Main exports: Nutmeg, cocoa, bananas, mace & textiles

GUATEMALA
República de Guatemala
The Republic of Guatemala

Area: 42,042 mi² / 108,889 km²

Highest point: Volcán Tajumulco

Population: 11,561,000 (1998)

Capital, population: Guatemala, 1,133,000 (1993)

Other important cities, population: Puerto Barrios, 338,000, Quezaltenango, 98,000, Escuintla, 66,000

Population growth per annum: 2.8%

Life expectancy at birth: 65 male, 70 female

Official Language: Spanish

Literacy: 63% male, 47% female

Religion: 75% Roman Catholic, 23% Protestant

Currency: one Quetzal = 100 centavos

Main exports: Coffee, sugar, bananas & cardamom

GUINEA
République de Guinée
The Republic of Guinea

Area: 94,926 mi² / 245,857 km²

Highest point: Mt Nimba

Population: 7,273,000 (1998)

Capital, population: Conakry, 950,000 (1991)

Other important cities, population: Kankan, 70,000, Labé, 110,000, Kindia, 80,000

Population growth per annum: 1.4%

Life expectancy at birth: 46 male, 47 female

Official Language: French

Literacy: 35% male, 13% female

Religion: 80% Muslim, Traditional

Currency: one Guinean franc = 100 centimes

Main exports: Bauxite, alumina, gold & coffee

GUINEA-BISSAU
Republica da Guiné-Bissau
The Republic of Guinea-Bissau

Area: 13,954 mi² / 36,125 km²

Highest point: Fanta Djallon

Population: 1,135,000 (1998)

Capital, population: Bissau, 1,178,584 (1997)

Other important cities, population: N/A

Population growth per annum: 2.0%

Life expectancy at birth: 44 male, 47 female

Official Language: Portuguese

Literacy: 50% male, 24% female

Religion: 65% Traditional, 30% Muslim, 5% Christian

Currency: one CFA franc = 100 centimes

Main exports: Cashew nuts, frozen fish and shrimps & timb

GUYANA
Co-operative Republic of Guyana

Area: 83,000 mi² / 214,969 km²

Highest point: Mt Roraima

Population: 857,000 (1998)

Capital, population: Georgetown, 188,000 (1983)

Other important cities, population: New Amsterdam, Linden, Rose Hall

Population growth per annum: 0.1%

Life expectancy at birth: 65 male, 70 female

Official Language: English

Literacy: 98% male, 97% female

Religion: 57% Christian, 33% Hindu, 9% Muslim

Currency: one Guyana dollar = 100 cents

Main exports: Sugar, gold, bauxite, rice, timber, rum & shrimps

HAITI
Républicque d'Haïti
The Republic of Haiti

Area: 10,700 mi² / 27,750 km²

Highest point: Pic La Selle

Population: 7,533,000 (1998)

Capital, population: Port-au-Prince, 1,402,000 (1991)

Other important cities, population: Les Cayes, 250,700, Jacmel, 237,700, Jérémie, 180,200

Population growth per annum: 1.9%

Life expectancy at birth: 57 male, 60 female

Official Language: French, Creole

Literacy: 69% male, 47% female

Religion: 90% Roman Catholic, Voodoo

Currency: one Gourde = 100 centimes

Main exports: Manufactured articles, coffee, essential oils & sisal

ONDURAS

pública de Honduras
e Republic of Honduras

a: 43,277 mi² / 112,088 km²

hest point: Cerro Las Minas

ulation: 6,145,000 (1998)

pital, population: Tegucigalpa, 775,300 (1994)

er important cities, population: San Pedro Sula, 460,600, luteca, 68,500, El Progreso, 64,700

ulation growth per annum: 2.8%

e expectancy at birth: 68 male, 72 female

icial Language: Spanish

eracy: 75% male, 71% female

igion: 97% Roman Catholic

rrency: one Lempira = 100 centavos

in exports: Bananas, coffee, shrimps and lobsters, fruit, d, zinc & meat

HUNGARY

Magyar Köztársaság
The Republic of Hungary

Area: 35,911 mi² / 93,032 km²

Highest point: Kékes

Population: 9,930,000 (1998)

Capital, population: Budapest, 1,930,000

Other important cities, population: Debrecen, 211,000, Miskolc, 182,000, Szeged, 169,000 (1995)

Population growth per annum: -0.6%

Life expectancy at birth: 67 male, 74 female

Official Language: Hungarian

Literacy: 99% male, 99% female

Religion: 68% Roman Catholic, 25% Protestant

Currency: one Forint = 100 fillér

Main exports: Raw materials, semi-finished products, consumer goods, foodstuffs & agricultural equipment

ELAND

öveldið Ísland
epublic of Iceland

ea: 39,758 mi² / 103,000 km²

ghest point: Hvannadalshnúkur

pulation: 276,000 (1998)

pital, population: Reykjavík, 105,458 (1996)

her important cities, population: Kópavogur, 18,550, narfjörður, 17,935, Akureyri, 115,015

pulation growth per annum: 1.0%

e expectancy at birth: 76 male, 81 female

icial Language: Icelandic

teracy: 99% male, 99% female

ligion: 91% Lutheran, Roman Catholic

rrency: one Króna = 100 aurar

in exports: Fish, shellfish, non-ferrous metals, animal ds & iron and steel

INDIA

Bharat
Republic of India

Area: 1,222,332 mi² / 3,165,596 km²

Highest point: Kangchenjunga

Population: 975,771,000 (1998)

Capital, population: New Delhi, 301,000 (1991)

Other important cities, population: Mumbai (Bombay), 12,596,000, Kolkata (Calcutta), 11,022,000. Delhi, 7,207,000

Population growth per annum: 2%

Life expectancy at birth: 63 male, 63 female

Official Language: 14 Various

Literacy: 62% male, 34% female

Religion: 82% Hindu, 12% Muslim, 2% Christian, 2% Sikh

Currency: one Rupee = 100 paisa

Main exports: Petroleum and petroleum products, machinery, gems and jewellery, clothing & engineering goods

INDONESIA
Republik Indonesia
The Republic of Indonesia

Area: 741,098 mi² / 1,919,443 km²

Highest point: Puncak Jaya

Population: 206,522,000 (1998)

Capital, population: Jakarta, 8,259,266 (1990)

Other important cities, population: Surabaya, 2,421,016, Bandung, 2,026,893, Medan, 1,685,972

Population growth per annum: 1.5%

Life expectancy at birth: 63 male, 67 female

Official Language: Bahasa Indonesia

Literacy: 84% male, 68% female

Religion: 87% Muslim, 10% Christian, 2% Hindu

Currency: one Rupiah = 100 sen

Main exports: Gas and oil, forestry products, manufactured goods, rubber, coffee, fishery products, coal, copper, tin, pepper, palm products & tea

IRAN
Jomhoori-e-Islami-e-Iran
The Islamic Republic of Iran

Area: 634,293 mi² / 1,648,000 km²

Highest point: Qolleh-ye Damavand

Population: 73,057,000 (1998)

Capital, population: Tehrān, 6,758,845 (1996)

Other important cities, population: Mashhad, 1,887,405, Esfahān, 1,266,072, Tabrīz, 1,191,043

Population growth per annum: 2.2%

Life expectancy at birth: 69 male, 70 female

Official Language: Farsi

Literacy: 89% male, 43% female

Religion: 99.8% Muslim (93.8% Shiite)

Currency: ten Rial = 1 toman

Main exports: Petroleum, crude oil & gas

IRAQ
Jumhouriya al'Iraqia
The Republic of Iraq

Area: 169,247 mi² / 438,317 km²

Highest point: Rawanduz

Population: 21,787,000 (1998)

Capital, population: Baghdād, 3,850,000 (1987)

Other important cities, population: Al Basrah, 616,700, Al Mawşil (Mosul), 570,926, Kirkūk, 570,000

Population growth per annum: 2.8%

Life expectancy at birth: 67 male, 70 female

Official Language: Arabic

Literacy: 77% male, 49% female

Religion: 96% Muslim (54% Shiite)

Currency: one Iraqi dinar = 1000 fils

Main exports: Crude oil

IRELAND
Poblacht na h'Eireann
Republic of Ireland

Area: 27,148 mi² / 70,283 km²

Highest point: Carrauntuohil

Population: 3,564,000 (1998)

Capital, population: Dublin (Baile Átha Cliath), 952,692 (1996)

Other important cities, population: Cork (Corcaigh), 179,9 Limerick (Luimneach), 75,729, Galway (Gaillimh), 57,363

Population growth per annum: 0.2%

Life expectancy at birth: 73 male, 79 female

Official Language: Irish, English

Literacy: 99% male, 99% female

Religion: 93% Roman Catholic, 3% Protestant

Currency: one Punt = 100 pence

Main exports: Machinery and transport equipment, chemica manufactured articles, live animals & food

164

ISRAEL

Medinat Israel
The State of Israel

Area: 8,473 mi² / 21,946 km²

Highest point: Har Meron (Mt Atzmon)

Population: 5,883,000 (1998)

Capital, population: Yerushalayim (Jerusalem), 591,400 (1995)

Other important cities, population: Tel Aviv-Yafo, 355,900, Hefa (Haifa), 252,300, Holon,163,900

Population growth per annum: 1.9%

Life expectancy at birth: 75 male, 79 female

Official Language: Hebrew, Arabic

Literacy: 97% male, 93% female

Religion: 82% Jewish, 14% Muslim, 2% Christian

Currency: one Shekel = 100 agorot

Main exports: Citrus fruits, diamonds, machinery, military hardware, foodstuffs, chemicals, textiles & clothing

ITALY

Repubblica Italiana
The Italian Republic

Area: 116,332 mi² / 301,302 km²

Highest point: Mt Bianco (Mt Blanc)

Population: 57,243,000 (1998)

Capital, population: Roma (Rome), 2,654,187 (1995)

Other important cities, population: Milano, 1,306,494, Napoli (Naples), 1,067,365, Torino, 923,106

Population growth per annum: 0.0%

Life expectancy at birth: 75 male, 81 female

Official Language: Italian

Literacy: 98% male, 98% female

Religion: 83% Roman Catholic

Currency: Euro / one Lira = 100 centesimi

Main exports: Metal products and machinery, textiles and leather goods, wood, paper, rubber goods, transport equipment & chemicals

JAMAICA

Jamaica

Area: 4,411 mi² / 11,425 km²

Highest point: Blue Mountain Peak

Population: 2,539,000 (1998)

Capital, population: Kingston, 683,700 (1995)

Other important cities, population: Spanish Town, 110,400, Portmore, 93,800, Montego Bay, 82,000

Population growth per annum: 0.9%

Life expectancy at birth: 72 male, 77 female

Official Language: English

Literacy: 98% male, 99% female

Religion: 70% Protestant, 8% Roman Catholic

Currency: one Jamaican dollar = 100 cents

Main exports: Alumina and bauxite, sugar, bananas, beverages & tobacco

JAPAN

Nippon
Japan

Area: 145,852 mi² / 377,727 km²

Highest point: Fuji-san

Population: 125,921,000 (1998)

Capital, population: Tōkyō, 7,968,000 (1995)

Other important cities, population: Yokohama, 3,307,000, Osaka, 2,602,000, Nagoya, 2,152,000

Population growth per annum: 0.2%

Life expectancy at birth: 77 male, 83 female

Official Language: Japanese

Literacy: 99% male, 99% female

Religion: 93% Shinto, 74% Buddhist

Currency: one Yen = 100 sen

Main exports: Machinery and transport equipment, metals and metal products, textile products & chemicals

JORDAN

Mamlaka Al Urduniya al Hashemiyah
Hashemite Kingdom of Jordan

Area: 37,738 mi² / 97,740 km²

Highest point: Jabal Ramm

Population: 6,956,000 (1998)

Capital, population: Ammān, 1,300,042 (1994)

Other important cities, population: Irbid, 379,844, Az Zarqā, 608,626

Population growth per annum: 3.2%

Life expectancy at birth: 64 male, 68 female

Official Language: Arabic

Literacy: 75% male, 70% female

Religion: 96% Sunni Muslim, 4% Christian

Currency: one Jordan dinar = 100 fils

Main exports: Phosphate, potash, fertilizers, foodstuffs, pharmaceuticals, fruit and vegetables, textiles, plastics & soaps

KAZAKHSTAN

Kazak Respublikasy
The Republic of Kazakhstan

Area: 1,049,155 mi² / 2,717,300 km²

Highest point: Khan Tängiri Shyngy

Population: 16,854,000 (1998)

Capital, population: Astana, 808,600 (1996)

Other important cities, population: Almaty (Alma-Ata), 2,141,100, Qaraghandy, 1,234,100

Population growth per annum: 0.1%

Life expectancy at birth: 67 male, 75 female

Official Language: Kazakh, Russian

Literacy: 97% male, 97% female

Religion: Muslim, Christian

Currency: one Tenge = 100 tiyn

Main exports: Metals, mineral products & chemicals

KENYA

Jamhuri ya Kenya
The Republic of Kenya

Area: 225,057 mi² / 582,646 km²

Highest point: Kirinyaga (Mt Kenya)

Population: 29,020,000 (1998)

Capital, population: Nairobi, 1,758,900 (1989)

Other important cities, population: Mombasa, 461,753, Kisumu, 192,733, Nakuru, 163,927

Population growth per annum: 2.2%

Life expectancy at birth: 57 male, 61 female

Official Language: Swahili

Literacy: 86% male, 70% female

Religion: 72% Christian, 18% Traditional, 6% Muslim

Currency: one Kenya shilling = 100 cents

Main exports: Tea, coffee & horticultural products

KIRIBATI

Ribaberikin Kiribati
The Republic of Kiribati

Area: 277 mi² / 717 km²

Highest point: Unnamed

Population: 77,000 (1995)

Capital, population: Tarawa, n/a

Other important cities, population: N/A

Population growth per annum: 1.9%

Life expectancy at birth: 51 male, 56 female

Official Language: English

Literacy: 90% male, 90% female

Religion: 53% Roman Catholic, 3% Protestant

Currency: one Australian dollar = 100 cents

Main exports: Copra, seaweed & fish

KUWAIT

Dowlat al Kuwait
The State of Kuwait

Area: 6,880 mi² / 17,818 km²

Highest point: Ash Shaqaya

Population: 1,809,000 (1998)

Capital, population: Al Kuwayt (Kuwait), 31,241 (1993)

Other important cities, population: Al Jahra, 139,476, as-Salimiya, 116,104, Hawalli, 84,478

Population growth per annum: 3.0%

Life expectancy at birth: 74 male, 78 female

Official Language: Arabic

Literacy: 61% male, 67% female

Religion: 92% Muslim, 6% Christian

Currency: one Kuwaiti dinar = 1000 fils

Main exports: Crude and refined oil & chemical fertilizer

KYRGYZSTAN

Kyrgyz Respublikasy
The Kyrgyz Republic

Area: 76,600 mi² / 198,500 km²

Highest point: Tengish Chokusu

Population: 4,497,000 (1998)

Capital, population: Bishkek, 641,400 (1991)

Other important cities, population: Osh, 238,200, Jalal-Abad, 74,200, Tokmok, 71,200

Population growth per annum: 0.4%

Life expectancy at birth: 67 male, 74 female

Official Language: Kirghiz

Literacy: 97% male, 97% female

Religion: 70% Sunni Muslim, Christian

Currency: one Som = 100 tyiyn

Main exports: Food and beverages, light industrial goods & non-ferrous metals

LAOS

Saathiaranarath Prachhathipatay
Prachhachhon Lao
Lao People's Democratic Republic

Area: 91,400 mi² / 236,800 km²

Highest point: Phou Bia

Population: 5,359,000 (1998)

Capital, population: Vientiane (Viangchan), 377,409 (1985)

Other important cities, population: Savannakhet, 50,690, Pakxé, 44,860, Luang Prabang, 44,244

Population growth per annum: 3.1%

Life expectancy at birth: 52 male, 55 female

Official Language: Lao

Literacy: 92% male, 67% female

Religion: 58% Buddhist, 34% Traditional, 2% Christian, 1% Muslim

Currency: one Kip = 100 at

Main exports: Electricity, timber, plywood, coffee & gypsum

LATVIA

Latvijas Republika
The Republic of Latvia

Area: 24,595 mi² / 63,700 km²

Highest point: Gaizinkalns

Population: 2,448,000 (1998)

Capital, population: Rīga, 820,577 (1996)

Other important cities, population: Daugavpils, 117,835, Liepāja, 97,917, Jelgava, 70,943

Population growth per annum: -1.1%

Life expectancy at birth: 64 male, 75 female

Official Language: Latvian

Literacy: 99% male, 99% female

Religion: Christian

Currency: one Lat = 100 santims

Main exports: Wood and wood products, textiles & foodstuffs

LEBANON

Jumhouriya-al-Lubnaniya
The Lebanese Republic

Area: 4,036 mi² / 10,452 km²

Highest point: Qurnat as-Sawda

Population: 3,194,000 (1998)

Capital, population: Bayrūt (Beirut), 1,500,000 (1991)

Other important cities, population: Tarābulus, 200,000, Zahlah, 700,000, Saydā, 100,000

Population growth per annum: 1.8%

Life expectancy at birth: 68 male, 72 female

Official Language: Arabic

Literacy: 88% male, 73% female

Religion: 53% Muslim, 38% Christian

Currency: one Lebanese pound = 100 piastres

Main exports: Paper, textiles, fruit, vegetables & jewellery

LESOTHO

The Kingdom of Lesotho

Area: 11,725 mi² / 30,355 km²

Highest point: Thabana Ntlenyana

Population: 2,184,000 (1998)

Capital, population: Maseru, 109,382 (1986)

Other important cities, population: Teyateyaneng, 14,251, Mafeteng, 12,667, Hlotse, 9,595

Population growth per annum: 2.5%

Life expectancy at birth: 61 male, 66 female

Official Language: Sesotho, English

Literacy: 62% male, 84% female

Religion: 44% Roman Catholic, (93% Christian)

Currency: one Loti = 100 lisente

Main exports: Cattle, wheat flour, tinned vegetables, wool, machinery and transport equipment, manufactured goods & mohair

LIBERIA

The Republic of Liberia

Area: 43,109 mi² / 111,370 km²

Highest point: Mt Nimba

Population: 2,748,000 (1998)

Capital, population: Monrovia, 425,000 (1984)

Other important cities, population: Buchanan, 24,000

Population growth per annum: 8.56%

Life expectancy at birth: 56 male, 69 female

Official Language: English

Literacy: 50% male, 29% female

Religion: 68% Christian, 18% Traditional, 14% Muslim

Currency: one Liberian dollar = 100 cents (US$ legal tender)

Main exports: Iron ore, rubber & sawn timber

LIBYA

Jamahiriya Al-Arabiya Al-Libiya
Al-Shabiya Al-Ishtirakiya Al-Uzma
The Great Socialist People's
Libyan Arab Jamahiriya

Area: 679,358 mi² / 1,759,540 km²

Highest point: Bette

Population: 5,980,000 (1998)

Capital, population: Tarābulus (Tripoli), 858,000 (1981)

Other important cities, population: Benghazi, 368,000, Miṣrātah, 117,000

Population growth per annum: 3.3%

Life expectancy at birth: 64 male, 68 female

Official Language: Arabic

Literacy: 75% male, 50% female

Religion: 97% Sunni Muslim

Currency: one Libyan dinar = 1000 millemes

Main exports: Crude oil & chemicals

LIECHTENSTEIN
Fürstentum Liechtenstein
The Principality of Liechtenstein

Area: 61.8 mi² / 160 km²

Highest point: Granspitze

Population: 31,000 (1996)

Capital, population: Vaduz, 4,870 (1990)

Other important cities, population: N/A

Population growth per annum: 1.4%

Life expectancy at birth: 78 male, 83 female

Official Language: German

Literacy: 99% male, 99% female

Religion: 86% Roman Catholic, 8% Protestant

Currency: one Swiss franc = 100 centimes

Main exports: Small machinery, dental materials, stamps, precision instruments & ceramics

LITHUANIA
Lietuvos Respublika
The Republic of Lithuania

Area: 25,170 mi² / 65,200 km²

Highest point: Juozapine

Population: 3,710,000 (1998)

Capital, population: Vilnius, 580,100 (1997)

Other important cities, population: Kaunas, 418,700, Klaipėda, 203,300, Šiauliai, 147,000

Population growth per annum: -0.3%

Life expectancy at birth: 65 male, 76 female

Official Language: Lithuanian

Literacy: 98% male, 98% female

Religion: 90% Roman Catholic

Currency: one Litas = 100 centas

Main exports: Meat, dairy products, spirits, e;ectricity, wood & wooden articles, iron & steel, TV sets

LUXEMBOURG
Grand-Duché de Luxembourg
The Grand Duchy of Luxembourg

Area: 999 mi² / 2,586 km²

Highest point: Huldange

Population: 421,000 (1998)

Capital, population: Luxembourg, 78,300 (1997)

Other important cities, population: Esch-sur-Alzette, 24,600, Differdange, 16,500, Dudelange, 16,200

Population growth per annum: 0.4%

Life expectancy at birth: 73 male, 80 female

Official Language: Letzebuergesch, French, German

Literacy: 99% male, 99% female

Religion: 95% Roman Catholic

Currency: Euro / one Luxembourg franc = 100 centimes

Main exports: Base metals, manufactured goods, mechanical and electrical equipment, rubber and plastics, textiles & clothing

MACEDONIA
Republika Makedonija
The Former Yugoslav
Republic of Macedonia

Area: 9,928 mi² / 25,713 km²

Highest point: Korab

Population: 2,205,000 (1998)

Capital, population: Skopje, 444,299 (1997)

Other important cities, population: Bitola, 77,464, Prilep, 68,148, Kumanovo, 71,853

Population growth per annum: 0.7%

Life expectancy at birth: 70 male, 76 female

Official Language: Macedonian

Literacy: 94%

Religion: 66% Eastern Orthodox, 30% Muslim

Currency: one Denar = 100 deni

Main exports: Manufactured goods, machinery, transport equipment, manufactured articles, sugar beet, vegetables, cheese, lamb & tobacco

MADAGASCAR
Repoblikan'i Madagasikara
The Democratic Republic of Madagascar

Area: 226,658 mi² / 587,041 km²

Highest point: Maromokotro Tsaratanana Massif

Population: 16,384,000 (1998)

Capital, population: Antananarivo, 1,052,835 (1993)

Other important cities, population: Toamasina, 127,441, Fianarantsoa, 99,005, Mahajanga, 100,807

Population growth per annum: 3.1%

Life expectancy at birth: 58 male, 61 female

Official Language: Malagasy

Literacy: 88% male, 73% female

Religion: 50% Traditional, 43% Christian

Currency: one Malagasy franc = 100 centimes

Main exports: Coffee, shrimps, cloves, vanilla, petroleum products, chromium & cotton fabrics

MALAWI
Dziko la Malaŵi
The Republic of Malawi

Area: 45,747 mi² / 118,484 km²

Highest point: Mt Sapitawa

Population: 10,377,000 (1998)

Capital, population: Lilongwe, 233,973 (1987)

Other important cities, population: Blantyre, 331,588, Muzuzu, 44,238, Zomba, 42,878

Population growth per annum: 2.5%

Life expectancy at birth: 44 male, 45 female

Official Language: Chichewa, English

Literacy: 52% male, 31% female

Religion: 64% Christian, 12% Muslim, Animist

Currency: one Kwacha = 100 tambala

Main exports: Tobacco, tea, sugar, cotton & groundnuts

MALAYSIA
Persekutuan Tanah Malaysia
Federation of Malaysia

Area: 127,317 mi² / 329,758 km²

Highest point: Gunong Kinabalu

Population: 21,449,000 (1998)

Capital, population: Kuala Lumpur, 1,231,500 (Fed. Terr.) (1997)

Other important cities, population: Ipoh, 382,853, George Town, 219,603, Johor Baharu, 328,436

Population growth per annum: 2.0%

Life expectancy at birth: 70 male, 74 female

Official Language: Bahasa Malaysia

Literacy: 86% male, 70% female

Religion: 53% Muslim, 17% Buddhist, 12% Chinese Folk, 7% Hindu,

Currency: one Ringgit = 100 sen

Main exports: Palm oil, rubber, crude oil, machinery and transport equipment, timber, tin, textiles & electronic goods

MALDIVES
Divehi Raajjeyge Jumhooriyyaa
Republic of the Maldives

Area: 115 mi² / 298 km²

Highest point: Unnamed

Population: 284,000 (1998)

Capital, population: Male, 62,973 (1995)

Other important cities, population: N/A

Population growth per annum: 3.4%

Life expectancy at birth: 66 male, 63 female

Official Language: Divehi

Literacy: 93% male, 93% female

Religion: Muslim

Currency: one Rufiyaa = 100 laari

Main exports: Marine products & clothing

MALI
République du Mali
The Republic of Mali

Area: 478,841 mi² / 1,240,192 km²

Highest point: Hombori Tondo

Population: 11,831,000 (1998)

Capital, population: Bamako, 740,000 (1984)

Other important cities, population: Ségou, 99,000, Mopti, 8,000, Sikasso, 70,000

Population growth per annum: 3.0%

Life expectancy at birth: 46 male, 50 female

Official Language: French

Literacy: 41% male, 24% female

Religion: 90% Muslim, 15% Animist

Currency: one CFA franc = 100 centimes

Main exports: Cotton, livestock, gold & manufactured articles

MALTA
Repubblika ta'Malta
The Republic of Malta

Area: 94.9 mi² / 246 km²

Highest point: Unnamed

Population: 374,000 (1998)

Capital, population: Valletta, 94,552 (1997)

Other important cities, population: Birkirkara, 21,551

Population growth per annum: 0.6%

Life expectancy at birth: 75 male, 79 female

Official Language: Maltese, English

Literacy: 86% male, 86% female

Religion: 96% Roman Catholic

Currency: one Maltese lira = 100 cents

Main exports: Machinery and transport equipment, manufactured articles, beverages, chemicals & tobacco

MARSHALL ISLANDS

Republic of the Marshall Islands

Area: 70 mi² / 181 km²

Highest point: Unnamed

Population: 63,000 (1998)

Capital, population: Dalap-Uliga-Darrit, 20,000 (1990)

Other important cities, population: N/A

Population growth per annum: 3.5%

Life expectancy at birth: 62 male, 65 female

Official Language: Marshallese

Literacy: 91% male, 90% female

Religion: 80% Independent Protestant Christian Church

Currency: US Dollar

Main exports: Coconut products, shells, copra, handicrafts, fish & live animals

MAURITANIA
République Islamique Arabe et Africaine de Mauritanie
The Islamic Republic of Mauritania

Area: 398,000 mi² / 1,030,700 km²

Highest point: Kediet ej Jill

Population: 2,454,000 (1998)

Capital, population: Nouakchott, 480,408 (1992)

Other important cities, population: Nouadhibou, 72,305, Kaédi, 35,241

Population growth per annum: 2.5%

Life expectancy at birth: 52 male, 55 female

Official Language: Arabic

Literacy: 47% male, 21% female

Religion: 99% Muslim

Currency: one Ouguiya = 5 khoums

Main exports: Fish & fish products, iron ore

MAURITIUS

The Republic of Mauritius

Area: 788 mi² / 2,040 km²

Highest point: Piton de la Rivière Noirè

Population: 1,154,000 (1998)

Capital, population: Port Louis, 146,322 (1996)

Other important cities, population: Beau Bassin-Rose Hill, 99,069, Vacoas-Phoenix, 96,928, Curepipe, 78,516

Population growth per annum: 1.1%

Life expectancy at birth: 68 male, 75 female

Official Language: English

Literacy: 87% male, 78% female

Religion: 52% Hindu, 26% Roman Catholic, 17% Muslim

Currency: one Mauritius rupee = 100 cents

Main exports: Sugar, clothing, tea, molasses & jewellery

MEXICO

Estados Unidos Mexicanos
The United Mexican States

Area: 756,198 mi² / 1,958,201 km²

Highest point: Volcán Citlaltepetl

Population: 95,831,000 (1998)

Capital, population: Mexico City, 16,674,000 (1995)

Other important cities, population: Guadalajara, 3,461,000, Monterrey, 3,022,000, Puebla, 1,222,000

Population growth per annum: 1.6%

Life expectancy at birth: 69 male, 75 female

Official Language: Spanish

Literacy: 89% male, 85% female

Religion: 93% Roman Catholic, 3% Protestant

Currency: one Peso = 100 centavos

Main exports: Manufactured products, crude oil and product & agricultural products

MICRONESIA

Federated States of Micronesia

Area: 271 mi² / 701 km²

Highest point: Mt Totolom

Population: 106,000 (1994)

Capital, population: Palikir, 5,549

Other important cities, population: Weno, 15,253, Kolonia, 6,169, Colonia, 3,456

Population growth per annum: 2.8%

Life expectancy at birth: 68 male, 73 female

Official Language: English

Literacy: 91% male, 88% female

Religion: Mostly Christian

Currency: US dollar

Main exports: Copra, pepper & fish

MOLDOVA

Republica Moldovenească
The Republic of Moldova

Area: 13,000 mi² / 33,700 km²

Highest point: Balaneshty

Population: 4,451,000 (1998)

Capital, population: Chişinău, 7,000,000 (1994)

Other important cities, population: Tiraspol, 186,000, Bălţi 161,000, Tighina, 133,000

Population growth per annum: 0.1%

Life expectancy at birth: 65 male, 72 female

Official Language: Moldavian

Literacy: 99% male, 99% female

Religion: Russian Orthodox, Evangelical

Currency: Leu

Main exports: Foodstuffs, machinery and equipment, textiles & clothing

MONACO
Principauté de Monaco
The Principality of Monaco

Area: 0.75 mi² / 1.95 km²

Highest point: Chemin de Révoirés

Population: 30,000 (1990)

Capital, population: Monaco

Other important cities, population: N/A

Population growth per annum: 1.1%

Life expectancy at birth: 74 male, 83 female

Official Language: French

Literacy: 99% male, 99% female

Religion: 90% Roman Catholic

Currency: French franc

Main exports: N/A

MONGOLIA
Mongol Uls
Mongolian Republic

Area: 604,250 mi² / 1,566,500 km²

Highest point: Mönh Hayrhan Uul

Population: 2,624,000 (1998)

Capital, population: Ulaanbaatar, 619,200 (1996)

Other important cities, population: Darhan, 89,900, Erdenet, 65,600

Population growth per annum: 2.1%

Life expectancy at birth: 64 male, 67 female

Official Language: Halh Mongol

Literacy: 88% male, 87% female

Religion: 31% Shamanist, 4% Muslim

Currency: one Tugrik = 100 möngö

Main exports: Minerals and metals, consumer goods, foodstuffs & agricultural products

MOROCCO
Mamlaka al-Maghrebia
The Kingdom of Morocco

Area: 177,192 mi² / 458,730 km²

Highest point: Jebel Toubkal

Population: 28,012,000 (1998)

Capital, population: Rabat, 1,220,000 (1993)

Other important cities, population: Dar el Beida (Casablanca), 3,200,000, Fès, 448,823, Marrakech, 602,000

Population growth per annum: 1.8%

Life expectancy at birth: 64 male, 68 female

Official Language: Arabic

Literacy: 61% male, 38% female

Religion: 98% Muslim

Currency: one Dirham = 100 centimes

Main exports: Phosphates, minerals, seafoods, citrus fruit, tobacco & clothing

MOZAMBIQUE
República de Moçambique
The Republic of Mozambique

Area: 308,642 mi² / 799,380 km²

Highest point: Binga

Population: 18,691,000 (1998)

Capital, population: Maputo, 2,000,000 (1993)

Other important cities, population: Beira, 294,197, Nampula, 232,670, Nacala, 125,208

Population growth per annum: 2.5%

Life expectancy at birth: 45 male, 48 female

Official Language: Portuguese

Literacy: 64% male, 37% female

Religion: 60% Traditional, 18% Roman Catholic, 13% Muslim

Currency: one Metical = 100 centavos

Main exports: Shellfish, cashew nuts, cotton, sugar & copra

MYANMAR
Myanmar Naingngandaw
The Union of Myanmar

Area: 261,228 mi² / 676,577 km²

Highest point: Hkakabe Razi

Population: 47,625,000 (1998)

Capital, population: Yangon (Rangoon), 2,458,712 (1983)

Other important cities, population: Mandalay, 532,985, Moulmein, 219,991, Pegu, 150,447

Population growth per annum: 1.8%

Life expectancy at birth: 59 male, 62 female

Official Language: Burmese

Literacy: 89% male, 72% female

Religion: 89% Buddhist, 5% Christian, 4% Muslim

Currency: one Kyat = 100 pyas

Main exports: Teak, rice, pulses, rubber, hardwood, base metals & gems

NAMIBIA
Republic of Namibia

Area: 318,275 mi² / 824,268 km²

Highest point: Brandberg

Population: 1,653,000 (1998)

Capital, population: Windhoek, 125,000 (1990)

Other important cities, population: Swakopmund, 15,500, Rehoboth, 15,000, Rundu, 15,000

Population growth per annum: 2.4%

Life expectancy at birth: 60 male, 63 female

Official Language: English

Literacy: 38%

Religion: 90% Christian

Currency: one Namibia dollar = 100 cents

Main exports: Diamonds, fish, live animals, meat & uranium

NAURU
The Republic of Nauru

Area: 8 mi² / 21.3 km²

Highest point: Unnamed

Population: 11,000 (1996)

Capital, population: No official capital

Other important cities, population: Yaren

Population growth per annum: 2.6%

Life expectancy at birth: 64 male, 69 female

Official Language: Nauruan, English

Literacy: 99% male, 99% female

Religion: Christian (Roman Catholic, Nauruan Protestant Church)

Currency: Australian dollar

Main exports: Phosphates

NEPAL
Nepal Adhirajya
The Kingdom of Nepal

Area: 56,831 mi² / 147,181 km²

Highest point: Qomolangma Feng (Mt Everest)

Population: 23,168,000 (1998)

Capital, population: Kathmandu, 419,073 (1991)

Other important cities, population: Patan, 117,203, Morang 130,129, Bhaktapur, 61,122

Population growth per annum: 2.5%

Life expectancy at birth: 57 male, 57 female

Official Language: Nepali

Literacy: 38% male, 13% female

Religion: 89% Hindu, 5% Buddhist, 3% Muslim

Currency: one Nepalese rupee = 100 paisas

Main exports: Carpets, clothing, hides and skins, grain, jute, oil seeds, ghee, potatoes, herbs & cattle

ETHERLANDS

oninkrijk der Nederlanden
he Kingdom of The Netherlands

ea: 16,170 mi² / 41,863 km²

ighest point: unnamed

opulation: 15,739,000 (1998)

apital, population: Amsterdam, 1,101,850 (1996), Seat of overnment, s'-Gravenhage, 694,895

her important cities, population: Rotterdam, 1,076,878, recht, 548,464

opulation growth per annum: 0.5%

fe expectancy at birth: 75 male, 81 female

ficial Language: Dutch

teracy: 99% male, 99% female

eligion: 89% Roman Catholic, 7% Dutch Reformed Church

urrency: Euro / one Guilder = 100 cents

ain exports: Machinery and transport equipment, foodstuffs, troleum, natural gas, chemicals, plants & cut flowers

---

NEW ZEALAND

New Zealand

Area: 104,461 mi² / 270,534 km²

Highest point: Mt Cook

Population: 3,680,000 (1998)

Capital, population: Wellington, 335,468 (1996)

Other important cities, population: Auckland, 997,940, Christchurch, 331,443, Dunedin, 112,279

Population growth per annum: 1.1%

Life expectancy at birth: 73 male, 79 female

Official Language: English, Maori

Literacy: 99% male, 99% female

Religion: 42% Protestant, 15% Roman Catholic

Currency: one New Zealand dollar = 100 cents

Main exports: Meat, dairy products, wool, fish, wood, fruit and vegetables, aluminium & machinery

---

ICARAGUA

epública de Nicaragua
he Republic of Nicaragua

rea: 50,456 mi² / 130,682 km²

ighest point: Mogotón

opulation: 4,464,000 (1998)

apital, population: Managua, 682,111 (1985)

ther important cities, population: León, 100,982, Granada, 8,636, Masaya, 74,946

opulation growth per annum: 2.6%

ife expectancy at birth: 67 male, 70 female

fficial Language: Spanish

iteracy: 64% male, 66% female

eligion: 87% Roman Catholic

urrency: one Córdoba = 100 centavos

ain exports: Coffee, meat, cotton, sugar, sea food, bananas chemical products

---

NIGER

République du Niger
Republic of Niger

Area: 489,401 mi² / 1,267,000 km²

Highest point: Mt Gréboun

Population: 10,119,000 (1998)

Capital, population: Niamey, 398,265 (1988)

Other important cities, population: Zinder, 120,900, Maradi, 113,000, Tahoua, 51,600

Population growth per annum: 3.3%

Life expectancy at birth: 47 male, 50 female

Official Language: French

Literacy: 40% male, 17% female

Religion: 97% Muslim

Currency: one CFA franc = 100 centimes

Main exports: Uranium, live animals, hides and skins, peas & cotton

NIGERIA

Federal Republic of Nigeria

Area: 356,669 mi² / 923,773 km²

Highest point: Dimlang

Population: 121,773,000 (1998)

Capital, population: Abuja, 305,900 (1992)

Other important cities, population: Lagos, 1,347,000, Ibadan, 1,295,000, Kano, 699,900

Population growth per annum: 2.8%

Life expectancy at birth: 51 male, 54 female

Official Language: English

Literacy: 62% male, 39% female

Religion: 48% Muslim, 17% Protestant, 17% Roman Catholic

Currency: one Naira = 100 kobo

Main exports: Petroleum, cocoa beans, rubber, palm products, minerals & fish

NORTH KOREA

Chosun Minchu-chui Immin Konghwa-guk

People's Democratic Republic of Korea

Area: 47,402 mi² / 122,762 km²

Highest point: Paekut-san

Population: 23,206,000 (1998)

Capital, population: P'yŏngyang, 2,639,448 (1984)

Other important cities, population: Ch'ŏngjin, 754,128, Namp'o, 691,284, Sinŭiju, 500,000

Population growth per annum: 1.6%

Life expectancy at birth: 69 male, 75 female

Official Language: Korean

Literacy: 99% male, 99% female

Religion: 16% Traditional, 14% Ch'ondogyo, 2% Buddhist, 1% Christian

Currency: one Won = 100 chon

Main exports: Metal ores and products

NORWAY

**Kongeriket Norge
The Kingdom of Norway**

Area: 125,050 mi² / 323,878 km²

Highest point: Galdhøpiggen

Population: 4,379,000 (1998)

Capital, population: Oslo, 459,292 (1990)

Other important cities, population: Bergen, 212,944, Trondheim, 137,846, Stavanger, 98,109

Population growth per annum: 0.4%

Life expectancy at birth: 74 male, 81 female

Official Language: Norwegian

Literacy: 99% male, 99% female

Religion: 88% Lutheran

Currency: one Norwegian Krone = 100 øre

Main exports: Petroleum, natural gas, fish products, metals, wood pulp & paper

OMAN

**Sultanat 'Uman
Sultanate of Oman**

Area: 119,507 mi² / 309,500 km²

Highest point: Jabal ash-Sham

Population: 2,504,000 (1998)

Capital, population: Masqat (Muscat), 380,000 (1990) (Capital Area)

Other important cities, population: Sohar, 91,521, Rustaq, 66,205, Nizwa, 62,880

Population growth per annum: 4.2%

Life expectancy at birth: 69 male, 73 female

Official Language: Arabic

Literacy: 52% male, 34% female

Religion: 88% Muslim, Hindu

Currency: one Omani rial = 1000 baiza

Main exports: Petroleum, metals and metal goods, textiles &

PAKISTAN

Islami Jamhuriya e Pakistan
Islamic Republic of Pakistan

Area: 307,293 mi² / 796,095 km²

Highest point: K2 (Mt Godwin Austen)

Population: 147,812,000 (1998)

Capital, population: Islamabad, 340,268 (1994)

Other important cities, population: Karachi, 10,000,000, Lahore, 5,500,000, Faisalabad, 2,000,000

Population growth per annum: 2.7%

Life expectancy at birth: 63 male, 65 female

Official Language: Urdu

Literacy: 47% male, 21% female

Religion: 97% Muslim

Currency: one Pakistan rupee = 100 paisas

Main exports: Cotton, textiles, petroleum and petroleum products, clothing, leather, rice, foodstuffs & live animals

PALAU

Republic of Palau

Area: 188 mi² / 488 km²

Highest point: Unnamed

Population: 17,000 (1996)

Capital, population: Koror, 11,500 (1995)

Other important cities, population: N/A

Population growth per annum: 2.3%

Life expectancy at birth: 68 male, 74 female

Official Language: English, Palauan

Literacy: 92%

Religion: Mostly Roman Catholic

Currency: US dollar

Main exports: Copra, coconut oil, handicrafts & tuna

PANAMÁ

República de Panamá
The Republic of Panama

Area: 29,761 mi² / 77,082 km²

Highest point: Volcán Barú

Population: 2,767,000 (1998)

Capital, population: Panamá, 658,102 (1995)

Other important cities, population: San Miguelito, 290,919, Colón, 156,289, David, 113,527

Population growth per annum: 1.6%

Life expectancy at birth: 72 male, 76 female

Official Language: Spanish

Literacy: 88% male, 88% female

Religion: 85% Roman Catholic, 5% Protestant

Currency: one Balboa = 100 centesimos

Main exports: Bananas, shellfish, sugar, clothing & coffee

PAPUA NEW GUINEA

The Independent State of
Papua New Guinea

Area: 178,780 mi² / 462,840 km²

Highest point: Mt Wilhelm

Population: 4,602,000 (1998)

Capital, population: Port Moresby, 193,242 (1990) (Nat. Capital Dist.)

Other important cities, population: Lae, 80,655, Madang, 27,057, Wewak, 23,224

Population growth per annum: 2.2%

Life expectancy at birth: 57 male, 59 female

Official Language: English

Literacy: 65% male, 38% female

Religion: 58% Protestant, 32% Roman Catholic

Currency: one Kina = 100 toea

Main exports: Gold, copper ore, crude oil, timber, coffee beans, copra & coconut products

PARAGUAY
República del Paraguay
Republic of Paraguay

Area: 157,115 mi² / 406,752 km²

Highest point: Cerro Tatug

Population: 5,223,000 (1998)

Capital, population: Asunción, 945,000 (1992)

Other important cities, population: Ciudad del Este, 134,000, Pedro Juan Caballero, 80,000, Encarnación, 31,445

Population growth per annum: 2.6%

Life expectancy at birth: 69 male, 73 female

Official Language: Spanish

Literacy: 92% male, 88% female

Religion: 96% Roman Catholic

Currency: one Guaraní = 100 céntimos

Main exports: Oil seeds, cotton, timber and wood products, hides, skins & meat

PERU
República del Perú
Republic of Peru

Area: 496,093 mi² / 1,285,216 km²

Highest point: Nevado Huascarán

Population: 24,797,000 (1998)

Capital, population: Lima (metropolitan area) , 5,706,127 (19

Other important cities, population: Arequipa, 619,156, Trujil 509,312, Chiclayo, 411,536

Population growth per annum: 1.7%

Life expectancy at birth: 66 male, 69 female

Official Language: Spanish, Quechua

Literacy: 92% male, 88% female

Religion: 92% Roman Catholic

Currency: one Nuevo sol = 100 cénts

Main exports: Copper, fishmeal, zinc, gold & refined oil products

PHILIPPINES
Republika ng Pilipinas
Republic of The Philippines

Area: 115,830 mi² / 300,000 km²

Highest point: Mt Apo

Population: 72,164,000 (1998)

Capital, population: Manila, 1,655,000 (1995)

Other important cities, population: Quezon City, 1,667,000, Davao, 850,000, Caloocan, 761,000

Population growth per annum: 2.0%

Life expectancy at birth: 67 male, 70 female

Official Language: Pilipino

Literacy: 90% male, 89% female

Religion: 84% Roman Catholic, 6% Aglipayan, 4% Muslim, 4% Protestant

Currency: one Peso = 100 centavos

Main exports: Electronic products, fruit and seafood, lumber and wood products, chemicals & coconut oil

POLAND
Rzeczpospolita Polska
Republic of Poland

Area: 120,628 mi² / 312,683 km²

Highest point: Rysy

Population: 38,664,000 (1998)

Capital, population: Warszawa (Warsaw), 1,638,300 (1995)

Other important cities, population: Łódź, 825,000, Kraków, 745,400, Wrocław, 642,700

Population growth per annum: 0.1%

Life expectancy at birth: 68 male, 76 female

Official Language: Polish

Literacy: 99% male, 99% female

Religion: 94% Roman Catholic

Currency: one Złoty = 100 groszy

Main exports: Machinery and transport equipment, textiles, chemicals, coal, coke, copper, sulphur, steel, foodstuffs, clothing, leather products, wood & paper products

PORTUGAL

República Portuguesa
The Portuguese Republic

Area: 35,516 mi² / 91,985 km²

Highest point: Punta do Pico

Population: 9,798,000 (1998)

Capital, population: Lisboa (Lisbon), 830,500 (1987)

Other important cities, population: Porto, 350,000, Amadora, 95,518, Setúbal, 77,885

Population growth per annum: -0.1%

Life expectancy at birth: 72 male, 79 female

Official Language: Portuguese

Literacy: 89% male, 81% female

Religion: 95% Roman Catholic

Currency: Euro / one Escudo = 100 centavos

Main exports: Textiles, clothing, pulp and paper, wood, tinned fish, electrical equipment, wine & refined oil

QATAR

Dawlat Qatar
State of Qatar

Area: 4,418 mi² / 11,437 km²

Highest point: Dukham Heights

Population: 579,000 (1998)

Capital, population: Ad Dawḥah (Doha), 217,294 (1986)

Other important cities, population: Dukhan, Umm Said, Ruwais

Population growth per annum: 1.8%

Life expectancy at birth: 70 male, 75 female

Official Language: Arabic

Literacy: 78% male, 78% female

Religion: Mostly Muslim

Currency: one Qatari riyal = 100 dirhams

Main exports: Petroleum

ROMANIA

România
Romania

Area: 91,699 mi² / 237,500 km²

Highest point: Vârful Moldoveanu

Population: 22,573,000 (1998)

Capital, population: Bucureşti (Bucharest), 2,339,156 (1994)

Other important cities, population: Constanţa, 348,575, Iaşi, 339,889, Timişoara, 327,830

Population growth per annum: -0.2%

Life expectancy at birth: 67 male, 73 female

Official Language: Romanian

Literacy: 97% male, 97% female

Religion: 70% Romanian Orthodox, 10% Greek Orthodox

Currency: one Leu = 100 bani

Main exports: Metals, textiles and clothing, machinery and equipment, minerals & foodstuffs

RUSSIA

Rossiiskaya Federatsiya
The Russian Federation

Area: 6,592,657 mi² / 17,075,000 km²

Highest point: Gora El'brus

Population: 147,231,000 (1998)

Capital, population: Moskva (Moscow), 8,600,000 (1995)

Other important cities, population: Sankt-Peterburg, 4,800,000, Nizhniy Novgorod, 1,443,000, Novosibirsk, 1,442,000

Population growth per annum: -0.3%

Life expectancy at birth: 62 male, 74 female

Official Language: Russian

Literacy: 99% male, 99% female

Religion: Russian Orthodox, Christian, Muslim

Currency: one Ruble = 100 kopeks

Main exports: Mineral fuels, metals, precious stones, chemicals, machinery and transport equipment, weapons, timber

RWANDA
Republika y'u Rwanda
The Republic of Rwanda

Area: 10,169 mi² / 26,338 km²

Highest point: Mt Karisimbi

Population: 6,527,000 (1998)

Capital, population: Kigali, 234,500 (1993)

Other important cities, population: Butare, 21,691, Ruhengeri, 16,025, Gisenyi, 12,436

Population growth per annum: 7.8%

Life expectancy at birth: 45 male, 48 female

Official Language: Kinyarwanda, French

Literacy: 64% male, 37% female

Religion: 65% Roman Catholic, 9% Protestant

Currency: one Rwanda franc = 100 centimes

Main exports: Coffee, tea, tin, pyrethrum and quinquina

SAINT KITTS-NEVIS

The Federation of St Christopher & Nevis

Area: 100 mi² / 261 km²

Highest point: Nevis Peak

Population: 42,000 (1996)

Capital, population: Basse-Terre, 12,605 (1994)

Other important cities, population: Charlestown, 1,411

Population growth per annum: -0.1%

Life expectancy at birth: 66 male, 72 female

Official Language: English

Literacy: 98% male, 86% female

Religion: Christian

Currency: one East Caribbean dollar = 100 cents

Main exports: Sugar, manufactured products & postage stam

SAINT LUCIA
Saint Lucia

Area: 238 mi² / 617 km²

Highest point: Mt Gimie

Population: 144,000 (1996)

Capital, population: Castries, 53,883 (1992)

Other important cities, population: Vieux Fort, 13,140

Population growth per annum: 1.4%

Life expectancy at birth: 68 male, 75 female

Official Language: English

Literacy: 82% male, 72% female

Religion: 80% Roman Catholic, Protestant

Currency: one East Caribbean dollar = 100 cents

Main exports: Bananas, copra and coconut products, tobacco & beverages

ST VINCENT & THE GRENADINES

Saint Vincent and the Grenadines

Area: 150 mi² / 388 km²

Highest point: Mt Soufrière

Population: 112,000 (1996)

Capital, population: Kingstown, 26,542 (1991)

Other important cities, population: N/A

Population growth per annum: 0.9%

Life expectancy at birth: 70 male, 75 female

Official Language: English

Literacy: 92% male, 86% female

Religion: Christian

Currency: one East Caribbean dollar = 100 cents

Main exports: Bananas & other foods

SAMOA
Malotute'atasi e Samoa i Sisifo
The Independent State of Samoa

Area: 1,094 mi² / 2,831 km²

Highest point: Mauga Silisli

Population: 170,000 (1998)

Capital, population: Apia, 32,196 (1986)

Other important cities, population: N/A

Population growth per annum: 1.2%

Life expectancy at birth: 68 male, 71 female

Official Language: Samoan, English

Literacy: 92% male, 88% female

Religion: 62% Protestant, 22% Roman Catholic

Currency: one Tala = 100 sene

Main exports: Palm products, timber, bananas, cocoa, beer & cigarettes

SAN MARINO
Repubblica di San Marino
The Republic of San Marino

Area: 24.1 mi² / 61.19 km²

Highest point: Mt Titano

Population: 25,000 (1995)

Capital, population: San Marino, 4,372 (1996)

Other important cities, population: Serravalle, 8,026

Population growth per annum: 1.2%

Life expectancy at birth: 75 male, 81 female

Official Language: Italian

Literacy: 98% male, 98% female

Religion: Roman Catholic

Currency: Italian currency

Main exports: Lime, building stone, ceramics, machinery, chemicals, wine, olive oil & textiles

SÃO TOMÉ AND PRÍNCIPE
República Democrática de São Tomé e Príncipe
The Democratic Republic of São Tomé & Príncipe

Area: 387 mi² / 1,001 km²

Highest point: Pico Gago Coutinho

Population: 127,000 (1995)

Capital, population: São Tomé, 34,997 (1984)

Other important cities, population: São António, 1,000

Population growth per annum: 2.0%

Life expectancy at birth: 67 male, 73 female

Official Language: Portuguese

Literacy: 85% male, 62% female

Religion: 90% Roman Catholic

Currency: one Dobra = 100 centimos

Main exports: Cocoa, copra, coffee, bananas & palm products

SAUDI ARABIA
Mamlaka al-'Arabiya as-Sa'udiya
The Kingdom of Saudi Arabia

Area: 849,400 mi² / 2,200,000 km²

Highest point: Razikh

Population: 20,206,000 (1998)

Capital, population: Ar Riyad (Riyadh), 1,500,000 (1994)

Other important cities, population: Jiddah, 1,400,000, Makkah (Mecca), 618,006, Al Madīnah (Medina), 500,000

Population growth per annum: 3.4%

Life expectancy at birth: 70 male, 73 female

Official Language: Arabic

Literacy: 73% male, 48% female

Religion: 98% Muslim

Currency: one Rial = 100 halalas

Main exports: Crude and refined oil, petrochemicals & wheat

SENEGAL
République du Sénégal
The Republic of Senegal

Area: 76,129 mi² / 197,161 km²

Highest point: Mt Gounou

Population: 9,001,000 (1998)

Capital, population: Dakar, 1,729,823 (1992)

Other important cities, population: Thiès, 201,350, Kaolack, 179,894, Ziguinchor, 148,831

Population growth per annum: 2.7%

Life expectancy at birth: 50 male, 52 female

Official Language: French

Literacy: 52% male, 25% female

Religion: 90% Muslim

Currency: one CFA franc = 100 centimes

Main exports: Fish, refined oil products, chemicals & groundnuts

SEYCHELLES

Republic of Seychelles

Area: 175 mi² / 455 km²

Highest point: Morne Seychellois

Population: 76,000 (1996)

Capital, population: Victoria

Other important cities, population: N/A

Population growth per annum: 1.0%

Life expectancy at birth: 69 male, 78 female

Official Language: Creole, English, French

Literacy: 86% male, 82% female

Religion: 92% Roman Catholic, 8% Anglican

Currency: one Seychelles rupee = 100 cents

Main exports: Fish, cinnamon & refined oil products

SIERRA LEONE

Republic of Sierra Leone

Area: 27,925 mi² / 73,326 km²

Highest point: Bintimani Peak

Population: 4,576,000 (1998)

Capital, population: Freetown, 469,776 (1988)

Other important cities, population: Bo, 26,000, Kenema, 13,000, Makeni, 12,000

Population growth per annum: 3.0%

Life expectancy at birth: 40 male, 43 female

Official Language: English

Literacy: 31% male, 11% female

Religion: 51% Traditional, 39% Muslim, 6% Protestant, 2% Roman Catholic

Currency: one Leone = 100 cents

Main exports: Diamonds, rutile, bauxite, gold, coffee & cocoa beans

SINGAPORE

Republic of Singapore

Area: 247.5 mi² / 641 km²

Highest point: Bukit Timah

Population: 3,491,000 (1998)

Capital, population: Singapore

Other important cities, population: N/A

Population growth per annum: 1.5%

Life expectancy at birth: 74 male, 79 female

Official Language: Chinese, Malay, Tamil, English

Literacy: 93% male, 79% female

Religion: 54% Buddhist, 13% Christian, 15% Muslim

Currency: one Singapore dollar = 100 cents

Main exports: Machinery and transport equipment, petroleum products, chemicals, rubber, foodstuff, clothing, metal products, iron and steel, plants & aquarium fish

SLOVAKIA
Slovenská Republica
The Slovak Republic

Area: 18,932 mi² / 49,035 km²

Highest point: Gerlachovsky

Population: 5,360,000 (1998)

Capital, population: Bratislava, 448,000 (1993)

Other important cities, population: Košice, 239,000, Zilina, 86,000, Nitra, 87,000

Population growth per annum: 0.1%

Life expectancy at birth: 67 male, 75 female

Official Language: Slovak

Literacy: 99% male, 99% female

Religion: 50% Roman Catholic, 20% Protestant

Currency: one Koruna = 100 haléru

Main exports: Manufactured goods, machinery & transport equipment

SLOVENIA
Republika Slovenija
The Republic of Slovenia

Area: 7,819 mi² / 20,251 km²

Highest point: Triglav

Population: 1,920,000 (1998)

Capital, population: Ljubljana, 330,000 (1997)

Other important cities, population: Maribor, 105,400, Celje, 42,000, Kranj, 37,100

Population growth per annum: -0.1%

Life expectancy at birth: 69 male, 78 female

Official Language: Slovene

Literacy: 96% male, 96% female

Religion: 75% Roman Catholic

Currency: one Tolar = 100 lipa

Main exports: Raw materials, machinery and transport equipment, foodstuffs, clothing, cosmetics & pharmaceuticals

SOLOMON ISLANDS

Solomon Islands

Area: 10,644 mi² / 27,556 km²

Highest point: Mt Makarakomburu

Population: 426,000 (1998)

Capital, population: Honiara, 33,749 (1989)

Other important cities, population: N/A

Population growth per annum: 3.2%

Life expectancy at birth: 70 male, 74 female

Official Language: English

Literacy: 60% male, 60% female

Religion: 75% Protestant, 19% Roman Catholic

Currency: one Solomon Island dollar = 100 cents

Main exports: Timber, fish & palm products

SOMALIA
Jamhuriyadda Dimugradiga
ee Soomaaliya
The Somali Democratic Republic

Area: 246,201 mi² / 637,657 km²

Highest point: Surud Ad

Population: 10,653,000 (1998)

Capital, population: Muqdisho (Mogadishu), 1,000,000 (1987)

Other important cities, population: Hargeysa, 400,000, Kismaayo, 200,000, Marka, 100,000

Population growth per annum: 3.9%

Life expectancy at birth: 47 male, 51 female

Official Language: Arabic, Somali

Literacy: 36% male, 14% female

Religion: 99% Muslim

Currency: one Somali shilling = 100 cents

Main exports: Livestock, skins and hides, bananas & fish

SOUTH AFRICA
Republiek van Suid-Afrika
Republic of South Africa

Area: 471,647 mi² / 1,221,037 km²

Highest point: Injasuti

Population: 44,296,000 (1998)

Capital, population: Pretoria, 1,080,187. Seat of Government Cape Town

Other important cities, population: Johannesburg, Durban, Bloemfontein

Population growth per annum: 2.2%

Life expectancy at birth: 62 male, 68 female

Official Language: Afrikaans, English

Literacy: 81% male, 81% female

Religion: 54% Protestant, 15% Roman Catholic, 3% Hindu

Currency: one Rand = 100 cents

Main exports: Metal and metal products, gold and gemstones, minerals and chemicals, pearls, machinery, wool, maize, fruit & sugar

SOUTH KOREA
Daehan Min-kuk
Republic of Korea

Area: 38,332 mi² / 99,274 km²

Highest point: Halle-san

Population: 46,115,000 (1998)

Capital, population: Sŏul (Seoul), 10,627,790 (1990)

Other important cities, population: Pusan, 3,797,566, Taegu, 2,228,834, Inch'ŏn, 1,818,293

Population growth per annum: 0.7%

Life expectancy at birth: 69 male, 70 female

Official Language: Korean

Literacy: 99% male, 96% female

Religion: 24% Buddhist, 16% Protestant, 5% Roman Catholic

Currency: one Won = 100 chon

Main exports: Transistors and chips, textiles, clothing, ships, cars, iron and steel, telecommunications equipment, office machines & chemicals

SPAIN
Reino de España
The Kingdom of Spain

Area: 194,884 mi² / 504,750 km²

Highest point: Pico del Tiede

Population: 39,754,000 (1998)

Capital, population: Madrid, 3,029,734 (1995)

Other important cities, population: Barcelona, 1,614,571, Valencia, 763,299, Sevilla, 719,588

Population growth per annum: 0.1%

Life expectancy at birth: 75 male, 81 female

Official Language: Spanish

Literacy: 97% male, 93% female

Religion: 97% Roman Catholic

Currency: Euro, one Peseta = 100 céntimos

Main exports: Motor vehicles, machinery and electrical equipment, metals & foodstuffs

SRI LANKA
Sri Lanka Prajathanthrika
Samajavadi Janarajaya
Democratic Socialist
Republic of Sri Lanka

Area: 25,343 mi² / 65,610 km²

Highest point: Pidurutalagala

Population: 18,450,000 (1998)

Capital, population: Colombo, 587,647 (1981)

Other important cities, population: Dehiwala-Mount Lavinia 173,529, Moratuwa, 134,826, Jaffna, 118,224

Population growth per annum: 1.0%

Life expectancy at birth: 71 male, 75 female

Official Language: Sinhala, Tamil

Literacy: 93% male, 83% female

Religion: 73% Buddhist, 15% Hindu, 7% Muslim, 5% Christian

Currency: one Sri Lankan rupee = 100 cents

Main exports: Tea, clothing and textiles, gem stones, coconuts & rubber

SUDAN

**Jamhuryat es-Sudan
The Republic of Sudan**

Area: 967,500 mi² / 2,505,813 km²

Highest point: Kinyeti

Population: 28,527,000 (1998)

Capital, population: Al Khartūm (Khartoum), 476,218 (1983)

Other important cities, population: Umm Durmān (Omdurman), 526,287, Al Khartūm Bahrı, 341,146, Būr Sūdān, 206,727

Population growth per annum: 2.2%

Life expectancy at birth: 54 male, 56 female

Official Language: Arabic

Literacy: 43% male, 12% female

Religion: 73% Muslim, 6% Roman Catholic, 2% Protestant

Currency: one Sudanese pound = 100 piastres

Main exports: Cotton, sesame seed, gum arabic, sorghum, livestock, hides & skins

SURINAME

Republic of Suriname

Area: 63,278 mi² / 163,820 km²

Highest point: Julianatop

Population: 443,000 (1998)

Capital, population: Paramaribo, 200,970 (1993)

Other important cities, population: N/A

Population growth per annum: 1.2%

Life expectancy at birth: 69 male, 74 female

Official Language: Dutch

Literacy: 95% male, 95% female

Religion: 27% Hindu, 23% Roman Catholic, 20% Muslim, 19% Protestant

Currency: one Suriname guilder = 100 cents

Main exports: Aluminium and alumina, shrimps, bananas, plantins, rice, timber & wood products

SWAZILAND

**Umbuso weSwatini
Kingdom of Swaziland**

Area: 6,705 mi² / 17,400 km²

Highest point: Emlembe

Population: 932,000 (1998)

Capital, population: Mbabane, 38,290 (1986)

Other important cities, population: Manzini, 18,084, Big Bend, 9,676, Mhlume, 6,509

Population growth per annum: 2.8%

Life expectancy at birth: 58 male, 62 female

Official Language: siSwati, English

Literacy: 76% male, 73% female

Religion: 60% Christian, 40% Traditional

Currency: one Lilangeni = 100 cents

Main exports: Sugar, wood pulp, cotton yarn, tinned fruit, coal, diamonds & gold

SWEDEN

**Konungariket Sverige
The Kingdom of Sweden**

Area: 173,806 mi² / 449,964 km²

Highest point: Kebnekaise

Population: 8,863,000 (1998)

Capital, population: Stockholm, 718,462 (1996)

Other important cities, population: Göteborg, 454,016, Malmö, 248,007, Uppsala, 184,507

Population growth per annum: 0.3%

Life expectancy at birth: 76 male, 82 female

Official Language: Swedish

Literacy: 99% male, 99% female

Religion: 89% Lutheran, 2% Roman Catholic

Currency: one Swedish krona = 100 öre

Main exports: Wood, pulp and paper, machinery, motor vehicles, chemicals, iron & steel

SWITZERLAND

Schweizerische Eidtgenossenschaft
Confédération Suisse
Confederazione Svizzera
The Swiss Confederation

Area: 15,943 mi² / 41,293 km²

Highest point: Dufourspitze (Mt Rosa)

Population: 7,325,000 (1998)

Capital, population: Bern, 134,129 (1994)

Other important cities, population: Zürich, 353,361, Basel, 360,400, Genève, 394,800

Population growth per annum: 0.7%

Life expectancy at birth: 75 male, 82 female

Official Language: German, French, Italian

Literacy: 99% male, 99% female

Religion: 46% Roman Catholic, 47% Protestant

Currency: one Swiss franc = 100 centimes

Main exports: Machinery and equipment, chemicals and pharmaceuticals, foodstuffs, precision instruments & metals

SYRIA

Jumhuriya al-Arabya as-Suriya
The Syrian Arab Republic

Area: 71,498 mi² / 185,180 km²

Highest point: Jabal ash Shaik (Mt Hermon)

Population: 15,335,000 (1998)

Capital, population: Dimashq (Damascus), 1,444,000 (1994)

Other important cities, population: Halab (Aleppo), 1,542,000, Hims (Homs), 558,000, Al Lādhiqīyah (Latakia), 303,000

Population growth per annum: 2.5%

Life expectancy at birth: 67 male, 71 female

Official Language: Arabic

Literacy: 53% male, 51% female

Religion: 90% Muslim

Currency: one Syrian pound = 100 piastres

Main exports: Crude oil, textiles, fruit and vegetables, cotton & phosphates

TAIWAN

Chung Hua Min Kuo
Republic of China

Area: 13,969 mi² / 36,179 km²

Highest point: Yu Shan

Population: 21,465,900 (1996)

Capital, population: T'ai-pei, 2,610,000 (1996)

Other important cities, population: Kao-hsiung, 1,430,000

Population growth per annum: 0.9%

Life expectancy at birth: 72 male, 78 female

Official Language: Chinese (Mandarin)

Literacy: 95% male, 93% female

Religion: 43% Buddhist, 21% Taoist, 7% Christian

Currency: one Taiwan dollar = 100 cents

Main exports: Electronic equipment, metal and metal products, textiles and clothing, plastic and rubber products, vehicles and transport equipment, toys, games & sports equipment

TAJIKISTAN

Respublika i Tojikiston
Republic of Tajikistan

Area: 55,240 mi² / 143,100 km²

Highest point: Pik Imeni Ismail Samani

Population: 6,161,000 (1998)

Capital, population: Dushanbe, 592,000 (1991)

Other important cities, population: Khudjand, Qūrghonteppa, Külob

Population growth per annum: 1.9%

Life expectancy at birth: 69 male, 74 female

Official Language: Tajik

Literacy: 97% male, 97% female

Religion: Mostly Muslim

Currency: one Tajik Rouble = 100 tanga

Main exports: Aluminium & cotton

TANZANIA
Jamhuri ya Muungano wa Tanzania
United Republic of Tanzania

Area: 364,881 mi² / 945,037 km²

Highest point: Kilimanjaro

Population: 32,189,000 (1998)

Capital, population: Dodoma, 203,833 (1988)

Other important cities, population: Dar es Salaam, 1,360,850, Mwanza, 223,013, Tanga, 187,634

Population growth per annum: 2.3%

Life expectancy at birth: 50 male, 53 female

Official Language: Swahili, English

Literacy: 79% male, 54% female

Religion: 34% Christian, 33% Muslim

Currency: one Tanzanian shilling = 100 cents

Main exports: Coffee beans, raw cotton, tobacco, tea, cloves, cashew nuts, minerals & petroleum products

THAILAND
Prathet Thai
Kingdom of Thailand

Area: 198,114 mi² / 513,115 km²

Highest point: Doi Inthanon

Population: 59,611,000 (1998)

Capital, population: Krung Thep (Bangkok), 5,572,000 (1993)

Other important cities, population: Chiang Mai, 164,382, Hat Yai, 139,357, Khon Khaen, 131,472

Population growth per annum: 0.8%

Life expectancy at birth: 65 male, 72 female

Official Language: Thai

Literacy: 96% male, 90% female

Religion: 95% Buddhist, 4% Muslim, 1% Christian

Currency: one Baht = 100 satang

Main exports: Clothing and textiles, electronic goods, rubber, gem stones, sugar, tapioca, fish, machinery & manufactured goods

TOGO
République Togolaise
Republic of Togo

Area: 21,934 mi² / 56,785 km²

Highest point: Pic Baumann

Population: 4,434,000 (1998)

Capital, population: Lomé, 470,000 (1997)

Other important cities, population: Sokodé, 55,000, Lama Kara, 41,000, Kpalimé, 31,000

Population growth per annum: 2.7%

Life expectancy at birth: 55 male, 59 female

Official Language: French

Literacy: 56% male, 31% female

Religion: 18% Christian, many traditional

Currency: one CFA franc = 100 centimes

Main exports: Cotton, coffee & cocoa beans

TONGA
The Kingdom of Tonga

Area: 289 mi² / 748 km²

Highest point: Kao

Population: 98,000 (1996)

Capital, population: Nuku'alofa, 29,018 (1986)

Other important cities, population: N/A

Population growth per annum: 0.4%

Life expectancy at birth: 67 male, 71 female

Official Language: Tongan, English

Literacy: 95% male, 89% female

Religion: Christian

Currency: one Pa'anga = 100 seniti

Main exports: Coconut products, clothes, vegetables & water melons

TRINIDAD & TOBAGO

The Republic of Trinidad & Tobago

Area: 1,978 mi² / 5,124 km²

Highest point: Cerro Aripo

Population: 1,318,000 (1998)

Capital, population: Port of Spain, 45,284 (1995)

Other important cities, population: San Fernando, 55,784, Arima, 24,874, Point Fortin, 20,084

Population growth per annum: 0.8%

Life expectancy at birth: 71 male, 75 female

Official Language: English

Literacy: 97% male, 95% female

Religion: 49% Christian, 24% Hindu, 6% Muslim

Currency: one Trinidad & Tobago dollar = 100 cents

Main exports: Mineral fuels, lubricants, chemicals, manufactured goods & foodstuffs

TUNISIA
Jumhuriya at-Tunisiya
The Tunisian Republic

Area: 63,378 mi² / 164,150 km²

Highest point: Jabal ash-Shanabi

Population: 9,497,000 (1998)

Capital, population: Tūnis, 674,100 (1994)

Other important cities, population: Ṣafāgis (Sfax), 230,900, Aryanah, 152,700, Bizerta, 98,900

Population growth per annum: 1.8%

Life expectancy at birth: 68 male, 71 female

Official Language: Arabic

Literacy: 74% male, 56% female

Religion: 99% Muslim

Currency: one Tunisian dinar = 1000 millimes

Main exports: Clothing and textiles, crude oil, fertilizers, olive oil, fruit, leather and footware, fish products, machinery & electrical equipment

TURKEY
Türkiye Çumhuriyeti
Republic of Turkey

Area: 300,947 mi² / 779,452 km²

Highest point: Ağri Daği (Mt Ararat)

Population: 63,762,000 (1998)

Capital, population: Ankara, 3,022,236 (1990)

Other important cities, population: İstanbûl, 6,407,215, İzmir, 2,665,105, Adana, 1,429,677

Population growth per annum: 1.6%

Life expectancy at birth: 67 male, 71 female

Official Language: Turkish

Literacy: 90% male, 71% female

Religion: 99% Muslim

Currency: one Turkish lira = 100 kuruş

Main exports: Clothing and textiles, foodstuffs, tobacco, leather, glass, refined oil & petroleum products

TURKMENISTAN
Turkmenostan Respublikasy
Turkmenistan

Area: 186,400 mi² / 448,100 km²

Highest point: Firyuza

Population: 4,315,000 (1998)

Capital, population: Ashgabat (Ashkhabad), 411,000 (1990)

Other important cities, population: Chärjew, Mary, Nebitdag

Population growth per annum: 2.0%

Life expectancy at birth: 64 male, 70 female

Official Language: Turkmen

Literacy: 98%

Religion: Mostly Muslim

Currency: one Manat = 100 tenesi

Main exports: Natural gas, cotton, electricity, petroleum & petroleum products

TUVALU

Tuvalu

Area: 9.5 mi² / 24 km²

Highest point: Unnamed

Population: 10,000 (1996)

Capital, population: Fongafale

Other important cities, population: N/A

Population growth per annum: 1.4%

Life expectancy at birth: 63 male, 65 female

Official Language: Tuvaluan, English

Literacy: 95%

Religion: Christian

Currency: Australian dollar

Main exports: Copra

UGANDA

Republic of Uganda

Area: 93,072 mi² / 241,038 km²

Highest point: Ngaliema

Population: 21,318,000 (1998)

Capital, population: Kampala, 874,241 (1996)

Other important cities, population: Jinja, 65,169, Mbale, 53,634, Masaka, 49,585

Population growth per annum: 2.6%

Life expectancy at birth: 42 male, 44 female

Official Language: English

Literacy: 62% male, 47% female

Religion: 62% Christian, 6% Muslim

Currency: one Uganda shilling = 100 cents

Main exports: Coffee and tea, cotton, tobacco, oil seed, fruit, textiles, hides & skins

UKRAINE
Ukraina
Ukraine

Area: 231,990 mi² / 603,700 km²

Highest point: Hora Hoverla

Population: 51,218,000 (1998)

Capital, population: Kyyiv (Kiev), 2,600,000 (1993)

Other important cities, population: Kharkiv, 1,623,000

Population growth per annum: -0.4%

Life expectancy at birth: 64 male, 74 female

Official Language: Ukrainian

Literacy: 99% male, 99% female

Religion: Ukrainian Orthodox

Currency: one Hryvna = 100 kopiykas

Main exports: Grain, coal, oil & minerals

UNITED ARAB EMIRATES

The United Arab Emirates

Area: 32,300 mi² / 83,657 km²

Highest point: Al-Hajar

Population: 2,354,000 (1998)

Capital, population: Abu Zaby (Abu Dhabi), 928,360

Other important cities, population: Dubayy, 674,101, Sharjah, 400,339, Ra's al Khaymah, 144,430

Population growth per annum: 2.0%

Life expectancy at birth: 74 male, 77 female

Official Language: Arabic

Literacy: 78% male, 78% female

Religion: Mostly Muslim

Currency: one Dirham = 100 fils

Main exports: Crude oil & natural gas

UNITED KINGDOM

United Kingdom of Great Britain and Northern Ireland

Area: 94,548 mi² / 244,880 km²

Highest point: Ben Nevis

Population: 58,249,000 (1998)

Capital, population: London, 6,679,699 (1991)

Other important cities, population: Manchester, 2,582,600, Birmingham, 1,007,500, Leeds, 710,500

Population growth per annum: 0.1%

Life expectancy at birth: 75 male, 79 female

Official Language: English

Literacy: 99% male, 99% female

Religion: 60% Protestant, 13% Roman Catholic

Currency: one Pound = 100 pence

Main exports: Machinery, computers, motor vehicles, petroleum, chemicals, manufactured products, agricultural products, foodstuffs & maps

UNITED STATES OF AMERICA

The United States of America

Area: 3,620,334 mi² / 9,372,614 km²

Highest point: Mt McKinley

Population: 273,754,000 (1998)

Capital, population: Washington, 543,213 (1996)

Other important cities, population: New York, 7,380,906, Los Angeles, 3,553,638, Chicago, 2,783,726

Population growth per annum: 0.8%

Life expectancy at birth: 73 male, 80 female

Official Language: English

Literacy: 99% male, 99% female

Religion: 55% Protestant, 30% Roman Catholic, 3% Jewish

Currency: one Dollar = 100 cents

Main exports: Machinery, motor vehicles, foodstuffs, aircraft, weapons, chemicals & electronic goods

URUGUAY

República Oriental del Uruguay
The Oriental Republic of Uruguay

Area: 68,037 mi² / 176,215 km²

Highest point: Cerro de las Animas

Population: 3,239,000 (1998)

Capital, population: Montevideo, 1,247,920 (1985)

Other important cities, population: Salto, 80,787, Paysandú, 75,081, Rivera, 56,335

Population growth per annum: 0.6%

Life expectancy at birth: 70 male, 76 female

Official Language: Spanish

Literacy: 97% male, 96% female

Religion: 60% Roman Catholic, 3% Protestant, 2% Jewish

Currency: one Uruguayan Nuevo Peso = 100 centésimos

Main exports: Textiles, meat and live animals, hides and skins, cereals & footwear

UZBEKISTAN

Ozbekiston Respublikasy
Republic of Uzbekistan

Area: 172,741 mi² / 447,400 km²

Highest point: Bannovka

Population: 24,106,000 (1998)

Capital, population: Toshkent, 2,100,000 (1994)

Other important cities, population: Samarqand, Andijon, Namangan

Population growth per annum: 1.9%

Life expectancy at birth: 68 male, 73 female

Official Language: Uzbek

Literacy: 97% male, 96% female

Religion: 75% Muslim

Currency: one Som = 100 tiyin

Main exports: Cotton, textiles, machinery, foodstuffs & gold

VANUATU
Ripablik blong Vanuatu
The Republic of Vanuatu

Area: 4,706 mi² / 12,190 km²

Highest point: Mt Tabwebesana

Population: 183,000 (1998)

Capital, population: Port-Vila, 31,800 (1997)

Other important cities, population: Lugauville, 10,000

Population growth per annum: 2.5%

Life expectancy at birth: 66 male, 70 female

Official Language: Bislama, English, French

Literacy: 54% male, 23% female

Religion: 80% Christian

Currency: one Vatu = 100 centimes

Main exports: Copra, timber, cocoa & shells

VATICAN CITY STATE
Stato della Città del Vaticano
The Vatican City

Area: 0.17 mi² / 0.44 km²

Highest point: N/A

Population: 1,000 (1996)

Capital, population: N/A

Other important cities, population: N/A

Population growth per annum: 0.0%

Life expectancy at birth: N/A

Official Language: Latin, Italian

Literacy: N/A

Religion: Roman Catholic

Currency: one Lira = 100 centesimi

Main exports: N/A

VENEZUELA
República de Venezuela
Republic of Venezuela

Area: 352,295 mi² / 912,050 km²

Highest point: Pico Bolivar

Population: 23,242,000 (1998)

Capital, population: Caracas, 3,100,000

Other important cities, population: Maracaibo, 1,500,000, Valencia, Barquisimeto

Population growth per annum: 2.0%

Life expectancy at birth: 70 male, 76 female

Official Language: Spanish

Literacy: 87% male, 86% female

Religion: 94% Roman Catholic

Currency: one Bolívar = 100 céntimos

Main exports: Petroleum and petroleum products, metals, natural gas, chemicals, manufactured goods & motor vehicles

VIETNAM
Công Hòa Xã Hôi Chu Nghĩa
Viêt Nam
Socialist Republic of Vietnam

Area: 127,301 mi² / 329,566 km²

Highest point: Fan Si Pan

Population: 76,896,000 (1998)

Capital, population: Ha Noi, 1,088,862 (1989)

Other important cities, population: Ho Chi Minh (Saigon), 3,169,135, Haiphong, 456,049, Da Nang, 370,670

Population growth per annum: 1.8%

Life expectancy at birth: 65 male, 70 female

Official Language: Vietnamese

Literacy: 92% male, 84% female

Religion: 55% Buddhist, 7% Roman Catholic

Currency: one Dong = 10 hao

Main exports: Rice, crude oil, coal, coffee, handicrafts, nuts, rubber, tea, tin & clothing

YEMEN

Jamhuriya al Yamaniya
Republic of Yemen

Area: 205,035 mi² / 531,000 km²

Highest point: Jebel Hadhar

Population: 16,890,000 (1998)

Capital, population: San'a', 972,000 (1995)

Other important cities, population: Baladiyat 'Adan (Aden), 562,000, Ta'izz, 178,043, Al Hudaydah (Hodeida), 155,110

Population growth per annum: 3.7%

Life expectancy at birth: 52 male, 52 female

Official Language: Arabic

Literacy: 53% male, 26% female

Religion: 95% Muslim (40% Shiite)

Currency: one Riyal = 100 fils

Main exports: Petroleum and petroleum products, cotton, manufactured goods, clothing, live animals, hides and skins, fish, rice & coffee

YUGOSLAVIA (FORMER)

now Serbia & Montenegro
Savezna Republika Jugoslavija
Federal Republic of Yugoslavia

Area: 39,449 mi² / 102,173 km²

Highest point: Mt Durmitor

Population: 10,410,000 (1998)

Capital, population: Beograd (Belgrade), 1,601,373 (1995)

Other important cities, population: Novi Sad, 179,626, Niš, 175,391, Kragujevac, 147,305

Population growth per annum: 0.5%

Life expectancy at birth: 70 male, 75 female

Official Language: Serbian

Literacy: 97% male, 88% female

Religion: 65% Orthodox, 19% Muslim, 7% Catholic

Currency: one Dinar = 100 para

Main exports: Machinery, manufactured goods, transport equipment, clothing, foodstuffs & live animals

ZAMBIA

Republic of Zambia

Area: 290,586 mi² / 752,614 km²

Highest point: Muchinga Mountains (unnamed)

Population: 8,690,000 (1998)

Capital, population: Lusaka, 921,000 (1989)

Other important cities, population: Kitwe, 495,000, Ndola, 467,000, Kabwe, 210,000

Population growth per annum: 2.1%

Life expectancy at birth: 45 male, 47 female

Official Language: English

Literacy: 81% male, 65% female

Religion: 54% Christian

Currency: one Kwacha = 100 ngwee

Main exports: Metals & tobacco

ZIMBABWE

Republic of Zimbabwe

Area: 150,872 mi² / 390,759 km²

Highest point: Inyangani

Population: 11,924,000 (1998)

Capital, population: Harare, 1,184,169 (1992)

Other important cities, population: Bulawayo, 620,936, Chitungwiza, 274,035, Gweru, 124,735

Population growth per annum: 2.1%

Life expectancy at birth: 50 male, 52 female

Official Language: English

Literacy: 74% male, 60% female

Religion: 44% Christian, 40% Animist

Currency: one Zimbabwe dollar = 100 cents

Main exports: Metals, tobacco, textiles, cotton & clothing

Symbols for maps in scales:
1:10m (Europe) and 1:20m

Inhabitants

More than 5 million — **New York**

1 000 000 - 5 000 000 — **Seattle**

250 000 - 1 000 000 — **Mexicali**

100 000 - 250 000 — Tijuana

25 000 - 100 000 — Sparks

Less than 25 000 — Monterey

National capital (UPPERCASE) — **OTTAWA**

State capital — **Boise**

International boundary

Disputed international boundary

State boundary

Disputed state boundary

Major road

Other road

Road under construction

Seasonal road

Railway

Canal

Highest peak in continent — ▲ McKinley

Highest peak in country — △ Logan

Height in feet — 17000ft

Depth in feet — ▽ 185ρ

Coral reef

Dam — | Kainji Dam

Waterfall — | Niagara Falls

Pass —)(

International airport — ⊕

Historical site — ⊞

The small aeroplane on the scale bar shows the approximate distance covered over a certain amount of time by a modern passenger aircraft.

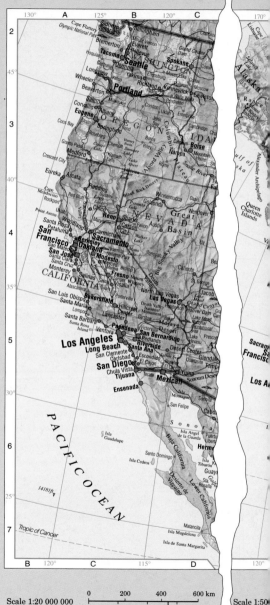

Scale 1:20 000 000

| 0 | 200 | 400 | 600 km |

| 0 | 100 | 200 | 300 miles |

½ hour's flight ✈

Scale 1:50

Symbols for maps in scales:
1:25m (Europe), 1:50m, 1:55m, 1:60m and 1:70m

Colour Key for Geographical Environments

Inhabitants

More than 5 million — Chicago

1 000 000 - 5 000 000 — Columbus

250 000 - 1 000 000 — Quebec

100 000 - 250 000 — Halifax

Less than 100 000 — Anderson

National capital (UPPERCASE) — NASSAU

International boundary

Disputed international boundary

Major road

Road under construction

Major railway

Canal

Highest peak in continent — McKinley

Highest peak in country — Logan

Heights in feet — 17000ft

Depths in feet — 185ft

Coral reef

Scientific station

Territorial claims in Antarctica

Disputed territorial claims in Antarctica

Tundra

Glacier, ice caps

Mountain

Coniferous forest

Mixed forest

Tropical rain forest

Savanna

Grassland, pasture

Steppe

Desert, sand desert

Rock desert

Lava field

Mangrove

Arable land

Marshland

Salt lake

Salt desert, salt pan, dry lake

Intermittent lake

Depression

Drift ice

North Pole — Arctic Circle
Tropic of Cancer — Latitudes
Equator
Longitudes
Tropic of Capricorn — Antarctic Circle
South Pole

The letters and numbers in the map edges are there to help you find names. Look for Las Vegas in the index **36 C4**. Turn to page 36 and look top or bottom for letter C and left or right for number 4. In this blue grid square you will find the city of Las Vegas.

Scale 1:50 000 000 means that a distance on the map is 50 000 000 times longer on the Earth's surface e.g. 1 cm on the map represents 500 km on the surface and 1 inch on the map represents 800 miles.

500   1000   1500 km

250   500   750 miles
hours flight ✈